An introduction to
systematic
political science

THE DORSEY SERIES IN POLITICAL SCIENCE

An introduction to systematic political science

DAVID H. EVERSON, Ph.D.
Sangamon State University

JOANN POPARAD PAINE, Ph.D.
Southern Illinois University, Carbondale

1973

THE DORSEY PRESS   *Homewood, Illinois   60430*

IRWIN-DORSEY INTERNATIONAL   *London, England   WC2H 9NJ*
IRWIN-DORSEY LIMITED   *Georgetown, Ontario   L7G 9NJ*

First printing, March 1973
Second printing, August 1973

ISBN 0-256-01199-0
Library of Congress Catalog Card No. 72-93549
Printed in the United States of America

FOR
Judith
Christopher
and
Tom
Robert
Tommy
Mary Kathryn
Elizabeth
Nicholas
Patrick

Preface

There is widespread disagreement among political scientists about the content of the introductory course in political science. Much of the disagreement revolves around two issues: (1) whether students should be provided the basic factual or substantive material of political science or whether the course should focus on how to inquire about the facts of politics; and (2) what should be the basic units or building blocks of political science. This book takes firm positions on these questions, which makes it different from most introductory texts in political science. First, we take the position that particular facts about politics are useless unless they are placed in a more general context. Second, we take exception to those who argue that an introduction to political science should be primarily devoted to descriptive material about politics and government. Third, we believe that questions about the nature of political inquiry—methodological questions—ought to be raised and treated at the introductory level. Indeed, we believe that it is crucial to introduce students to systematic political inquiry as early as students in other disciplines (psychology and economics come to mind) are introduced to the tools of those disciplines. Fourth, this does not mean that we believe that the basic course should be a course in the techniques of political inquiry; rather, we argue that general methodological questions should be raised within the framework of the important substantive questions about politics. Finally, we treat concepts as the basic building blocks or units of political science. This is in contrast to those who treat the subject matter by the area of inquiry, such as comparative politics, international relations, or state and local government. Discrete political facts, the "stuff" of politics, are understandable only when we define them in terms of concepts and put those concepts into generalizations and theories.

This book, therefore, is not a survey of the subfields of political science. Rather, we have described and analyzed those approaches to the study of politics which most frequently provide the organization for the substantive ideas contained in more advanced courses. The organization of the book reflects our desire to integrate the development of a critical capacity with the analysis of approaches. Parts I and II raise general methodological questions about the study of politics: (1) What is systematic political inquiry? (2) What is politics? (3) What are significant "political questions"? (4) What are the uses and limitations of systematic political inquiry? (5) How can we use our knowledge of the characteristics of systematic political inquiry to analyze research as well as the behavior and statements of politicians? In Part III, the emphasis changes to an examination of various approaches to the study of politics. We divide approaches by levels of analysis, macro and micro. Each approach is described and critically examined in terms of related substantive questions. We then treat the problems of integrating levels of analysis. Finally, in the last chapter, we take up the question of the relevance of systematic political inquiry for the development of public policy.

This book is not intended for the passive consumer. It invites active and independent participation in the discovery, formulation, testing, interpretation, and evaluation of ideas about political behavior. If, in the process, more questions are raised than answered, it is only because political scientists have more questions than answers. By learning how to estimate and evaluate the risks associated with political decisions, we may approximate the ideal of making decisions on matters of fact independent of the way we want things to be.

Thus, we have deliberately chosen to emphasize methodological considerations in an introductory text in political science. We have also kept before the reader the purpose of methodology: it is a tool facilitating inquiry into significant political questions.

A final comment, by way of a caveat, should be made here. Particularly in the first section of the book, we have taken positions on issues in the philosophy of science which we have not had the inclination to defend in detail in an introductory text not primarily devoted to an examination of these philosophical issues. Examples of such issues which we recognize to be controversial include the fact-value controversy and the question of the nature of scientific explanation in the social sciences. We have attempted, however, to indicate briefly our reasons for taking the positions that we do and to indicate some sources for further inquiry.

Acknowledgments

This volume is a joint response to a problem encountered in the classroom teaching of introductory political science. The problem was that there seemed to us to be little relationship between the text for the introductory course and the rest of the subject matter of political science. The common assumption of the introductory text seemed to be that our students were not ready for the real "stuff" of the contemporary study of politics. This assumption did not square either with our own inclinations or with our observation of what goes on in introductory courses in the other social sciences.

A number of people have offered constructive criticism about this effort. We wish to thank especially John C. Wahlke, Walter Rosenbaum, Michael R. King, Marie Barovic Rosenbaum, and Edward C. Uliassi. Where we persisted in the error of our ways, we accept responsibility.

We also wish to acknowledge the indirect contributions of two outstanding teachers, Robert Y. Fluno, of Whitman College, and Milton Hobbs, of the University of Illinois.

February 1973

DAVID H. EVERSON
JOANN P. PAINE

Contents

part I

Introduction

1

The uses and limitations of political science

In this chapter we examine both the uses and limitations of political science. It is because we feel strongly that political science does have a contribution to make, both to academic knowledge and to human betterment, that we argue for the uses of the study of politics. At the same time, it is important to spell out the realistic limitations of political inquiry, particularly in light of the fact that our age seems to swing between millennial hopes about perfection in the application of knowledge to human problems and irrational despair about the relevance of academic pursuits to the human condition. We seek a middle course between these extremes.

THE USES OF POLITICAL SCIENCE

What are the compelling reasons for studying politics, and in particular, for studying politics the way we will say it should be studied? The continuing interest of many attentive observers in political phenomena, such as elections, the workings of Congress, or the latest Middle East crisis, certainly suggests a reason for learning more about political behavior. Of course, politics does influence directly or indirectly the lives of almost everyone. The mere mention of public education, abortion laws, and the draft sufficiently illustrates the influence of political decisions and nondecisions. And certainly there are many interesting questions about the degree of influence in the other direction—how much impact do people have on governmental decisions? Notwithstanding the interest of students in politics and the manifest significance of political decisions, it has not automatically followed that students have found *political science* a fascinating and relevant subject. While we would not claim that the study of politics provides a panacea for all of our social and political ills, we believe that individuals of all political persuasions and temperaments can benefit from the study of politics.

Initially, our argument rests on the observation that every person is his own political decision maker and political scientist. All of us, regardless of whether we are self-conscious about what we are doing, engage in activities which resemble the behaviors of political decision makers and political scientists. We all gather (at least in some minimum sense) political data, analyze it, draw conclusions from it, use political information to evaluate political events, and decide to act or not to act as a result of our evaluations and conclusions. As in many facets of life, there is a degree of correspondence between what a layman does and what an "expert" does with respect to an area of concern, in this case, politics. The principle benefit people can gain from a study of political science is an increased capacity to be systematic political decision makers by learning to estimate the risks they are running in accepting or rejecting statements and courses of action relative to politics. We shall, therefore, focus our attention on how to make use of the knowledge of political scientists when thinking about politics—not what to think.

In the preceding paragraph, we mentioned several activities which political decision makers, political scientists, and other citizens engage in to one degree or another. We shall now outline and discuss briefly the major activities which political scientists undertake, show how these activities are interrelated, and discuss how people in general do many of these same things.

We will divide these activities into three categories: descriptive, analytic, and prescriptive. In the descriptive category, we find political scientists gathering specific and general facts about politics. In analysis, political scientists try to predict and explain political events. Prescriptive activities of political scientists include policy recommendations and stating political preferences.

One of the major things that political scientists do is to gather *specific facts* about politics, and, sometimes almost unintentionally, almost everyone else does also. In this context, we use the term "specific fact" to refer to a statement about politics which can be demonstrated to be true or false by evidence obtained from observation of a single object or event. For example, Senator Kennedy voted for the foreign aid bill of 1971, true or false? Presumably, as we will indicate in more detail below, there ought to be something purposeful and systematic about the ways in which political scientists gather specific facts about politics. Nevertheless, the facts which political scientists do gather vary in terms of the degree of difficulty of acquisition, reliability, and significance. In a moment we will be in a position to see how important the gathering of specific facts is to the accomplishment of the other objectives of political scientists.

A second major thing that political scientists do is to combine specific facts about politics in particular ways to make general statements or *generalizations* about politics. A generalization is developed from, but goes beyond, a set of specific facts: "Every generalization . . . is based on a number of concrete observations."[1] However, when we generalize, we go beyond the specific facts we have observed to make assertions about the relationships between classes of objects. An illustration may help to make the point. Suppose we observe that among our friends, all (or nearly all) vote for the same political party as their parents do. These observations consist of a set of specific facts: Tom votes the same way as his parents, Mary does also, and so on. From these specific facts, we may leap[2] to the generalization: all children (or most children) vote the same way as their parents. Note that the generalization does not refer to specific people, but to general classes (parents and children). In this instance, of course, the leap would be dubious, because we would be generalizing solely on the basis of personal experience. Much of this book is devoted to the examination of the questions: (1) How do we judge the accuracy of generalizations? and (2) How do we use generalizations in the study of politics?

Virtually everyone generalizes about politics. For example, someone may identify the Republican Party as a "party of depression" or the Democratic Party as a "party of war." These comments may be reformulated as hypothetical generalizations (hypothetical here means taking an "if . . . then" form): if the Republicans come to power, the likelihood of a depression is increased; or, if the Democrats come to power, the likelihood of a war is increased.

Human beings are not content with discrete, singular facts; they try to arrange these facts in meaningful patterns. Indeed, we could not be content with specific facts; for they are, in isolation, meaningless and uninterpretable. A red traffic signal would have no meaning for us in the absence of the context of generalizations about traffic laws or the behavior of other drivers. The capacities we develop for systematic generalization about politics are critical for the other activities of political scientists.

Political scientists try to explain and predict political events. Virtually everyone else does, too. We shall not give a complete explication of "explain" and "predict" here—that will come later.[3] Rather, we will indicate by an example what we mean. Frequently, we are asked (or we ask ourselves) to explain certain facts about politics: Why didn't

---

[1] Alan C. Isaak, *Scope and Methods of Political Science* (Homewood, Ill.: Dorsey Press, 1969), p. 92.

[2] This leap is sometimes called "induction." *Ibid.*

[3] Our discussion of explanation and prediction may be found in Chapter 6.

Lyndon Johnson seek reelection in 1968? One might begin an answer
with reference to certain facts, or alleged facts, like LBJ's standing in
presidential popularity polls. If pressed, however, a normal response
would be to draw a connection between the observed facts and more
general observations about behavior: candidates who perceive they have
no chance of winning withdraw from elections.[4] Note that we have
gone beyond the specific facts of this case to invoke a generalization
about politics which does not refer specifically to LBJ or the 1968 election, but to "candidates" and "elections."

We normally think of prediction in ordinary discourse in terms of
future events, i.e., can we predict the state of the United States economic
system six months from now? It is important to note that a predictive
statement involving a generalization (such as the following: if an American political party nominates for the presidency someone perceived to
be a political extremist by the voters, that candidate will lose the election)
may refer to any moment in time—past, present, or future. Predicting
the past is sometimes called "postdiction." Prediction involves the same
process of invoking generalizations. If asked to suggest why one outcome
is more likely than another, we almost invariably generalize from past
events and assumptions about the continuation of present conditions.
Thus, we will argue in the course of this book that explanation and
prediction are dependent upon reliable generalizations.

It may not be precisely clear why political scientists seek to be able
to explain and predict political events. Part of the answer is simply human
curiosity—we want to know why things happen the way they do or
what will happen under certain conditions. There also may be more
pragmatic considerations. The capacities of explaining and predicting
help political scientists and others concerned with political outcomes make
policy recommendations and political evaluations when they wish to influence and control political events.

Political scientists, decision makers, and other citizens also make value
judgments or statements. Any time we express a subjective preference
about anything, we are making a value statement. Some of our value
judgments are policy recommendations, proposing that government do
something, continue with present policy, or refrain from doing something.
Someone may say that the federal government should turn over some
of its revenue to the states without strings attached. If asked to defend
this recommendation, the individual might well offer *explanations* of why
the current system functions inadequately and why the desired policy
consequences would follow from the proposed changes. The latter statements would involve *predictions*. That is, the recommendation of an
alternative policy over a present one necessarily involves a comparison

---

[4] This illustrative generalization is not always true.

between what the consequences (outcomes) of the present policy are and what the consequences of the alternative would be. For such an argument to be convincing, an individual would have to demonstrate an understanding of how the present policy functions to produce the outcomes it does and why the alternative would be expected to produce different (and better) outcomes. If, as we argued previously, explanation and prediction involve the invoking of generalization, and policy recommendations assume explanation and prediction, it follows that policy recommendations require generalizations.

Finally, political scientists make other types of political evaluations or value statements about politics. Almost everyone does the same thing. We say that certain political actions are good and that others are bad; we judge political events and actors as desirable or undesirable. Such value statements assert a moral or ethical judgment about something. On what basis do we make such judgments? What if someone questions our assertion that "the seniority system in Congress is a bad thing" or that "abolishing the electoral college would be a good thing"? If we wish to avoid endless argument, we might say that what is "bad" about the seniority system is making the length of time in the Congress the sole criterion for appointing chairmen to important committees, leaving the most recently elected members without much say in deciding which bills will get to the floor for a vote. Deciding that these things are bad is a subjective judgment with which others may disagree. However, the discussion now can move on to offering facts, generalizations, and predictions in support of our evaluation. With respect to the seniority system, we might refer to additional facts about the numbers of Southern Congressmen in positions of leadership in key committees, generalizations about the presumed impact of this situation, and predictions about the expected consequences of changing the system to some other form of leadership selection. The same process would probably be followed with reference to the abolishment of the electoral college. The point we are making is that the defense of a political value judgment often takes structurally the same form as the defense of a policy recommendation—it turns out that the evaluation is often made because it is seen as a means to some other desired end. In the case of the seniority system in Congress, the end or goal might well be a different (more liberal) set of public policies.[5]

To tie this discussion together, we now note an additional consideration. Earlier we suggested that facts in themselves were not very meaningful. They are not intrinsically useful but, rather, are useful as they serve to confirm, modify, or refute generalizations. Suppose that we have a

---

[5] We use the seniority system as an example of public policy analysis in the final chapter of this book.

generalization that says that all white, Anglo-Saxon Protestants (WASPs) vote Republican. In order to refute that generalization, we need to find one specific fact; namely, we need to find one WASP who voted for a Democrat. If we find him, as we surely will, then we will have to modify our generalization.[6] There are, of course, countless facts about an individual which would *not* be relevant for this particular generalization. It follows that all facts about politics are not equally useful, and the relevance of particular facts depends upon the problem at hand.

The student who has followed the foregoing discussion will now recognize the conclusion—that he is a political decision maker and that to be a more systematic and self-conscious decision maker, he has to be a political scientist of sorts: that is, he needs to apply the critical tools of political analysis to areas of his concern. Moreover, we have argued that sound generalizations leading to explanations and predictions are the keys to accomplishing what many political scientists, political decision makers, and other citizens want to do: namely, the critical examination of policy recommendations and political value statements. This book, then, is directed toward illuminating methods for discovering, testing, and using political generalizations to predict and explain political events and to analyze statements about these events.

THE LIMITATIONS OF POLITICAL SCIENCE

Everything sounds simple so far. All we need to do is to gather a fund of reliable general information, and we can confidently recommend policy solutions to our social and political problems, make sound political evaluations, and change the world in the desired direction. If political scientists have gotten their hands on this secret, why haven't they let everyone else in on it? The inevitable answer is that it is not that simple. There are many problems in "doing political science." These problems include: (1) practical difficulties of access to the data of political science, (2) difficulties related to the kinds of generalizations which political scientists are likely to be able to make, and (3) difficulties related to the fact that political scientists as scientists cannot tell us which values to prefer in guiding our policy recommendations and political evaluations.

The first point is relatively straightforward, even though it has enormous consequences for political science. Just as the historian, for reasons completely beyond his control (the courthouse that burned down, the memoirs not written) is often shut off from data which is needed for his particular problem, so too the political scientist often finds himself

---

[6] That is, our generalization may now refer not to all WASPs, but perhaps it refers to "most" or "some."

unable to gather the best data simply because it is inaccessible.[7] Political scientists can and do study decision making in the Soviet Union, but they cannot make first-hand observations of the process. Political scientists can and do study elections in the 19th and early 20th centuries in the United States, but they cannot interview many of the voters in those elections. The obvious consequence is that political scientists often have to make do with data which is less satisfactory than the ideal in terms of forming their basic generalizations.[8]

A second problem, and a more interesting one from a theoretical point of view, is that political scientists study human behavior, and human behavior is complex and difficult to predict and explain.[9] One consequence is that generalizations about human political behavior usually (if not always) admit of exceptions. For example, we find that most, but not all, people who "strongly identify" with the Republican Party vote for Republican presidential candidates.[10] However, we cannot predict the behavior of particular members of the set of Republican strong identifiers; that is, we know that well over 90 percent of those who strongly identify with the Republican Party vote for Republican presidential candidates, but we do not know what a particular Republican strong identifier will do. The result is that our generalizations are often statistical or probabilistic,[11] i.e., the statement is not universal or true for all cases. What is the import of this fact? The reader will recall that we suggested that generalizations form the basis for prediction and explanation. But if generalizations refer only to the set, can we make confident predictions or explanations about the behavior of a particular member of the set? The answer, of course, is "no"; for that particular member might be one of the exceptions to the generalization.

There is a final difficulty and consequent limitation. We are among the social scientists who distinguish factual questions from value ques-

---

[7] It is well to point out here that changes in technology may make previously inaccessible data accessible. For example, the invention of sample survey techniques allowed investigators to study mass voting behavior in ways not available to them before. At the same time, new technology may direct attention to areas of inquiry not previously investigated.

[8] We discuss problems of data collection in Chapter 4.

[9] We do not want to get into the argument here as to whether the physical or social sciences are more difficult. All we safely assert is that the study of human behavior is as difficult as the study of any other phenomena.

[10] Angus Campbell *et al., The American Voter* (New York: John Wiley & Sons, 1964), p. 81. In 1952 and 1956, 99 percent of all "strong Republicans" voted for Eisenhower!

[11] Some would argue that this is because the world is by nature a probabilistic world (i.e., some things happen by chance), while others would argue that the world is deterministic but we lack knowledge of all the relevant variables. Since, at this time, the outcome is the same, it does not matter which assumption you wish to make about the nature of the real world.

tions.[12] Factual statements involve assertions about the world that are amenable to empirical investigation: "They deal with what is and not with what ought to be."[13] Value statements, on the other hand, express preferences for "what ought to be, endorsing ends, purposes, or norms."[14] Value questions, then, cannot be decided on the same basis as factual questions—by appeals to the evidence. This is not to suggest that decisions on questions of fact are always easy or straightforward. Rather, decisions involving such questions rest on the way the world *is*, not on the way we want it to be.

This observation does not contradict our earlier comments about the relevance of facts and generalizations for political evaluation because "political evaluations are usually a mixture of factual and moral judgments."[15] When value questions are framed in terms of *means-ends* relationships, these questions can be treated as factual statements. For example, "abolishing the seniority system in Congress would be a good thing, because (as a means) it would lead to the passage of more liberal legislation by Congress (desired end)" is a statement which can be translated for purposes of empirical analysis. Would the suggested means in fact lead to the desired end? That is why empirical political science is usually necessary for the analysis of value questions. However, ultimate value questions, those which do not assert some kinds of means-ends relationship, cannot be decided by reference to facts. An ultimate value statement is, by definition, one which stands on its own and is not made with reference to some other, higher goal. In this case we might say that we value human life in and of itself, not as a means to something else.

We are not proclaiming a value-free political science. It should be clear from what we have said previously that values are important in political inquiry, both in terms of the selection of topics for study and, perhaps more importantly, in the commitment to the quest for knowledge and human betterment. What we do insist on is a clear distinction be-

---

[12] We are aware of the rich controversy over the position we have taken, and we are also aware that we have not even begun to develop the argument which would have to be made to uphold the distinction between facts and values. For the reader who wishes to pursue the topic, we suggest the following sources: Felix Oppenheim, *Moral Principles in Political Philosophy* (New York: Random House, 1968) for a statement of the position we would endorse, and Donald Van-DeVeer, "Oppenheim's Defense of Noncognitivism," *American Political Science Review*, Vol. 65 (December 1971), pp. 1105–14, for a critique of our position; other relevant works include Robert Dahl, *Modern Political Analysis* (Englewood Cliffs, N.J.: Prentice-Hall, 1963), pp. 93–110, and Leo Strauss, *Natural Right and History* (Chicago: University of Chicago Press, 1953).

[13] Vernon Van Dyke, *Political Science: A Philosophical Analysis* (Stanford, Cal.: Stanford University Press, 1960), p. 8. This does not preclude the probability that there can be several constructions of what the world is. In other words, there may be more than one empirically valid description, because different factors may be selected by different investigators.

[14] *Ibid.*

[15] Dahl, *op. cit.*, p. 103.

tween factual and value questions and that, as much as possible, the decisions investigators make in their research involving value judgments be made explicit.

At this point, it may appear that the limitations we have suggested are insuperable. It is not our intent to convey such a gloomy prospect. Rather, we wish to stress that political explanations, predictions, policy recommendations, and evaluations carry with them hazards and degrees of uncertainty. The recognition that we might be wrong cannot deter us from making decisions, even if the decision is to postpone action. A prominent political scientist, Robert Dahl, has expressed the position in this manner:

> A person who refuses to make political decisions unless they are based on empirical knowledge at a high level of scientific validity will be paralyzed. Yet in politics, "refusing to decide" is simply deciding to let others decide for you.[16]

Therefore, we seek to show how more valid empirical knowledge can be developed and how to estimate the risks of deciding or refusing to decide.

SUMMARY AND CONCLUSIONS

In this chapter we laid a foundation for what follows through a discussion of the uses and limitations of political science. We have stressed that a study of political science which focuses on the methods of acquisition of political data and how to think about political questions has potential benefits for everyone, especially those who are interested in political evaluations and policy recommendations. We have argued that these activities are in large measure dependent upon the accumulation of accurate generalizations about politics. In studying the assumptions which political scientists make and the methods of systematic inquiry they employ, it is hoped that the payoff will be an increased capability for critical analysis of the political process.

Political science cannot, however, claim to be able to cure the world's ills. A commitment to the systematic study of politics (or any other science for that matter) means that one must eschew certainty for uncertainty and be prepared for imperfect and changing knowledge. As we have indicated, practical difficulties are raised by the intransigence of the data with which we must deal—human behavior, and the limitation that empirical political science cannot decide the most important questions, the ones about ultimate values. Even with these limitations, we believe that the study of politics can be challenging, exciting, and personally rewarding.

---

[16] *Ibid.*, p. 105.

chapter

2

Political science and the eternal issues

In the last chapter, we discussed some of the uses and limitations of the systematic study of politics. Our arguments for the uses were based on the contention that we all gather specific facts about politics, generalize about politics, try to explain and predict political events, and, perhaps most importantly, make political evaluations and policy recommendations. In order to perform the latter activities systematically and with a minimum of risk, it is necessary to discover reliable generalizations about politics. To do this, we will need to first consider the nature of the subject matter of political science. In doing so, our strategy will be to try to identify and illustrate some eternal political issues.

WHAT IS POLITICAL?

To systematically study something, we like to know what that something is. If we were to look at what political scientists actually study, we would find a bewildering variety of phenomena in terms of the subjects of inquiry. Currently, political scientists examine such traditional areas of inquiry as constitutions, political institutions, and laws in terms of the three divisions made in the previous chapter: description, analysis, and prescription. But political scientists may also be found examining the socialization (learning) of children, the distribution of power in local communities and in nongovernmental organizations, the factors explaining rebellion, or the attitudes of citizens about authority in terms of those same three divisions.[1]

This range of topics studied suggests both the interdisciplinary interests of political scientists and the absence of common agreement about the

[1] Of course, this list of areas of inquiry is illustrative, not exhaustive, of areas that political scientists have investigated.

precise nature of their discipline. There is little agreement about the proper boundaries of political science. We can probably identify two distinctive schools of thought among political scientists on this boundary problem, although the variation within each school may be quite large. One school would identify the "political" with activity directed toward or taking place within the formal institutions we call government.[2] This approach appears to make good sense—politics is usually tied to the institutions of government when we use the term in everyday language. However, this resolution of the question ultimately forces us to consider what we mean by "government."[3]

A second approach identifies the "political" with a distinctive set of processes or relationships wherever they might occur. We also recognize this approach in ordinary language through the use of phrases such as "office politics." In this view, there are certain human behaviors which are defined as political regardless of the institutional or organizational context in which they take place, or even if they take place outside of an institutional context. Such distinctive processes or relationships might be called "conflict," "power," or the "allocation of scarce values."[4]

At first glance, the approach identifying the political with the institutions of government might appear to be more restrictive, and the second, identifying politics with distinctive human relationships, broader. This is true to a certain extent; for with the latter approach, political behavior may occur anywhere, in the family, the trade union, the church, and so on. There is a sense, however, in which the adoption of the former approach, taken literally, would involve a further expansion of the concerns of political scientists. Vernon Van Dyke has commented that focusing on government "opens up too vast a terrain" even though that focus "traditionally has had connotations that are too narrow. . . ."[5] What he means is that government is so pervasive in modern society that to focus on the activities of government is to quite literally focus on almost everything.[6]

[2] Charles Hyneman, for example, has stated: "The central point of attention in American political science . . . is that part of the affairs of state which centers in government, and that kind or part of government which speaks through law." Quoted by Vernon Van Dyke, "The Optimum Scope of Political Science," in James C. Charlesworth (ed.), *A Design for Political Science: Scope, Objectives, and Methods* (Philadelphia: American Academy of Political and Social Science, 1966), pp. 9–10. Note that Hyneman's statement is descriptive, about what political scientists do, and is limited to American political science.

[3] Alan C. Isaak, *Scope and Methods of Political Science* (Homewood, Ill.: Dorsey Press, 1969), p. 16.

[4] For a more extensive discussion of these conceptual approaches to political science, see *ibid.*, pp. 14–21.

[5] "The Optimum Scope of Political Science," *op. cit.*, pp. 10–11.

[6] Political scientists in fact deal with public education, public health, crime, agriculture, space exploration, and any other area where governmental agencies or politicians are found.

Which is the right orientation to a definition of politics? Although we prefer to use the term "political" to mean a process or relationship involving conflict, power, or decision making, this question is neither very meaningful nor very important. It is not meaningful because, as we will argue later, matters of definition are not matters of truth or falsity in the same way that factual assertions are. In addition, the question is not that important. A precise definition of politics, which is of necessity inclusive of some things and exclusive of others, is not necessary for our discussion; "politics" or "political" are not usually included in empirical generalizations.[7] Words such as this, which delineate general areas of inquiry have been called "chapter heading" words or "global" terms.[8] There is no need for precision or exactness if all we are doing with a word is indicating a broad area of interest, and we think that this is all one can reasonably expect to do with a term such as "political."

THE ETERNAL ISSUES OF POLITICS

Our discussion of what politics is suggests our response to the question of whether or not there are eternal political issues. If politics is to be found virtually everywhere and involves the authoritative allocation of those things we value, conflict, and power relationships, it follows that certain key political questions probably have always been with us and have been addressed by political thinkers for a long time. We will now describe some of these questions to show how these concerns permeate the activities of contemporary political scientists.

Following the classification of activities described in Chapter 1, we will divide these questions into three types: (1) those related to the *description* of political events, (2) those related to the explanation and prediction of political events (*analysis*), and (3) those related to the evaluation of political events (*prescription*).

Eternal descriptive questions

There are many descriptive questions in politics, and many of these questions are recurring ones. As an illustration of this type of question, let us examine the characteristics of a political system. Since the inception of the study of politics, political observers have felt the need to classify and label kinds of political systems. Although we will discuss the topic of definition more completely in the next chapter, we should note here that in order to generalize about politics (or anything else), we need to develop criteria by which to distinguish some kinds of things from

---

[7] Of course, if these words do appear, then they must be defined precisely, as we will discuss later.

[8] Robert Dubin, *Theory Building* (New York: Free Press, 1969), pp. 60–63.

others—in this case, observers have felt the need to distinguish some kinds of political systems from others. Once this task has been accomplished, an observer may move to record systematically the generalizations about the various kinds of systems, to attempt to explain and predict the occurrence of various kinds of systems, and to evaluate them. But all of these activities are subsequent to the identification, classification, and enumeration of various types of systems.

We shall briefly examine two of these attempts and indicate their relationship to the descriptive problem of identifying types of political systems. In the fifth century B.C., Aristotle developed a typology of political systems based on two criteria: (1) the number of rulers and (2) whether the ruling group ruled in their self-interest or in the interest of all.[9] This two-factor scheme resulted in the typology shown in Table 2–1.[10] There is clearly a "value" aspect of Aristotle's typology of political

TABLE 2–1
Aristotle's Classification of Types of Political Systems

| | System Ruled in the Interest Of: | |
Number of Rulers	All	Rulers
One............	Monarchy	Tyranny
Few............	Aristocracy	Oligarchy
Many..........	Polity	Democracy

systems. The systems which are governed in the interest of all are the good systems (those to be preferred), and those governed in the interest of the rulers are the bad systems (those not to be preferred). Typologies often implicitly or explicitly reflect the value preferences of those who develop them. This is not necessarily undesirable, but the reader should be alert to the ways in which such preferences are expressed. With reference to Aristotle's typology, it is interesting to note that democracy was not a good system, because the majority ruled solely in its own interest—democracy was not a good word to the Greeks.

What kinds of descriptive questions are suggested by a typology such as Aristotle's? One, investigated by Aristotle, is an enumeration of the relative frequencies of various types of systems. What is the most frequently occurring type of political system? What is the least frequently

[9] Ernest Barker (trans.), *The Politics of Aristotle* (New York: Oxford University Press, 1962), pp. 157–79.

[10] A typology is a classification system for objects (such as political systems) which divides the objects on the basis of explicit criteria into mutually exclusive and collectively exhaustive categories. For a discussion of problems of definition, see Chapter 3.

occurring type? Asking this deceptively simple descriptive question may provoke additional interesting inquiries which move beyond the mere number of different types of systems. For example, we may then ask what kinds of social characteristics are found in conjunction with certain types of political systems. Aristotle was very interested in the conditions underlying the various systems in his typology.[11]

Political thinkers have never ceased creating typologies of various political systems. We shall now use a more recent typology to indicate the continuity between the past and some modern developments. In the past 200 years, political parties have developed in nearly all political systems. Consequently, a number of people have attempted to classify political systems in terms of the character of the political parties in those systems. Gabriel Almond's typology, shown in Table 2–2, is based on

TABLE 2–2
Almond's Classification of Party Systems

Number of Parties	Type of Party		
	Authoritarian	*Dominant*	*Competitive*
1	"Authoritarian"	"Dominant"	
2			Two-party competitive
More than 2			Multiparty competitive

the number of parties and the degree to which competition is allowed in the system.[12] The types of party systems are: (1) authoritarian, (2) dominant nonauthoritarian, (3) competitive two-party, and (4) competitive multiparty. Note that both the authoritarian and dominant nonauthoritarian party systems have fundamentally one party. The basis of distinction between the two is the degree to which the party dominates the society. Note that the two-party and multiparty sysems are both competitive. Systems (1) and (2) are distinguished from (3) and (4) by the number of parties and by the competitiveness of the system. By definition, it seems that there are no multiparty systems which are not competitive.

In any case, there is a degree of correspondence between Aristotle and Almond and Coleman. Numbers remain a criterion for distinguishing the systems. There is also an implicit value orientation in the Almond and Coleman scheme. Competitive systems are to be preferred to non-

---

[11] See *The Politics of Aristotle, op. cit.,* pp. 181–83, on the role of the middle class.

[12] Gabriel A. Almond and James Coleman (eds.), *The Politics of Developing Areas* (Princeton, N.J.: Princeton University Press, 1960).

competitive ones. It is also clear that the additional descriptive questions we considered with respect to Aristotle's typology of political systems can be addressed to Almond and Coleman. The major break with the classical past is the selection of the political party as a major element in classifying political systems.[13] Finally, it should be mentioned that such descriptive research, both in Aristotle's time and in ours, depends upon our being able to gather the data which would allow us to make the distinctions implied by the typologies.[14]

Eternal explanatory questions

We have noted that one eternal descriptive question concerns the characteristics of types of political systems (and the questions which flow from that central question). Explanatory questions also recur. Certainly, one of the most significant sets of questions has to do with the explanation of political stability and political instability or change.[15] One specific illustration of an explanatory question relating to the general questions of stability and instability is this: Why do revolutions occur? Again, we will look at both a classical and a modern attempt to deal with that explanatory question.

Aristotle was not content to classify political systems. Among other things, he was also very interested in why political systems change. In doing so, he suggested "the *policies* likely to ensure the stability of constitutions. . . ."[16] We shall briefly examine his discussion of the general causes[17] of revolution.[18] Aristotle divides the general causes of revolution into three categories: (1) psychological motives, (2) the objects of the motives, and (3) the immediate origins. The psychological causes are attitudes on the part of citizens relating to inequality and equality in political systems. Thus, Aristotle comments:

There are some who stir up sedition because their minds are filled by a passion for equality. . . . There are others who do it because their minds are filled with a passion for inequality. . . . Thus inferiors become revolutionaries in order to be equals, and equals in order to be superiors.[19]

---

[13] One reason for this is that many writers regard competitive parties as a distinctive aspect of democratic political systems. It is a fact that no national representative democratic system has ever functioned in the absence of parties.

[14] For a discussion of these problems, see Chapters 3 and 4.

[15] We ignore prediction for the moment. In a later chapter, we will argue that good explanation should allow for good prediction.

[16] *The Politics of Aristotle, op. cit.*, p. 203.

[17] We discuss the concept of cause in some detail in Chapter 4.

[18] Aristotle also discusses the specific causes of revolution in the various types of constitutions (e.g., oligarchies). *Op. cit.*, pp. 214–54.

[19] *Ibid.*, p. 207.

For example, in line with Aristotle's typology of constitutions mentioned in the previous section, oligarchies are changed to democracies through the passion for equality and democracies are changed to oligarchies through the passion for inequality.

Aristotle then suggests that "the objects which are at stake are profit and honour" and their opposites. That is, it is inequality or equality with respect to those objects which is the reason for the passion for change. Finally, he enumerates the "occasions and origins of disturbances. . . ."[20] These are the events or conditions which arouse passions. We shall not list all of the instances which Aristotle mentions; but, as an example, he states that "insolence" on the part of the rulers may lead to revolution: "[W]hen those who are in office show insolence, and seek their personal advantage, the citizens turn seditious—not only attacking other persons, but also attacking the constitution which gives such persons power."[21] Following from his discussion of the causes of revolution, Aristotle suggests how to avoid revolution and promote stability. For example, he cautions rulers in democracies to "spare the rich" and in oligarchies to have special regard for the poor.[22]

A more recent attempt to explain revolution is that of Crane Brinton in his study of *The Anatomy of Revolution.*[23] Brinton's study is based on an analysis of four revolutions: the English (of 1688), the American, the French, and the Russian. We cannot do justice in any sense to the full richness and complexity of Brinton's fine study, but we can summarize his general explanation for the outbreak of revolution. He presents three broad categories of conditions leading to revolution: (1) economic and political weaknesses, (2) the desertion of the intellectuals, and (3) class antagonisms. We shall illustrate the flavor of his argument with examples from each category.

With regard to economic and political weaknesses, Brinton notes that revolutions do not appear to occur in countries that are "economically retrograde; on the contrary, they took place in societies economically progressive."[24] However, the governments of the societies found themselves in financial difficulty and "certain groups [in the societies] feel that governmental policies are against their particular economic interests. . . ." Brinton also observes a breakdown in the effectiveness of the government: "In our four societies the governments seem to have been relatively inefficient. . . ."[25] With respect to the second category, Brinton

---

[20] *Ibid.*
[21] *Ibid.*, p. 208.
[22] *Ibid.*, p. 229.
[23] New York: Vintage Books, 1965.
[24] *Ibid.*, p. 32.
[25] *Ibid.*, p. 36.

observes that: "Quantitatively, we may say that in a society markedly unstable there seem to be absolutely more intellectuals, at any rate comparatively more intellectuals, bitterly attacking existing institutions and desirous of a considerable alteration in society, business and government."[26] Finally, Brinton finds sharp class antagonisms (ruling classes versus subordinate classes) symptomatic of revolution. It is perhaps here that Brinton's diagnosis most closely parallels that of Aristotle. As a final comment, in fairness to Brinton, he is extremely cautious in warning that his explanations are limited to four cases and are tentative.[27]

Doubtless this brief review of two explanations of revolution has raised important questions in your mind. Not the least of such questions would be this: How do we evaluate the quality of various explanations? In a broad sense, this entire book is devoted to that question. In a more specific sense, that question is taken up in detail in Chapter 6.

Eternal evaluative questions

Some value questions about politics are eternal as well. Perhaps the most general question, and one which combines a value preference with a broad policy recommendation, is: What is the best kind of political system? Again, many political thinkers have addressed this question, and a large number of answers have been presented. Again, by way of illustration, we shall examine one classical and one more modern answer.

We have already found Aristotle a fruitful source in the areas of description and explanation, and we shall turn to him again for an example of political evaluation of the best kind of political system. Recall that Aristotle distinguished six types of political systems. Which did he prefer? First, we should note that here we are considering Aristotle's preferred "practical" political system, not the ideal which can never (or infrequently) be realized. Aristotle judges constitutions in the light of the principle "that goodness consists in a mean. . . ."[28] From this general principle, Aristotle deduces that "in the ownership of all gifts of fortune a middle condition will be best."[29] That is, the best society is one in which the middle class predominates. In such a society, political power will also rest in the middle class. In effect, Aristotle argues that a large middle class will have a moderating effect on politics, and therefore,

---

[26] *Ibid.*, pp. 42–43.

[27] He says: ". . . we must infer from what we have just done that in its earlier stages diagnosis of revolution is extremely difficult, and certainly cannot be reduced to a neat formula, a recipe, a set of rules." *Ibid.*, p. 65.

[28] *The Politics of Aristotle, op. cit.*, p. 180. By the "mean," Aristotle meant the avoidance of excesses or extremes.

[29] *Ibid.*, p. 181.

a large middle class is a social condition conducive to the establishment of a polity, his preferred form of government.

> It is clear from our argument, first, that the best form of political society is one where power is vested in the middle class, and secondly, that good government is attainable in those states where there is a large middle class. . . . It is therefore the greatest of blessings for a state that its members should possess a moderate and adequate property. . . . it is clear that the middle type of constitution polity is best. It is the one type free from faction; where the middle class is large, there is least likelihood of faction and dissension among the citizens.[30]

In effect, Aristotle's choice of a polity as the most preferred system is a policy recommendation (based on certain conditions): if you want to achieve a given objective (the mean, moderation), and if conditions are appropriate (a large middle class), then the best form of government is a polity.[31] Incidentally, in this discussion Aristotle suggests a relationship which continually recurs in discussions of the conditions underlying democracy: that a large middle class is supportive of democratic survival.[32]

For a modern example of political evaluation, let us turn to Robert Dahl's analysis of the American political system in the mid 1950s.[33] Aristotle's "best" political system was one which he felt was practicable for the majority of citizens. Dahl's treatment is of an actual political system which not only deviates from the ideal, but which may not even be the best system from a practical point of view; nevertheless, Dahl does not find it "so obviously a defective system as some of its critics suggest."[34] The organization of Dahl's analysis is instructive for our purposes. He begins with the construction of an idealized political system which he calls a "polyarchy," by which he means something like representative democracy.[35] He then gives a descriptive account of the American political system, emphasizing some of the ways in which it approximates or deviates from the ideal of polyarchy. Some of the characteristics used to compare polyarchy with the American political system are shown in Table 2–3.

---

[30] *Ibid.*, p. 182.

[31] For Aristotle, a polity is an example of the mean, because it is a "mixed" constitution, containing elements of democracy and oligarchy. *Ibid.*, p. 175.

[32] Seymour Martin Lipset, *Political Man: The Social Bases of Politics* (Garden City, N.Y.: Doubleday & Co., 1960), p. 45–50.

[33] *A Preface to Democratic Theory* (Chicago: University of Chicago Press, 1956), chap. 5.

[34] *Ibid.*, p. 150. This is not necessarily Dahl's current evaluation of the American political system.

[35] *Ibid.*, p. 84.

TABLE 2–3
Selected Comparisons: Polyarchy versus the American Political System

Polyarchy	American Political System
Policies are selected in accordance with majority rule, i.e., "the alternative with the greatest number of votes is declared the winner."*	". . . specific policies tend to be products of 'minorities rule.' "‡
Elections are controlling with respect to policies.†	". . . in no large nation state can elections tell us much about the preferences of majorities. . . ."§

* Robert Dahl, *A Preface to Democratic Theory* (Chicago: University of Chicago Press, 1956), p. 84. The statement refers to voting both on representatives in elections and on policies in representative bodies.
    † *Ibid.*
    ‡ *Ibid.*, p. 133.
    § *Ibid.*, pp. 129–30.

Dahl's descriptive account of the American political system emphasizes the fact that "active and legitimate" groups (normally minorities) can influence decisions that affect them at some point in the decision-making process.[36] He also explains the survival of the American system by reference to the "social balance of power" in American society, rather than by the American constitutional system as such.[37] Finally, he evaluates the American political system favorably in terms of certain criteria:

With all its defects, it does nonetheless provide a high probability that any active and legitimate group will make itself heard effectively at some stage in the process of decision. This is no mean thing in a political system . . . so long as the social prerequisites of democracy are substantially intact in this country, it appears to be a relatively efficient system for reinforcing agreement, encouraging moderation, and maintaining social peace in a restless and immoderate people operating a gigantic, powerful, diversified, and incredibly complex society.[38]

Thus, Dahl sees the American system as a means to several desirable goals: (1) representation of active and legitimate groups, (2) reaching agreement, (3) moderation, and (4) "maintaining social peace." The important point here is not whether Dahl is correct or not, but rather how we might evaluate his evaluation. Note that we could criticize him on two grounds: factual and normative (value). In a factual sense, we could ask if the system actually produces the consequences he claims? For example, is it true that all "active and legitimate" groups get heard

[36] *Ibid.*, pp. 137–38.
[37] *Ibid.*, pp. 142–43.
[38] *Ibid.*, pp. 150–51.

in the process?[39] Is it true that we have "social peace"? Second, in a value sense, we could criticize him for offering us the wrong goals. We might prefer some other outcomes even if we agreed that factually he was right. We may not believe that political moderation is the answer for the pressing problems of our time.[40]

SUMMARY AND CONCLUSIONS

In this chapter we have tried to indicate the key questions in the study of politics. First, we defined politics as a process which occurs in virtually all human relationships and as a relationship among people involving conflict or the resolution of conflict over things that are values. Politics is significant, for it determines, in Lasswell's classic words, "who gets what, when, how."[41] Political scientists may study political processes or relationships wherever they occur, but the bulk of attention, in societies like the United States, will probably be centered on activities in and around the institutions we call government.

Second, we asked the question: Are there eternal questions with which political scientists deal, and if so, what kinds of questions are these? Again, our purpose is to indicate what political scientists are ultimately about. We noted that the kinds of questions which political scientists address themselves to can be divided into three types: (1) descriptive, (2) explanatory (and predictive), and (3) evaluative. Using classical and modern examples, we illustrated recurring questions political analysts have examined. The descriptive question we illustrated was the problem of distinguishing types of political systems. The explanatory question was explaining revolutionary change, while the evaluative question was evaluating types of political systems (e.g., what is an ideal political system?).

Third, we should reemphasize the way in which the various types of questions are interrelated. In order to have something to explain, we must have good descriptions. To evaluate political objects and events, we need accurate description and good explanation (or prediction). If we evaluate the American political system as good or bad, we will generally do so on the basis of the descriptive characteristics of the system (e.g., that all "active and legitimate" groups can be heard), and on the

---

[39] We must also be concerned with what is meant by an "active and legitimate" group, and who defines the legitimacy of a group.

[40] For both normative and empirical criticisms of Dahl (and others), see Jack Walker, "A Critique of the Elitist Theory of Democracy," *American Political Science Review*, Vol. 60(1966), pp. 285–95. For Dahl's reply, see "Further Reflections on the Elitist Theory of Democracy," *American Political Science Review*, Vol. 60(1966), pp. 296–305.

[41] Harold Lasswell, *Politics: Who Gets What, When, How* (New York: McGraw-Hill, 1936).

basis of our explanations of the way in which the system operates (e.g., that operation of the political system helps to maintain "social peace"). Finally, our desire to evaluate political things often leads us to descriptive and explanatory activities. Aristotle's attempts to classify political systems and to explain revolutions probably both stemmed from his normative concerns with the "good life" and with the best kind of political system. We are saying that the types of questions with which political scientists deal, and have been dealing for some time, are connected, and that all are critically important for the multiple goals of political scientists.

It may be worth while to conclude this chapter with a rather arbitrary list of some additional major, general questions, within the categories of description, explanation, and evaluation. This list, shown as Table 2–4, does not exhaust the significant concerns of political scientists, and

TABLE 2–4
An Illustrative List of Major Political Questions

Descriptive	Explanatory	Evaluative
1. What are the types of political systems? How frequently do they occur? What social conditions are associated with the various types?	1. Why does political change occur?	1. What is the ideal political system? Given real world constraints, what is the best practical political system?
	2. Why does political change fail to occur (why are some systems stable)?	
2. What is the distribution of power within political systems?	3. Why does political violence occur? Within systems? Between systems?	2. When are acts of political violence justifiable?
3. What are the actual outcomes within various types of political systems? What is the distribution of rewards and costs? What is the relationship between the power distribution and the outcomes?	4. Why do people participate in politics?	3. Is a particular policy desirable or undesirable?
		4. Should people participate in politics?
4. Who participates in politics?		

we cannot pretend that political scientists necessarily have good answers to any or all of these questions. These are some of the important areas of concern. In the following chapters, we will be concerned with how political scientists attempt to answer such questions.

part II

The characteristics of a systematic study of politics: Exposition and examples

chapter
3

Concepts and generalizations

Having discussed many of the questions that stimulate the activities of political scientists, we are ready to describe the ways that one can proceed to develop "answers" to these and other questions. Since our questions generally ask how one set of similar events or behaviors affects another and different set of similar events or behaviors, we are actually consciously or unconsciously formulating our questions after putting together a number of discrete facts and labeling them with concept names. Therefore, we will begin our discussion of the characteristics of a systematic study of politics with concepts and generalizations. This discussion will move us toward considering in later chapters how we discover and test hypotheses about politics.

CONCEPTS AND DEFINITIONS

Everyone carries around with him a large number of political concepts: revolution, democracy, totalitarianism, power, equality, and so on. Concepts refer to properties of things or to relationships among things. That is, they subsume the characteristics which are common to several entities. They can be contrasted to proper names, which identify particular, unique things such as Christopher Everson or Nicholas Paine. Both Christopher and Nicholas are *boys*. Concepts may also refer to relationships among entities, as when we say that Chris is *older than* Nicholas or the President is *more powerful than* a United States Senator.

Why are concepts important for the systematic study of politics? The answer is that concepts are the building blocks for the generalizations we make about politics. Generalizations relate concepts to one another. Therefore, to understand how to discover and test political generalizations, we need to know something about the nature of concepts.

As a primary example of a political science concept, we are going to use the notion of partisan identification which has been developed in the study of voting behavior in the United States.[1] "Partisan identification" means the psychological identification an individual has with a political party.[2] In a rough sense, it may be taken as analogous to religious identification—the sense of psychological identification or attachment to a particular church. When we apply a term such as partisan identification to a property of something (in this case, persons), what are we doing? Essentially, we are giving a shorthand label which stands in place of a set of related characteristics. We are saying: Let the words "partisan identification" stand for a set of characteristics which distinguish partisan identifiers from others. Some people consider themselves Democrats or Republicans (partisan identifiers) while others consider themselves independents (nonpartisans). This is like a definition in a mathematical equation: partisan identification equals psychological identification with a political party. A concept stands in place of a coherent set of characteristics, including relationships, which make up the *definition* of the concept. And these are the characteristics that are sometimes derived from the discrete facts of politics and, therefore, serve as one of the major links between the world of political science and the world of politics.

Earlier, we indicated a position with respect to matters of definition which we should elaborate here. The position asserts that definitions are neither true nor false in a factual sense but are stipulated by the user. In other words, the acceptability of the definition is not contingent on its factual truth. Such definitions are called nominal definitions. Robert Dahl has commented with respect to nominal definitions:

Nominal definitions do not, by themselves, tell us anything about "fact," about what goes on in the "real" world. Nothing can be shown to be true or false about the real world of politics (or economics, or whatever) simply by defining a term. Definitions may help us to understand our language; they do not, unaided, help us to understand what is going on in the world.[3]

This means that if we use the term "partisan identification" to mean a psychological tie to a political party and you use it to mean the way in which an individual votes in a given election, there are no strictly factual grounds on which to decide who is right and who is wrong; in fact, the question is misleading. This position is not taken by all political

---

[1] For a more extensive discussion of the concept and findings relative to it, see Angus Campbell *et al.*, *The American Voter* (New York: John Wiley & Sons, 1964) chap. 5. A readable treatment of the history of the concept can be found in William Buchanan, *Understanding Political Variables* (New York: Charles Scribner's Sons, 1969), pp. 151–55.

[2] Campbell *et al.*, *op. cit.*, pp. 67–68.

[3] Robert Dahl, *Modern Political Analysis* (Englewood Cliffs, N.J.: Prentice-Hall, 1963), p. 8.

scientists or philosophers, but it is one which is very compatible with other positions taken in this book. It should be clear that the position does not suggest that definitions are solely the whim of the definer. There are a number of characteristics of useful scientific concepts which limit the freedom to define at will.

What are the characteristics of useful scientific concepts? When we refer to scientific concepts, we are referring to concepts which appear in *empirical generalizations*. While we intend to discuss generalizations more fully in the latter half of this chapter, it is necessary to indicate briefly here what we mean by the term. Vernon Van Dyke has noted: "Before we generalize, we classify. We put items possessing shared attributes into one category."[4] This process of classification is concept development or concept formation.[5] A generalization, then, relates two or more concepts: people who identify with a political party generally tend to vote for that party's presidential candidates.[6] The concepts which are related in that generalization are *identification* with a party and *voting* for that party. Now, what are empirical generalizations? Empirical refers to "something that can, at least in principle, be confirmed or refuted by experience."[7] Empirical generalizations are true or false depending upon the way the world is: either identifiers tend to vote for their party or they do not. Thus, generalizations contrast with definitions which are neither true or false.

The first requirement of useful scientific concepts[8] flows directly from our discussion of empirical generalizations. Before we can determine the truth or falsity of a generalization, the concepts in empirical generalizations must be linked to empirical observations. In more technical language, we must have *operational definitions* of the concepts.[9] Why? Let us take the example of the generalization suggested above: those who iden-

---

[4] *Political Science: A Philosophical Analysis* (Stanford, Cal.: Stanford University Press, 1960), p. 20.

[5] Carl G. Hempel, *Philosophy of Natural Science* (Englewood Cliffs, N.J.: Prentice-Hall, 1966), chap. 7.

[6] Note that if we had defined partisan identification as voting for a particular party's candidates our statement would not be an empirical generalization; for voting for a party's candidates would then be the same thing as identifying with the party. Concepts must be independently defined in empirical generalizations.

[7] Dahl, *op. cit.*, p. 8.

[8] We also call these variables.

[9] We want to make quite clear what we are and are not asserting by this claim. We are asserting that generalizations we want to test (we will call them hypotheses) must contain concepts which are operationalized. By operationalized, we mean that the concepts must be measured, i.e., linked to observations, in such a way that other observers could repeat the measurements and get the same results. We are not asserting that all concepts must be directly linked to observables; only those in testable hypotheses must be. We are also not claiming that a concept such as partisan identification may not be measured in a number of different ways which may or may not yield substantially the same results.

tify with a party tend to vote for that party's presidential candidates. How can we know if the statement is true or not if we cannot distinguish those who identify with the party from those who do not, and if we cannot distinguish those who vote for the party's candidates from those who do not? This means that our definitions of "identification with the party" and "voting for the party presidential candidates" must be operational, i.e., sufficiently precise, physically possible, empirically grounded, and replicable; so that any competent observer could carry out the operations necessary to test the generalization in question. As an illustration, a common method of operationalizing partisan identification is to ask individuals the following question: "Generally speaking, do you usually think of yourself as a Republican, a Democrat, an independent, or what?"[10] A follow-up to this question focuses on *degree* or *strength* of partisan attachment, and we will consider this refinement of the concept below.

The process of operationalizing concepts may be better comprehended pictorially, as in Figure 3–1. The important point to keep in mind is

FIGURE 3–1
Operationalizing Concepts

Conceptual Level: *Concepts*	*Partisan Identification*	*Voting for Party*
	↓	↓
Empirical or "real world" level: variables	Response of individual to question asking him to report whether he thinks of himself as a Republican, Democrat, whatever.	Voting for Democratic or Republican presidential candidates, e.g., the response of an individual to a question: How did you vote in the last presidential election?

that verbal or conceptual definitions must be translated into empirical or operational indicators by specifying how and what is to be measured if concepts are to be useful in empirical generalizations. Sometimes this requirement is referred to as the "empirical import" of a concept.[11]

It is not sufficient, however, that useful scientific concepts merely exhibit empirical import or be operational. Why not? It is easy to see that we may empirically define a host of concepts which will be relatively meaningless in terms of helping us to explain or predict political behavior. For example, we might operationalize partisan predispositions according

---

[10] Buchanan, *op. cit.*, p. 153.

[11] Hempel, *op. cit.*, p. 96.

to the style of tie which an individual wears, but we might be highly skeptical of this empirical indicator in terms of predicting voting behavior.[12] We not only want concepts with empirical import, but also concepts which are linked in meaningful fashion to other concepts in generalizations which help us to explain and predict. In a more formal sense, this requirement is sometimes referred to as "significance":

A concept is neither true nor false, only propositions are. . . . Yet there is a distinction of "good" and "bad" among defined descriptive concepts. To have a name for it I shall say that a concept is or is not *significant*. A concept is significant if and only if it occurs, together with others, in statements of lawfulness which we have reason to believe are true.[13]

The significance of "partisan identification" has been established by the fact that it can be used to predict the direction of voting, political activity, and political attitudes.[14]

Thus, we have argued that although the definitions of concepts are neither true nor false, there are standards which circumscribe the freedom to arbitrarily stipulate any definition for a scientific concept. These are the complementary requirements of "empirical import" and "significance." There are several additional considerations, however, which we must discuss with respect to concepts. Two of the most important have to do with levels of measurement of concepts and levels of analysis. We shall deal with the levels of measurement first.

Whenever we define a concept, such as partisan identification, we are distinguishing some kinds of things from others. In the same way that a biologist uses a set of characteristics (which make up a definition) to distinguish one species of animals from another, so must our definitions allow us to classify objects (including people) by various useful categories. Our definition tells us how to distinguish those who, for example, have a partisan identity from those who do not. We can divide the responses to the question asking people to tell us whether they consider themselves to be Republicans or Democrats into five categories: (1) Democratic identifiers, (2) Republican identifiers, (3) independents, (4) those who identify with another party (e.g., Prohibitionists), and (5) those who do not identify themselves politically. Our classification

---

[12] Although one critic of voting studies has asked the question: "What is the connection between wearing hand-painted ties and party choice?" Leslie A. Fiedler, "Voting and Voting Studies," in Eugene Burdick and Arthur J. Brodbeck, *American Voting Behavior* (New York: Free Press, 1959), p. 195.

[13] This comment is from the distinguished philosopher of science, Gustav Bergmann, quoted in Robert Dubin, *Theory Building* (New York: Free Press, 1969), p. 28. Hempel uses the term "systematic import" to refer to significance (*op. cit.*, pp. 96–97).

[14] Campbell *et al.*, *op. cit.*, chap. 5.

should be *exhaustive* in that all individuals should fit in one of the categories, and *mutually exclusive* to eliminate ambiguity about trying to fit a given person into a single category. Concepts which meet these minimum criteria are at the lowest level of measurement. The concepts are called *classificatory* and the level of measurement is called *nominal*.[15]

Once we have established a proper classification system, we may discover that a case exhibits more or less of the property in question than another case. Suppose we examine the cases which fit into the category of Democratic identifiers. You will remember that we suggested a follow-up question which asked for the degree or strength of partisan attachment. Based on this question, individuals could be ranked or ordered as either strong Democrats or weak Democrats. Applying this kind of reasoning to the first three categories in our classification of partisan identifiers, we could arrive at measures of the strength of partisan identification such as those illustrated in Figure 3–2. Concepts which can be used for such comparisons are called *comparative* concepts and the corresponding level of measurement is called *ordinal*.[16]

FIGURE 3–2
Strength of Partisan Identification as Comparative Concepts

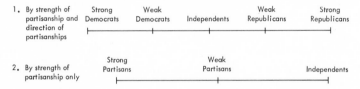

The next level of measurement of a concept is to be able to say how much more or less of the property a particular case has. With respect to our example, this would mean that not only could we say that one individual was a stronger partisan than another, but how much stronger in terms of a unit of measurement. That is, if we could determine the "distance" between a strong Democrat and a weak Democrat and an independent, and so on, we would have an interval scale. If concepts meet this kind of criterion (and our measure of partisan identification does not), they are called *quantitative* concepts and the level of measurement is *interval*.[17]

The final level of measurement is called a *ratio scale*. The ratio scale

[15] Alan C. Isaak, *Scope and Methods of Political Science* (Homewood, Ill.: Dorsey Press, 1969), pp. 72–73, and Hayward R. Alker, *Mathematics and Politics* (New York: Macmillan Co., 1965), pp. 19–20.

[16] Isaak, *op. cit.*, pp. 73–75; Alker, *op. cit.*, pp. 20–21.

[17] Isaak, *op. cit.*, pp. 75–77, and Alker, *op. cit.*, pp. 21–22.

is like the interval scale except that it has a true rather than an arbitrary zero point. An example may help to clarify the distinction. A temperature scale, such as Farenheit or centigrade, is an interval scale, because the zero point is arbitrary. For these scales, the idea of a complete absence of temperature does not make any sense. On the other hand, personal income can be considered a ratio scale; it is possible to define and measure a zero income. Normally, in contrast to temperature, the concept of "negative income" (income below zero) is not meaningful.

A concept is not intrinsically one type of concept or another.[18] Then how do we decide whether a concept definition is one level or another? The simple answer is that this is determined by how we measure the phenomena. However, this simple answer is not sufficient; for how we measure the concept depends upon our operational definition, and there may be a number of such acceptable definitions. In addition, we may feel some uncertainty regarding the level we are measuring. Are four violent acts, measured by the number of fatalities counted, four times one violent act? The difference between one violent act and zero violent acts for individuals may be greater than that between one and two violent acts. That is, it may be easier for individuals to initiate second and third violent acts after having initiated the first one than it would be for them to initiate the first violent act. Therefore, we might decide to assign the number zero to no violent acts, but the number four to two violent acts.

It is probably not immediately apparent why the level of measurement of a concept is important. The reason is that the arithmetical operations that can be performed on the numbers measuring the concepts are determined by the level of measurement. Perhaps some examples may clarify the point. Suppose that we had the following distribution of cases in the following nominal level categories: Republican identifiers, 25; independents, 15; Democratic identifiers, 60. How would we respond if someone asked for an average for these cases? Because the nominal level of measurement consists only of categories which are mutually exclusive and collectively exhaustive (there is no order to the categories and no "distance" between them), the only permissible arithmetic operation is to count the number of cases in each category. The average for these cases, then is the most frequently occurring category, Democratic identifiers. The term for this average is the mode. Now, suppose that we had the following ranking of cases in an ordinal scale: strong Democrat,

---

[18] We are only scratching the surface here of an ongoing controversy between the "purists" and others who disagree on the importance and the possibility of always being able to unambiguously determine the level of measurement. The importance of preserving the pure distinctions will be affected by finding that our conclusions differ with the level of measurement selected. Right now, research findings indicate that sometimes it does and sometimes it does not.

20; moderate Democrat, 25; weak Democrat, 30. Since this is a ranking, the appropriate average, called the median, is the middle case. In this instance, the middle case would occur among the 25 individuals grouped as moderate Democrats. Finally, suppose that we had the following data on income for six individuals: Robert, $2,000; Elizabeth, $2,500; Mary, $2,160; Judy, $2,100; Tom, $1,900; Chris, $2,300. Since income is at least an interval scale, all arithmetical operations are permissible. This means that we can add the scores together, divide by the number of individuals, and arrive at an average called the mean: $2,160 in this case. It should be apparent from these examples that interval and ratio scales are more desirable; nevertheless, they are difficult to achieve in the social sciences.

We must also distinguish the levels of analysis of the concepts we are working with. Concepts may refer to *micro* properties or *macro* properties. The term "micro" refers to the smallest unit that is being defined in a particular investigation; that unit may be an individual, a group, or a nation. Whatever the unit might be, it is "micro" because no smaller unit is being examined—for purposes of a given study, it is indivisible. "Macro" concepts, then, are those which are developed from the characteristics of individual micro units or the relationships among such units. We can use our example concept of partisan identification to illustrate the distinction. Suppose that the micro units under investigation were the registered voters of Sangamon County, Illinois. The partisan identification of each individual voter would be a micro property of that voter. A macro property of Sangamon County would be the distribution of partisan identification among the registered voters, i.e., the percentages of Democratic identifiers, Republican identifiers, independents, and so on, in that county.

Macro concepts are always relative to corresponding micro concepts and vice versa. Therefore, whether a concept is macro or micro depends on how you are looking at the problem. Using our same illustration, if the smallest unit of investigation were the counties of the state of Illinois, then a micro property of Sangamon County would be the distribution of partisan preferences and a macro property of the state of Illinois would be the distribution of partisan preferences for all voters in the state aggregated from the individual counties. Figure 3–3 illustrates the possible relationships between macro and micro concepts as determined by the units under consideration.

It would be misleading to conclude from these examples that macro concepts are always constructed through the simple aggregation of micro concepts. That is, in the examples, the macro properties are always the sums (or proportions of the totals) of the corresponding micro properties. Often some other rule of combination may make more sense. For example, if we want to be able to relate the partisanship of a particular macro unit to its tendency to vote for a certain candidate, we may want to

FIGURE 3–3
Levels of Analysis: Macro and Micro Concepts

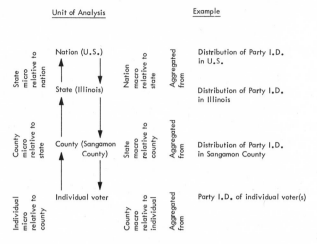

weight certain categories of partisans differentially because the groups have different voter turnout rates.

Although we will discuss at some length the importance of distinguishing macro from micro concepts later on, we will give some indication of the reasons for doing so here. The most important reason is that we often want to try to explain something which goes on at a macro level by something which goes on at a micro level (or vice versa). We try to explain, for example, characteristics of national political systems by the characteristics of the individuals who live in that system.[19] There are, however, potential fallacies in making easy inferences from one level to another. We must be aware of the macro-micro distinction and the fallacies associated with moving from one level to the other in order to avoid incorrect predictions and explanations.

A final set of distinctions must be made about concepts. We may speak of concepts as being either *attributes* or *variables*. An attribute is a property or characteristic of something which is either present or absent. For example, a person is either a male or he is not. An illustration of a political characteristic which is an attribute would be whether someone was a Democrat (Democratic Party identifier) or not.[20] A variable is a characteristic or property of something which varies in degree. For example, a thermometer measures the temperature of objects by degrees.

---

[19] As an illustration, we might explain the "aggressiveness" of a nation by the "aggressive nature" of its people. A little reflection should indicate the dangers of such an explanation. Is "aggressiveness" at the international level the same thing as "aggressiveness" among individuals?

[20] An attribute corresponds to what we have called the nominal level of measurement, and the same rules apply.

An illustration of a political characteristic which is a variable would be the percentage of Democratic Party identifiers in the years 1952 through 1972 in the United States.[21]

GENERALIZATIONS

To review: in the initial chapter, we suggested that the discovery of valid political generalizations is critical for accomplishing the goals of explanation, prediction, evaluation, and policy recommendation. In this chapter we began examining the characteristics of a systematic study of politics. Having considered the forms and requirements of concepts, the building blocks for the development of generalizations, we can now specifically consider the characteristics of scientific generalizations.

Earlier we defined empirical generalizations as being statements which relate two or more concepts and which, at least in principle, can be confirmed or refuted by experience (by reference to observable evidence). When we say that a generalization relates two or more concepts, our attention is directed to the question: What do we mean by a relationship? To explain this idea, we are going to introduce the important ideas of joint occurrence and concomitant variation. Let us examine joint occurrence first. Joint occurrence refers to relationships among attributes. Suppose that our generalization suggests that partisanship is related to voting behavior, i.e., that Democratic identifiers vote for the Democratic Party and Republican identifiers vote for the Republican Party. Verbally, this means that where the attribute "Democratic identifier" occurs, the attribute "voting Democratic" also occurs, and vice versa. It also means that where the attribute "Republican identifier" occurs, the attribute "Republican voter" also occurs, and vice versa. Visually, such a relationship can be seen in Table 3–1. In the table, all Democratic identifiers

TABLE 3–1
An Illustration of Joint Occurrence of Attributes

Voting	Partisan Identity	
	Democrat	Republican
Democratic.........	100%	0
Republican.........	0	100%

---

[21] A variable corresponds to the ordinal, interval, and ratio scales of measurement. Note that in the example given, the percentage of Democratic Party identifiers in the years 1952 through 1972 is a variable at the macro level. At an individual or micro level, whether one was a Democratic identifier or not would be an attribute. Can you think of a political variable at the individual level?

vote Democratic and all Republican identifiers vote Republican. This is an extreme, perfect (and unlikely) example of joint occurrence.

The idea of concomitant variation refers to the relationship among variables. Again, let us refer to an illustrative generalization: the degree of partisanship is positively related to the level of political activity. Let us suppose that scores on the variables of degree of partisanship and level of political activity range from zero to five, with five being a high score.[22] The hypothesis, in verbal translation, is predicting that as the degree of partisanship increases (as partisanship scores are higher), the level of political activity will also increase (the scores on partisanship will be higher). Visually, such a relationship can be seen in Figure 3–4. If the scores in Figure 3–4 had been measured on an interval scale, we

FIGURE 3–4
An Illustration of Concomitant Variation

Individuals	Score on Variable 1 (Partisanship)	Score on Variable 2 (Activity)
1	1	2
2	2	3
3	5	4
4	3	4
5	4	5

could plot them as in Figure 3–5. The pattern of the plots suggests that there is a regular, although imperfect, tendency for increases in partisanship to be related to increases in activity and vice versa. This is what is meant by concomitant variation. Notice that the third individual (3) does not fall on a straight line that we might draw going through the points.[23]

Generalizations in a given area (such as voting behavior) are ideally related or connected to each other—there is an ordering of generalizations from higher level ones to lower level ones. That is, generalizations vary in the scope of phenomena to which they refer. Thus, a generalization with more limited scope would be: individuals who strongly identify with the Republican Party tend to vote for presidential candidates of that party. "Individuals who strongly identify with any party tend to

---

[22] Our level of measurement is ordinal here, so the difference between scores of one and five is not defined to be the same as the difference between scores of one and two. This should be kept in mind with regard to the plotting of concomitant variation in Figure 3–5.

[23] Three questions may help you to understand concomitant variation better. First, what would no relationship look like? Second, what would a negative or inverse relationship look like? Finally, what would a perfect positive relationship look like?

FIGURE 3–5
Plotting Concomitant Variation

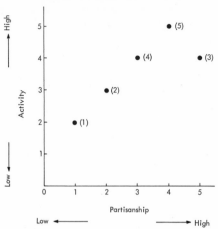

vote for candidates of that party" is a generalization of broader scope or applicability, because it does not refer to a specific political party or to a particular political office. More kinds of behavior can be subsumed under generalizations with broader scope than can be subsumed under generalizations with less scope. Again, if the generalization had been: individuals who strongly identify with the Republican Party in Illinois tend to vote for candidates of the Republican Party in Illinois, we would say that it had less scope because the range of phenomena which is covered has been significantly restricted to the state of Illinois.

We have just mentioned the scope of generalizations, and now we must introduce another distinction relative to the form of generalizations. This is the distinction between *universal* generalizations and *statistical* generalizations. A universal generalization has the form: all A's are B's. The claim of the generalization is that all members of a set relate to all members of another set: all Republican identifiers vote Republican. In contrast to the universal generalization, there is the statistical generalization of the form: some percent of A's are B's.[24] The claim is that some members of a set are related to some members of the other set: 90 percent of Republican identifiers vote Republican. Statistical generalizations, sometimes called probabilistic generalizations or tendency statements, may be more or less precise in their claims.[25] As we noted in

---

[24] Of course, a universal generalization is a special case of a statistical generalization; that is, a universal generalization is one which holds 100 percent of the time.

[25] Some might argue that this statement is unacceptable, for they require that all statistical statements include exact probabilities or percentages and reject the form, "Some Republican identifiers vote Republican." Generally, social scientists consider both forms to be statistical statements.

the first chapter of this book, virtually all of the generalizations we deal with in political science are statistical.

In concluding this brief section on generalizations, we need to distinguish three types of empirical generalizations: axioms, hypotheses, and laws. In any theoretical system,[26] there are generalizations which are not tested but which are taken as given. These may be called premises, assumptions, or axioms. They constitute the highest order of generalizations, most often those with the greatest scope, in a theoretical system. They are assumed to be true and are not tested directly.[27] An example of an axiom might be the assumption, common in some economic and political theories, that human behavior is basically guided by self-interest. Such a statement is never directly tested, but the implications of it are.

Hypotheses are lower order generalizations, which may be derived from axioms. Hypotheses are subjected to empirical scrutiny or testing.[28] Such an hypothesis might be: the strength of partisan identification is related to the consistency of party voting of individuals. In examining this hypothesis, we would, of course, have to follow the requirements that concepts be operationally defined and independent of each other. In Chapter 4 we examine the techniques by which political scientists subject hypotheses to empirical scrutiny. We refer to the rules and procedures by which we examine hypotheses as the "context of justification."

Some hypotheses are confirmed, or more accurately, not disconfirmed. If this is the case after extensive testing, we may call the generalization a law. A law is a very frequently confirmed empirical generalization. Laws may either be universal or statistical. It is sometimes assumed that statistical laws are somehow less "scientific" than universal ones. Since most of our generalizations are statistical, this assumption would reduce the scientific character of political science. One reason the assumption might seem plausible is that with statistical laws, we cannot explain or predict individual behavior. The "law" that 99 percent of strong Republicans vote for Republican candidates for President does not allow us to predict the behavior of an individual who strongly identifies with the Republican Party. Statistical laws, however, can be used to predict the outcome of collective events. Suppose that we know the statistical laws which relate degrees of partisan attachment to the Republican and Democratic parties to the propensity to vote Republican or Democratic and suppose that nothing else influences voting behavior.[29] Given the knowl-

---

[26] Theoretical systems will be examined in some detail in Chapter 6.

[27] They are still, in principle, empirical generalizations, and in other contexts could be tested.

[28] We say "may be derived from axioms" because axioms are frequently not discovered until a number of hypotheses have been repeatedly tested and confirmed.

[29] This is, of course, a dubious assumption.

edge of these laws and the turnout for each group, we could predict the outcome of the collective event—that is, the total vote for the Republican candidate. Thus, we could, with the knowledge of the appropriate statistical laws, predict the outcome of the election—no small achievement.

SUMMARY AND CONCLUSION

In this chapter we have discussed the nature of concepts and generalizations in political science. There are a series of important points to keep in mind from this chapter as we turn our attention to the techniques of inquiry in the next chapter:

1. Definitions of concepts are neither true nor false; they are more or less useful to the degree that they meet the requirements of "empirical import" and "significance."
2. Concepts may be distinguished by (1) their measurement properties (classificatory-nominal, comparative-ordinal, quantitative-interval, and ratio); (2) by the level of analysis (macro or micro); and (3) by the nature of the concepts (attribute or variable).
3. Generalizations relate concepts. Generalizations vary in scope and form (joint occurrence or concomitant variation, universal or statistical). Axioms are generalizations which are assumed within a theoretical system; hypotheses are testable generalizations; laws are confirmed generalizations.
4. The "context of justification" refers to the rules and procedures whereby we subject hypotheses to empirical scrutiny.

With these ideas in mind we will move to the consideration of hypothesis testing.

*attribute — only two possible values
up or down.*

chapter

4

Hypothesis testing and
analysis of examples

In the last chapter, we spoke of hypotheses as being testable generalizations. Now we are going to spell out the implications of that statement by examining some specific illustrations of how political scientists go about testing hypotheses. We will examine the specific techniques which are used in order to discuss the underlying logic of research. We do not intend to teach research methods here, but rather to suggest criteria for the evaluation of the substantive literature of political science employing these methods.

A LOGICAL SEQUENCE OF TESTING

At this point, we shall outline a series of steps in a *logical* sequence that a political scientist might move through. This same sequence provides a series of questions for you to ask as you approach any report of research. These steps are as follows:[1]

1. The specification of a general problem or problem area.
2. The development of hypotheses which relate to the general problem and its resolution.
3. The spelling out of the meanings of the key concepts. This includes both the conceptual and operational definitions of the concepts.
4. The selection of methods of investigating the hypotheses.
5. The analysis and interpretation of the data which has been collected.

---

[1] For a good discussion of the major steps of research, see Claire Selltiz *et al., Research Methods in Social Relations* (New York: Holt, Rinehart & Winston, 1951), especially chaps. 1 and 2.

6. The establishment of conclusions which relate the evidence to the general problem area.

This sequence is, of course, an idealized pattern and is not necessarily followed in particular research situations.[2]

In order to introduce hypothesis testing in political science, we are going to examine two particular pieces of research which are reprinted here. The first is Seymour Martin Lipset's pathbreaking study of economic development and political stability.[3] Let us turn to the article in Appendix A following this chapter and dissect it in terms of the sequence of hypothesis testing we just suggested.

Lipset's specification of the problem

Research has to begin somewhere, and often it begins with a problem or question—often a nagging problem (and, it is hoped, a problem of some theoretical or social significance). What is the problem that Lipset is attempting to deal with? As we examine the first part of the article, we note that Lipset begins by specifying a set of characteristics which *define* "democracy in a complex society." He is evidently interested in democratic political systems. He is not, however, merely interested in the problem of describing the incidence of democracy in political systems; i.e., the problem is not just one of description. What is really of concern to Lipset is the "problem of *stable* democracy." Fundamentally, Lipset is interested in an explanatory question: Why are some democratic systems stable and others unstable? What are the conditions which make for democratic stability? This problem becomes significant when we consider the fact that stable democratic systems are the exception, not the rule, in the history of democratic systems.

Lipset's hypotheses

The first difficulty in research is the conversion of general problems into more specific hypotheses. Seldom is a problem stated in researchable terms initially. At this point, a question may occur. Where do our hypotheses come from? Lipset tells us, for example, that "the more well-to-do a nation, the greater the chances that it will sustain democracy." This is the principal hypothesis which we will follow through our analysis

---

[2] For a discussion of recurring patterns in social research which do not necessarily fit the pattern we have indicated here, see Robert K. Merton, "The Bearing of Empirical Research upon the Development of Social Theory," *American Sociological Review*, Vol. 13 (October 1948), pp. 505–15.

[3] *Political Man: The Social Bases of Politics* (Garden City, N.Y.: Doubleday & Co., 1960).

of this research.[4] Lipset indicates that this hypothesis is derived from a long stream of literature on democratic societies going back at least to Aristotle. To point to the literature as a source for a hypothesis is probably a shortcut way of saying that either: (1) there is a theory which leads us to expect the hypothesis to be true or (2) there are observations of empirical relationships which suggest that the hypothesis is true. In reality, the source for a hypothesis is likely to be both of those approaches. In a later chapter, we will discuss "theory" in greater detail. It is sufficient to note here that the theoretical justification for the hypothesis that wealth will be related to democracy is the more general expectation that "only in a wealthy society in which relatively few citizens lived at the level of real poverty could there be a situation in which the mass of the population intelligently participate in politics and develop the self-restraint necessary to avoid succumbing to the appeals of irresponsible demagogues." This statement suggests that democracies require (1) mass participation and (2) "self-restraint" in order to survive. It may also be supposed that the hypothesis is supported by the observation that wealth and democracy tend to co-vary. It is the objective of research to provide more systematic evidence for that which we believe to be true on the basis of casual observation.

Lipset's conceptualization of democracy

We have now arrived at a hypothesis for investigation. The next stage of research is to specify the meanings for the concepts which appear in the generalization. The hypothesis is: "democracy is related to the state of economic development." We are going to focus on the question: What does Lipset mean by "democracy"? Although we will concentrate here on democracy, the same problems apply to a definition of "economic development."

There is no single, agreed-upon definition of democracy in political science.[5] Lipset makes it clear that he is talking about democracy at the national system level. His definition specifies a set of conditions which characterize democracy:

(1) a 'political formula or body of beliefs specifying which institutions— political parties, a free press, and so forth—are legitimate (accepted as proper by all); (2) one set of political leaders in office; and (3) one or more sets of recognized leaders attempting to gain office.

---

[4] The other major hypothesis links legitimacy to democratic stability. We have not treated that aspect of Lipset's argument here.

[5] For a discussion of the problems of defining democracy, see Charles Cnudde and Deane Neubauer, *Empirical Democratic Theory* (Chicago: Markham, 1969), Part I.

In short, this definition suggests that the key defining characteristics of national system democracy are a widespread belief in the legitimacy (rightness) of democratic institutions[6] and political competition.

In terms of our discussion in the previous chapter about the levels of concepts, it should be noted here that both democracy and economic development are macro level concepts—they refer to properties of systems which are constructed from other, micro, properties. We will see this more clearly when we examine how Lipset operationalizes his concepts.

One other decision that Lipset makes at the conceptual level is important here. In terms of the level of measurement of the concept, he decides to treat democracy as a nominal scale:

The precise dividing line between "more democratic" and "less democratic" is also not basic, since presumably democracy is not a unitary quality of a social system, but a complex of characteristics which may be ranked in many different ways. For this reason I have divided the countries under consideration into general categories, rather than attempting to rank them from highest to lowest. . . .

Although he uses the terms "more" and "less," Lipset is rejecting the use of an ordinal scale of democracy because of the problem of combining the various characteristics of democracy into a single dimension. This problem may be illustrated with the characteristics which Lipset uses to define democracy. Suppose one nation is "high" on legitimacy but "low" on political competition, while another nation is "low" on legitimacy but "high" on political competition. How should we rank one nation in comparison to the other? Are the dimensions equal in their contribution to democracy (in which case, we would rank the nations as equal), or is one more important than the other? Lipset chooses not to attack that question, but rather to provide a cruder, nominal set of categories for the European and English-speaking nations of the world. The categories are "stable democracies" and "unstable democracies and dictatorships."[7]

Lipset's operationalization of democracy

The next difficult decision is the translation of concept definitions into operational (empirical) definitions. As we discussed in Chapter 3,

---

[6] The fact that Lipset uses the concept of legitimacy as part of the conceptual definition of democracy casts some question over his other major hypothesis relating legitimacy to democracy. If legitimacy is part of the meaning of democracy (by definition), then the relationship asserted between legitimacy and democracy is circular (true by definition).

[7] Lipset's work has been criticized for failing to develop a more refined scale of democracy. See Phillips Cutright, "National Political Development," in Cnudde and Neubauer, *op. cit.*, pp. 193–209. Lipset's nominal scale results in the anomaly, for example, that France and Albania are grouped together.

we cannot reject hypotheses if they are not stated in operational terms. Specifically, this means that for Lipset to divide nations into "stable democracies" and "unstable democracies and dictatorships," he must provide a set of specific, empirical criteria. Using these criteria, we too must be able to make the same assignment of nations into one of the two categories. Lipset says:

> The main criteria used to define European democracies are the uninterrupted continuation of political democracy since World War I *and* the absence over the past twenty-five years of a major political movement opposed to the democratic "rules of the game."

The first criterion evidently refers to the dimension of political competition.

It is operationally unclear, however, because the phrase "uninterrupted continuation of political democracy" contains the concept, "political democracy," for which we presumably are trying to specify the operational meaning. How much political competition is necessary for there to be political democracy? Lipset does not say explicitly. As for the criterion relating to legitimacy, Lipset is more specific. A "major movement opposed to the democratic 'rules of the game' " is defined in the following way: "no totalitarian movement, either fascist or communist, received 20 percent of the vote during this time."

This is probably a good place to make a general point about the relationship between conceptual and operational definitions. Lipset's criterion of legitimacy (belief in the democratic "rules of the game") is, presumably, an attitude or set of attitudes which are widely shared in the population. Nevertheless, his operational indicator of the presence of legitimacy is the absence of totalitarian movements. This indicator is indirect—it does not directly tap the citizens' attitudes. It may be a good guess that systems with low legitimacy are more likely to have totalitarian parties. But this method of operationalizing legitimacy involves making the *assumption* of such a connection. The general point, then, is that often we have to (for practical reasons) make do with very indirect indicators of the concepts we want to measure.

Lipset's methods of data collection

In discussing operationalization, we touched on the problems of selecting methods of data collection. In short, a researcher must specify what he is studying and how he is going to study it. The *what* is a deceptively simple issue. Remember that the hypothesis suggested a relationship between economic development and political democracy. Are we going to study all of the democracies that have ever existed? If not, what criteria are we going to use to select the cases which we will study? Lipset chooses to study nations which have been political democracies in the 20th century. In addition, he decides to study only European, English-speaking, and Latin American nations. Finally, he separates the European and English-speaking nations from the Latin American nations in terms of his analysis.

Why are the questions related to what you are studying important? There are two major, and related, reasons. We are investigating *generalizations*. The what specifies the scope of our generalization from a given study. We cannot conclude from Lipset's study that the generalization relating economic development and democracy (if supported) is necessarily true for African or Asian nations, or for nations in the future, or for nations in the past. Moreover, we may find that although our generalization is supported within certain clusters of cases (in this case, nations) in our study, it is not supported in others. Part of the task of research is to specify the conditions under which generalizations may or may not hold. Thus, the relationship between economic development and political democracy may be fairly strong for nations in one area but not in another, or may be stronger for nations with less democratic development than for nations with more democratic development.[8]

There are many methods of gathering data. In this book, we do not propose to introduce or discuss the various methods which are available.[9] Therefore, it is crucial to remember that the methods used in the materials we shall discuss are only examples and that other techniques are used as well.

The method which Lipset uses is called "aggregate data analysis." The essential characteristic of this method is the collection and analysis of data which relates to the macro properties of systems rather than to the micro properties of individuals. Specifically, in the Lipset study, the indicators of wealth and economic development refer to characteristics of systems, such as per capita (or average) income, rather than to individuals.[10] Often, aggregate data has been gathered by someone else (such as the United Nations or the U.S. government) for other purposes. A major methodological problem of aggregate data analysis will be discussed in the following section concerning the analysis and interpretation of findings in the Lipset study.

Lipset's analysis and interpretation of data

We now turn to the actual analysis of the statistical data which Lipset has collected. In order to examine the analysis, we will use the ideas

---

[8] Neubauer, "Some Conditions of Democracy," in Cnudde and Neubauer, *op. cit.*, p. 231.

[9] For example, content analysis of communications materials.

[10] Of course, this aggregate measure is constructed from individual incomes.

of association and co-variation which we introduced earlier. Lipset's hypothesis suggests a positive association between stable democracy and economic development. In operational terms, this means that stable democracies should have higher levels of economic development than unstable democracies and dictatorships. This predicted relationship is illustrated in Figure 4–1.

FIGURE 4–1
The Economic Development–Democracy
Hypothesis

Stable Democracies	Unstable Democracies and Dictatorships
Higher Economic Development	Lower Economic Development

To fill in the data for testing the hypothesis, Lipset uses the following strategies. First, he uses multiple indicators of economic development by breaking that concept down into indices (or variables) of wealth, industrialization, education, and urbanization. He does not rely on a single, or even a few, aggregate indicators of economic development. The more indicators used, the more convincing is the supportive evidence for a hypothesis. Second, Lipset presents averages and ranges for the measures of economic development. The averages indicate the central tendencies (means) for the nations in the two categories on a given indicator. For example, the per capita income for the European and English-speaking democracies is $695, versus $308 for the European and English-speaking unstable democracies and dictatorships. The ranges indicate the variations among the nations in the various categories. The stable democracies have a range in per capita income of $420 to $1,453, while the unstable democracies and dictatorships have a range of $128 to $482. Using the data in this manner, it is clear that the general hypothesis of a positive relationship between economic development and political democracy is given strong support.

At this point, a number of methodological issues are raised by the analysis. Fundamentally, these issues are all tied to the question: Can we move beyond description of the relationship between economic development and political democracy to explanation? In short, can we infer a causal relationship between economic development and democracy? In order to discuss this question, we need to digress briefly to explain our use of the term "cause."

Often, in political science as in other sciences, we want to be able to say more than that there is a relationship between two things. We want to say something about causal relationships: Does economic development cause democracy or does democracy cause economic development?

Questions relating to causality are exceedingly complex, but it is our intention to suggest some of the major considerations here.

What do we mean when we say that something "causes" something else? What can we observe which allows us to infer a causal relationship? Clearly, there is nothing called "cause" to observe directly. We see some things happening and then others. One of the first cues to a causal relationship is when we observe association: systems with high economic development tend to be democratic, while systems with low economic development tend to be nondemocratic. But this is what we have just observed, and we indicated that evidence of association, by itself, was insufficient to demonstrate cause. Why? One reason is that the concomitant variation of economic development and political democracy does not demonstrate which is causing which. It could just as well be that democracy causes economic development. This suggests a second criterion: time order. For a causal relationship to exist, the presumed causal variable must come before the presumed caused variable in time.[11] But again we cannot attribute cause solely on the basis of association and time order. We run the risk of commiting the "post hoc" fallacy—after this, therefore, because of this.

In order to demonstrate causality, we must seek additional evidence. One type of evidence we seek is to eliminate the possibility that other factors are producing the observed relationship. This is called the search for "spuriousness." For example, someone might claim that Protestant religious values produce both economic development and political democracy; thus, the associations produced by Lipset are spurious. This argument is illustrated in Figure 4–2.

FIGURE 4–2
An Example of Spuriousness

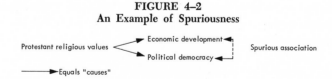

In order to determine whether an observed relationship is spurious, we need to introduce third factors which conceivably could be producing a spurious association. Because of the fact that we can never be certain that we have examined all of the possible disturbing factors, we also can never be certain that we have absolutely demonstrated a causal relationship.

---

[11] It is customary to call the causal variable the "independent" variable and the caused variable the "dependent" variable. This usage reflects the fact that the dependent variable depends on variations in the independent variable, but the independent variable is not dependent on the dependent variable—that is, the relationship is one-way or asymmetric.

Finally, even though we have demonstrated association, established time order, and checked for spuriousness, there is yet an additional criterion normally applied to causal relationships—that they make sense in some theoretical perspective. In effect, what this means is that we can provide an explanation for the presumed causal relationship. For example, if we assert that economic development has a causal role to play in producing political democracy, we want to have a reasonable explanation of why that should be the case. Nonsense correlations or correlations we cannot explain lead us to posit spuriousness or to look for the causal connections.

We return now to Lipset's interpretation of data. Three things are clear about that interpretation. First, Lipset's data will not support a causal interpretation that economic development causes political democracy. A major reason is that the time dimension is missing; we have static (single points in time) associations. Second, it is clear that Lipset does not attempt to use his data to demonstrate a causal relationship. By and large, he is careful to use the language of "association" or "relationship" in describing the findings.[12] Third, it is also clear that Lipset uses the data to speculate on causal relationships.

Lipset's interpretations of the causal relationships between economic development and political democracy are complex and subtle. His argument is that the relationships are reciprocal and multivariate. In simple terms, this means that, over time, economic development leads to political democracy, which in turn has other consequences which may facilitate economic development. In addition, once instituted, political democracy tends to have a life of its own. The concept of multivariate explanation means that Lipset feels (as do most contemporary social scientists) that political and social phenomena are likely to have multiple causes and multiple consequences. A simplified diagram of Lipset's argument can be found in Figure 4–3.[13]

FIGURE 4–3
Economic Development and Political Democracy: A Reciprocal and Multivariate Relationship

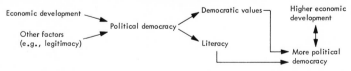

---

[12] The one exception is when he suggests that the evidence indicates that education is a "necessary condition" for democracy.

[13] One facet of Lipset's argument that is left out of the figure is his point that one of the consequences of democracy may be factors which actually weaken democracy in the long run. For example, he suggests that democracy may lead to increased bureaucracy, which may lead to less democracy.

Another important methodological point arises from a consideration of Lipset's interpretations. In order to explain the findings, he resorts to inferences about micro level phenomena. As an example, he speculates that "the general income level of a nation also affects its receptivity to democratic norms." In effect, he is arguing that it is easier to tolerate political defeat in a system characterized by more wealth than one characterized by less wealth. At the individual level, it might be argued that individuals with more income would be more receptive to democratic norms than those with less income. In fact, much evidence from data gathered on individuals would support that generalization. It would *not*, however, be legitimate to infer the micro level relationship from the observation of the macro level correlation or relationship between income and political democracy. The mistake of making such an inference is called an "ecological fallacy."[14] In this case, the fallacy is aggravated by the fact that it is not even legitimate to *assume* that democratic nations have higher proportions of people who subscribe to democratic norms. It is possible that the belief in democracy is not a necessary condition for democratic systems.[15]

One final methodological point can be teased out of an examination of Lipset's work. Although the regularity of the data supporting the hypothesis is impressive, Lipset recognizes that there are deviant cases which do not fit the general relationship. For example, he points out that "Germany and France have been among the best educated nations of Europe, but this by itself did not stabilize their democracies." This is an empirical illustration of the point that we have made previously: social science generalizations are likely to be probabilistic. It also reemphasizes the need to be concerned with multivariate explanations. Presumably, there were other factors which accounted for the "deviancy" of Germany and France.

Lipset's conclusions

What are the implications of the findings and interpretations of a study? It is at this point that research has its payoff. At least ideally, research is a cumulative and ongoing process. Specifically, Lipset was originally concerned with the problem of democratic stability. One important conclusion which he draws from his finding of the association

---

[14] William S. Robinson, "Ecological Correlations and the Behavior of Individuals," *American Sociological Review*, Vol. 15 (June 1950), pp. 351–57. Robinson points out, for example, that the macro level correlation between race and literacy (percentage black, percentage illiterate) was .95. At the individual level, the correlation was .20.

[15] See Herbert McClosky, "Consensus and Ideology in American Politics," *American Political Science Review*, Vol. 58 (June, 1964), pp. 361–82.

between economic development and democratic stability is that while it may appear that rapid industrialization and economic development is necessary for democratic development, such development induces strains in a society which may prevent democratic development. This view may ultimately lead us to be very pessimistic regarding the possibility for democratic development in the emerging nations, for they face a cruel dilemma: democracy requires economic development, but rapid economic development may threaten democracy.

A final comment on Lipset

Before we turn to the second study, we should stress that Lipset's research was an initial step in the process of investigating the relationship between economic factors and democratic stability. It was not the last word. A number of problems remained after this study was done, and a number remain still. In brief, these problems may be summarized as follows:

1. Studies need to be done which examine the relationships between economic development and political democracy over time.
2. Additional work needs to be done on the conceptualization and measurement of the concept "democracy."[16]
3. An assessment needs to be made of the *strength* of the relationship between economic development and democracy. Lipset's data merely shows that there is such a relationship.[17]
4. Work needs to be done connecting the macro level findings with micro phenomena such as democratic values.

To some degree, all of these questions have been studied. To some degree, the answers which we have are incomplete.

Lipset's study has served as a model for one type of hypothesis testing in political science. In particular, the Lipset study illustrates macro analysis, the problems of operationalization, some important methodological points, and comparative analysis. We turn now to a second research illustration to make some additional points about hypothesis testing.

McClosky's problem

The second article (in Appendix B of this chapter) used to illustrate hypothesis testing is by Herbert McClosky, Paul J. Hoffmann, and Rosemary O'Hara and concerns "Issue Conflict and Consensus among Party

---

[16] Cutright, *op. cit.*
[17] *Ibid.*

Leaders and Followers."[18] Again, we shall organize the analysis of this article using the logical sequence of research outlined at the beginning of this chapter. What is the general problem with which McClosky is concerned? As is typical, the general problem is specified early in the article. McClosky notes that a frequent criticism (or observation) of American political parties is that they do not differ from each other on significant political questions: "According to this view, each set of American party leaders is satisfied to play Tweedledee to the other's Tweedledum." McClosky points out that these observations are generally impressionistic, with "little systematic effort having been made to verify or refute them." The general problem flows directly from this observation: it is to *describe* the degree of ideological consensus or conflict between American party leaders and followers. This problem is significant, because we cannot make judgments about why American parties are the way they are until we are sure that they are the way we think they are. It might turn out that there are sharper differences between the parties than would be suggested by the stereotype of "Tweedledee and Tweedledum."

McClosky's hypotheses

McClosky expects the differences between American parties to be much sharper than commonly believed. Further, he differentiates between party leaders and followers and expects the leaders to differ more sharply than the followers. Therefore, two major descriptive hypotheses may be identified:

1. Republican Party adherents differ from Democratic Party adherents on significant public policy questions.
2. In comparison, Republican Party leaders differ more from Democratic Party leaders than Republican Party followers differ from Democratic Party followers.

As with Lipset, these hypotheses are not simply "pulled out of the air." McClosky bases these hypotheses on several theoretical expectations. For example, "We . . . thought that the competition for office, though giving rise to similarities between the parties, also impels them to diverge from each other in order to sharpen their respective appeals."

Conceptualization of party differences

The most important concept in the study is that of "differences on significant public policy questions." It is on these important questions

---

[18] Herbert McClosky, Paul J. Hoffman, and Rosemary O'Hara, "Issue Conflict and Consensus among Party Leaders and Followers," *American Political Science Review*, Vol. 54 (June, 1960), pp. 406–27. In referring to this article, we shall use the name of the senior author to avoid the tediousness of repeating three names.

that differences between the parties are expected to emerge. However, there is no single place in the article where the concept "significant public policy questions" is given a precise conceptual definition. This is in contrast to Lipset's early clarification of his use of the term "democracy." Nevertheless, it seems clear from the article that the differences are expected to be found on "major national issues" in five general areas: "public ownership, government regulation of the economy, equilitarianism and human welfare, tax policy and foreign policy." The criterion of selection seems to be that the "issues are so generalized as to encompass many other specific issues, and so highly charged as to awaken a profusion of symbolic and emotive associations." At the conceptual level, no attempt is made to spell out what "significant" differences are, and this will be an important point to consider below.

Operationalization of party differences

The operationalization of party differences offers us an opportunity to introduce another type of political research. Twenty-four specific issues were given to the subjects in the study, and they were asked to indicate "whether [they] believed support for each issue should be 'increased,' 'decreased,' or 'remain as is.'" Thus, the operationalization depended on measuring the preferences of the subjects in the study. This was done via a questionnaire.[19] At the outset, then, this study examines individual attitudes—the data is gathered on the *micro* level.

Ultimately, the measure of party differences is constructed from these micro level responses. As McClosky describes the construction, a "ratio of support" index is calculated for each issue in the following way. Suppose that on a given issue, out of 100 subjects, 75 people favored an increase in the program, 15 people favored a decrease, and 10 people said the program should remain as is. The index assigns a score of one to the "increase" responses, a score of zero to the "decrease" responses, and a score of one half to the "remain as is" response. Figure 4–4 shows how the ratio of support would be calculated for these hypothetical data. Ratio of support scores can vary between one (where everyone favored an increase) and zero (where everyone favored a decrease). The comparisons between groups (such as Republicans and Democrats) is then made by comparing the ratio of support scores for the two groups.

In terms of level of measurement, the ratio of support is an index which *assumes* that the intervals between "increase," "remain as is," and "decrease" are equal for the respondents. This assumption is made in the assignment of scores to the various categories to facilitate the computation of the average scores for the respective groups. Nevertheless, it

---

[19] For a discussion of the uses of questionnaires in social research, see William J. Goode and Paul K. Hatt, *Methods in Social Research* (New York: McGraw-Hill, 1952).

FIGURE 4–4
Calculation of the Ratio of Support

Subjects	No.	Score	Total
Increase	75	75 × 1	75
Decrease	15	15 × 0	0
As is	10	10 × 0.5	5
			80 = Total score for all subjects

$$\text{Ratio of support} = \frac{\text{Total score for all subjects}}{\text{Total number of subjects}} = \frac{80}{100} = 0.80$$

is the case that the index assumes an interval measure, but evidence is not presented that the weighting is justified.

The weighting system does, however, provide for a convenient interpretation of the ratio of support scores for the various groups: "0 to 0.25—strongly wish to reduce support; 0.26 to 0.45—wish to reduce support; 0.46 to 0.55—satisfied with the status quo; 0.56 to 0.75—wish to increase support; and 0.76 to 1—strongly wish to increase support." In effect, this interpretation collapses the interval scale index into a set of ordinal categories.[20]

Two other points are worth making about the operationalization of the idea of party differences. First, as Lipset does with economic development, McClosky uses multiple indicators which allow him to examine differences across a range of types of issues and a range of more specific items within the types. Second, the concept of party differences could, of course, have been operationalized in some other way. For example, McClosky might have examined party platforms, or party behavior in the government. What differences in interpretation might have resulted from a different operationalization of party differences?

McClosky's methods

In the case of this study, the questions about methods have to do with who is studied and how they are studied. The general hypotheses have to do with party differences and with party leaders versus party followers. To study party leaders, McClosky "turned to the Democratic and Republican national conventions, largely because they are the leading and most representative of the party organs, their delegates coming from every part of the United States and from every level of party and government activity." Questionnaires were distributed to all of the delegates

---

[20] It should be apparent that the choice of the precise dividing points depends in part on the scoring system, and therefore is also arbitrary.

and alternates to the 1956 national conventions, and somewhat less than half of them responded.[21] The concept of party follower was operationalized in the following way. Two national cross-sectional surveys were conducted which yielded a sample of approximately 1,500 people. These respondents were asked to indicate their partisan affiliation: "Forty respondents could not be identified as adherents of either party." Therefore, the "who" in this study can be summarized as in Figure 4–5. These

FIGURE 4–5
McClosky's Operationalization of Party Leaders and Followers

Democratic Party		Republican Party	
Leaders	Followers	Leaders	Followers
Delegates and alternates to the 1956 presidential nominating convention ($n = 1,788$)	National cross-sectional samples of Democratic partisans ("pure" Democrats, $n = 629$; "independent" Democrats, $n = 192$; total $n = 821$)	Delegates and alternates to the 1956 presidential nominating convention ($n = 1,232$)	National cross-sectional samples of Republican partisans ("pure" Republicans, $n = 479$; "independent" Republicans, $n = 144$; total $n = 623$)

are the groups which will be compared in the analysis of party differences. It is important to note that, as with the Lipset choices of what nations to study in what time period, these choices limit the generalizations which can be made in terms of time and respondents.

The method of study used by McClosky is the survey.[22] Surveys have become one of the most frequently used research techniques in the social sciences. Surveys enable one to gather relatively large amounts of information on relatively large numbers of people in a relatively efficient manner. A survey involves asking people questions in a systematic manner and providing a means of recording the responses. Fundamentally, there are two types of surveys: self-administered questionnaires (which were used in this study) and interviews. In the interview, the interviewer asks the questions and records the responses.

A number of problems arise with the use of surveys. One problem

---

[21] No evidence is presented on whether the delegate respondents are "representative" of the entire group of delegates. Such evidence is cited in support of the representatives of the cross-sectional samples on sex, age, region, size of city, and party affiliation.

[22] See Charles H. Backstrom and Gerald D. Hursch, *Survey Research* (Evanston, Ill.: Northwestern University Press, 1963).

is that of "sampling."[23] Often, we cannot interview the total group of people that we wish to generalize about in our conclusions. This is the case, for example, when we want to talk about Democratic and Republican Party followers. Patently, we cannot interview all of these individuals in the United States. We must, therefore, be concerned that our method of sampling will allow us to generalize to the larger population. Techniques have been developed which permit the generalization from a sample to a larger population. While the specific procedures for drawing a proper sample are best explored in sources devoted entirely to the subject,[24] we need to call attention to the problem of sampling, for it arises again in the interpretation of the findings.

A second problem of surveys is that the data gathered may either contain certain errors or may not permit the kinds of inferences which we wish to make. As an example of such errors, we may note that relying on the responses of the subjects does not eliminate the possibility of incorrect information due to faulty memory, distortion, or even outright lying. Many procedures have been developed to handle these problems.[25]

As an example of the possibility that the data may not be adequate to the problem, note that the attitudes expressed on the survey may not reflect behaviors which we wish to predict. McClosky was aware of this possible criticism of his study:

. . . one may wonder about the value of opinions stated on a questionnaire compared with the worth of views formally expressed by an organization or implicit in the actions of its leaders. . . . The beliefs expressed in official party statements or in legislative roll calls, it might be claimed, represent the *operating* beliefs of the organization. . . . Positions taken on issues on which a party stakes its future may be more valid evidence of what the party truly believes than are the opinions expressed by individual members under conditions of maximum safety. On the other hand, the responses to the issue and attitude questions in the PAB study represent the anonymous, private opinions of party leaders and followers, uncomplicated by a need to make political capital, to proselytize, to conciliate critics, or to find grounds for embarrassing the opposition at the next election. Hence they may for some purposes represent the most accurate possible reflection of the "actual" state of party opinion.

The resolution of this kind of problem depends upon whether you think that the survey method adequately taps the concept (in this case, party differences) which you want to study.[26]

---

[23] Sampling, of course, is not a problem peculiar to surveys. In the Lipset example, the selection of nations to study is also a sampling problem.

[24] For an introduction to the topic, see Backstrom and Hursh, *op. cit.*, chap. 2.

[25] For a good discussion of survey methodology and problems associated with it, see Herbert Hyman, *Survey Design and Analysis* (New York: Free Press, 1955).

[26] For example, is the concept "party difference" more concerned with "private" or "public" opinion of parties?

McClosky's analysis and interpretation of data

McClosky engages in extensive analysis of his data, and his interpretations are challenging, subtle, and important. We shall examine only a small, but basic, part of that analysis here, limiting our comments to findings reported in Table B–1 of his study. The table presents the average differences in ratio of support scores for the various groupings of the study across the five issue categories. Then, a summary measure is presented which is the average difference for all five categories. How are these data calculated? The steps may be summarized using differences between Democratic leaders and Republican leaders on the issue of "Public ownership of resources" as an example.

In Table B–2–A of McClosky's study, we find that there are two items relating to public ownership of resources, one having to do with natural resources and the other with atomic energy. A ratio of support score is calculated for each item. Then, an average ratio of support score is calculated for both Democratic and Republican leaders. Finally, the difference between the two is calculated and that figure becomes the first entry in the upper left-hand corner of Table B–1 of his study. Figure 4–6 outlines these steps. Each of the average differences in Table

FIGURE 4–6
Calculation of Differences in Ratios of Support for Public Ownership

	Leaders Favoring	
Public Ownership Issues	*Dem.*	*Rep.*
1. Natural resources...................	0.69	0.30
2. Atomic energy......................	0.83	0.65
Average support for public ownership........	0.76	0.48
Average difference: 0.76 − 0.48 = 0.28		

B–1 is calculated in the same way. The final, summary, measures at the bottom of the table are, as indicated previously, averages of the data for all five issue categories. It is these figures we wish to examine.

We began with two descriptive hypotheses. The first was that Republican Party adherents differ from Democratic Party adherents on significant public policy questions. This hypothesis directs us to look at the differences in Table B–1. Is the hypothesis supported? Figure 4–7 summarizes these comparisons. In all cases, the differences are greater than zero (a zero difference would be the expectation if the parties were precisely the same). Comparatively speaking, the differences between Democratic leaders and Republican leaders and between Republican lead-

FIGURE 4–7
Party Differences

	Dem. Leaders v. Rep. Leaders	Dem. Followers v. Rep. Followers	Dem. Leaders v. Rep. Followers	Rep. Leaders v. Dem. Followers
Average difference in ratio of support for all categories.......	0.21	0.04	0.08	0.20

ers and Democratic followers are the largest (approximately 0.20). But these observations only raise the question, what is a significant difference?

One approach to the question is to test for statistical significance. The idea of "statistical significance" relates to a problem created by sampling. The problem is that the differences we observe could be due to sampling error, the error which results from the process of selecting a sample instead of studying the whole group. Thus, the 0.04 difference between Democratic followers and Republican followers could simply be due to sampling error. The concept of statistical significance relates to the attempt to reject the hypothesis that the observed differences are only due to sampling error.[27] To say that a difference is statistically significant is to say that we can reject the hypothesis that the observed differences are due to sampling error (given a level of confidence expressed in probability terms) because the observed differences are sufficiently large. McClosky tells us (in footnote 13) that "unless otherwise indicated, all the differences reported are statistically significant at or beyond the .01 level." This means that there is just one chance in one hundred that the observed differences are an artifact of the sampling process.

Is it sufficient to know that the differences are statistically significant? Relatively small differences (in terms of the relative magnitudes) turn out to be statistically significant. In terms of other criteria, the differences between Democratic followers and Republican followers are not very sharp. First, as we noted, those differences are considerably less than others reported, e.g., those between Republican and Democratic leaders. Second, the support ratios for Democratic and Republican followers generally fall within the same ordinal categories which McClosky proposed for interpretation.[28] For example, in Table B–2–A of his article, both

---

[27] The hypothesis of "no difference" is called a "null hypothesis." For a discussion, see Herbert Blalock, *Social Statistics* (New York: McGraw-Hill, 1960), p. 121; or Dennis J. Palumbo, *Statistics in Political and Behavioral Science* (New York: Appleton-Century-Crofts, 1969), pp. 117–19.

[28] In fact, if we used these categories, on the assumption that the ratio of support was only an ordinal scale, we would conclude that there was no difference between Republican and Democratic followers. This is an instance where the measurement level makes a difference.

Democratic and Republican followers fall in the "wish to increase support" category on public ownership issues. Third, the differences are slight in comparison to what they theoretically might be under conditions of maximum party difference (what would the maximum party difference be?). These observations prompt two additional comments. One is that the decision on whether differences between Democrats and Republicans are significant within a system must, to some degree, be arbitrary—depending upon what we believe is a truly "significant" difference. The second is that the decision would be less arbitrary if we had some additional bases of comparison. We know that party leaders are more sharply divided than party followers. What do other political systems look like in terms of party differences?

On the basis of the descriptive evidence, we can say that Republicans and Democrats do generally differ on these policy questions. In examining the concept of difference, we have also noted that the second hypothesis is confirmed: party leaders diverge more sharply than party followers. It is this finding which forms the basis for a major conclusion of the McClosky article to which we will turn shortly.

McClosky interprets the findings of sharper differences among party leaders in the following vein:

1. The greater ideological sophistication and coherency of beliefs of the leaders.
2. The greater partisan commitment and political involvement of the leaders.
3. The relatively smaller size of the leadership group.
4. The effects of political competition.

McClosky's conclusions

McClosky's major conclusion is that the stereotype of the two parties (at the leadership level) as identical is not supported: "Examination of the opinions of Democratic and Republican leaders shows them to be distinct communities of co-believers who diverge sharply on many important issues." A secondary conclusion is that the party leadership diverges more sharply than does the general population. This provides the basis for the observation that "little support was found for the belief that deep cleavages exist in the electorate but are ignored by the leaders." The import of this finding is that those who argue that the parties ought to take sharp and opposing stands on public issues (the "choice, not an echo" argument) cannot rest their case on the argument that these stands would reflect divisions in the electorate submerged by the present party system. In fact, it could be argued from McClosky's data that the Republican Party actually deviates from its followers significantly in the conservative direction ("Republican followers, in fact, disagree far more with their own leaders than with the leaders of the Democratic Party").

A final comment on McClosky

This study was chosen because it illustrated survey research, construction of measures at the micro level, and some problems of sampling and sampling error. As with the Lipset article, additional questions are raised by the research. Included are these: (1) What would the findings be if we examined a different group of party leaders? and (2) Do the findings hold up over time? This research produced findings which not only are interesting from a theoretical and academic point of view, but which have implications for those interested in questions of party reform in the United States.

CONCLUSIONS

In this chapter, we have examined the logical sequence of research by focusing on two research reports in political science. We have not tried to illustrate all types of research, but these two articles are not unrepresentative of what you will find in the political science literature. Neither have we tried to cover every aspect of the articles. What we have done is to provide a general framework and, by example, an indication of some of the major problems which arise in research.

In conclusion, we can summarize this chapter by repeating the steps of analyzing research with the examples from the two articles:

Major Steps in Research	Lipset	McClosky
1. Specification of a general problem.	1. Explanation: What are the conditions of democratic stability?	1. Description: Do American parties differ?
2. Hypothesis development.	2. Economic development associated with democratic stability.	2. Parties do differ. Leaders differ more than followers.
3. Conceptualization.	3. Democracy.	3. Party differences.
4. Operationalization.	4. Competition, rules of the game.	4. Support ratios.
5. Methods.	5. Aggregate data analysis.	5. Survey.
6. Analysis and interpretation.	6. Hypothesis supported.	6. Hypothesis supported.
7. Conclusions.	7. Democracy difficult in emerging nations.	7. Party system does not suppress divisions in electorate.

The identification of the decision points must be made before attempting to understand why the decisions were made the way they were and what consequences these decisions have for the interpretation and applicability of the findings.

appendix
A

Economic development
and democracy*

SEYMOUR MARTIN LIPSET

The conditions associated with the existence and stability of democratic society have been a leading concern of political philosophy. In this paper[1] the problem is attacked from a sociological and behavioral standpoint, by presenting a number of hypotheses concerning some social requisites for democracy, and by discussing some of the data available to test these hypotheses. In its concern with conditions—values, social institutions, historical events—external to the political system itself which sustain different general types of political systems, the paper moves outside the generally recognized province of political sociology. This growing field has dealt largely with the internal analysis of organizations with political goals, or with the determinants of action *within* various political institutions, such as parties, government agencies, or the electoral process.[2] It

* This appeared as a portion of an article titled "Some Social Requisites of Democracy: Economic Development and Political Legitimacy" in *American Political Science Review*, Vol. 53 (March 1959), pp. 69–105. Reprinted by permission of the American Political Science Association.

[1] This paper was written as one aspect of a comparative analysis of political behavior in western democracies which is supported by grants from the Behavioral Sciences Division of the Ford Foundation and the Committee on Comparative Politics of the Social Science Research Council. Assistance from Robert Alford and Amitai Etzioni is gratefully acknowledged. It was originally presented at the September 1958 meetings of the American Political Science Association in St. Louis, Missouri.

[2] See my "Political Sociology, 1945–1955," in Hans L. Zetterberg, ed., *Sociology in the USA* (Paris: UNESCO, 1956), pp. 45–55, for a summary of the various areas covered by political sociology. For a discussion of intellectual trends in political sociology and the rationale underlying a focus on the problem of democracy, see my "Political Sociology," in R. K. Merton, *et al.*, eds., *Sociology Today* (New York: Basic Books, 1959), ch. 3.

has in the main left to the political philosopher the larger concern with the relations of the total political system to society as a whole.

INTRODUCTION

A sociological analysis of any pattern of behavior, whether referring to a small or a large social system, must result in specific hypotheses, empirically testable statements. Thus, in dealing with democracy, one must be able to point to a set of conditions that have actually existed in a number of countries, and say: democracy has emerged out of these conditions, and has become stabilized because of certain supporting institutions and values, as well as because of its own internal self-maintaining processes. The conditions listed must be ones which differentiate most democratic states from most others.

A recent discussion by a group of political theorists on the "cultural prerequisites to a successfully functioning democracy" points up the difference between the approach of the political sociologists and the political philosopher to a comparable problem.[3] A considerable portion of this symposium is devoted to a debate concerning the contribution of religion, particularly Christian ethics, toward democratic attitudes. The principal author, Ernest Griffith, sees a necessary connection between the Judeo-Christian heritage and attitudes which sustain democratic institutions; the other participants stress the political and economic conditions which may provide the basis for a consensus on basic values which does not depend on religion; and they point to the depression, poverty, and social disorganization which resulted in fascism in Italy and Germany, in spite of strongly religious populations and traditions. What is most striking about this discussion is its lack of a perspective which assumes that theoretical propositions must be subject to test by a systematic comparison of *all* available cases, and which treats a deviant case properly as one case out of many. In this symposium, on the contrary, deviant cases which do not fit a given proposition are cited to demonstrate that there are *no* social conditions which are regularly associated with a given complex political system. So the conflicts among political philosophers about the necessary conditions underlying given political systems often lead to a triumphant demonstration that a given situation clearly violates the thesis of one's opponent, much as if the existence of some wealthy socialists, or poor conservatives, demonstrated that economic factors were not an important determinant of political preference.

The advantage of an attempt such as is presented here, which seeks to dissect the conditions of democracy into several interrelated variables,

---

[3] Ernest S. Griffith, John Plamenatz, and J. Roland Pennock, "Cultural Prerequisites to a Successfully Functioning Democracy: A Symposium," *American Political Science Review*, Vol. 50 (1956), pp. 101–37.

is that deviant cases fall into proper perspective. The statistical preponderance of evidence supporting the relationship of a variable such as education to democracy indicates that the existence of deviant cases (such as Germany, which succumbed to dictatorship in spite of an advanced educational system) cannot be the sole basis for rejecting the hypothesis. A deviant case, considered within a context which marshals the evidence on all relevant cases, often may actually strengthen the basic hypothesis if an intensive study of it reveals the special conditions which prevented the usual relationship from appearing.[4] Thus, electoral research indicates that a large proportion of the more economically well-to-do leftists are underprivileged along other dimensions of social status, such as ethnic or religious position.

Controversy in this area stems not only from variations in methodology, but also from use of different definitions. Clearly in order to discuss democracy, or any other phenomenon, it is first necessary to define it. For the purposes of this paper, democracy (in a complex society) is defined as a political system which supplies regular constitutional opportunities for changing the governing officials. It is a social mechanism for the resolution of the problem of societal decision-making among conflicting interest groups which permits the largest possible part of the population to influence these decisions through their ability to choose among alternative contenders for political office. In large measure abstracted from the work of Joseph Schumpeter and Max Weber,[5] this definition implies a number of specific conditions: (a) a "political formula," a system of beliefs, legitimizing the democratic system and specifying the institutions—parties, a free press, and so forth—which are legitimized, i.e., accepted as proper by all; (b) one set of political leaders in office; and (c) one or more sets of leaders, out of office, who act as a legitimate opposition attempting to gain office.

The need for these conditions is clear. *First,* if a political system is not characterized by a value system allowing the peaceful "play" of

---

[4] A detailed example of how a deviant case and analysis advances theory may be found in S. M. Lipset, M. Trow, and J. Coleman, *Union Democracy* (Glencoe: The Free Press, 1956). This book is a study of the political process inside the International Typographical Union, which has a long-term two-party system with free elections and frequent turnover in office, and is thus the clearest exception to Robert Michels' "iron law of oligarchy." The research, however, was not intended as a report on this union, but rather as the best means available to test and amplify Michels' "law." The study could only have been made through a systematic effort to establish a basic theory and derive hypotheses. The best way to add to knowledge about the internal government of voluntary associations seemed to be to study the most deviant case. In the process of examining the particular historical and structural conditions sustaining the two-party system in the ITU, the general theory was clarified.

[5] Joseph Schumpeter, *Capitalism, Socialism and Democracy* (New York: Harper and Bros., 1947), pp. 232–302, esp. 269; Max Weber, *Essays in Sociology* (New York: Oxford University Press, 1946), p. 226.

power—the adherence by the "outs" to decisions made by "ins" and the recognition by "ins" of the rights of the "outs"—there can be no stable democracy. This has been the problem faced by many Latin American states. *Second,* if the outcome of the political game is not the periodic awarding of effective authority to one group, a party or stable coalition, then unstable and irresponsible government rather than democracy will result. This state of affairs existed in pre-Fascist Italy, and for much, though not all of the history of the Third and Fourth French Republics, which were characterized by weak coalition governments, often formed among parties which had major interest and value conflicts with each other. *Third,* if the conditions facilitating the perpetuation of an effective opposition do not exist, then the authority of officials will be maximized, and popular influence on policy will be at a minimum. This is the situation in all one-party states; and by general agreement, at least in the West, these are dictatorships.

Two principal complex characteristics of social systems will be considered here as they bear on the problem of stable democracy: economic development and legitimacy. These will be presented as structural characteristics of a society which sustain a democratic political system. After a discussion of the economic development complex (comprising industrialization, wealth, urbanization, and education) and its consequences for democracy, we shall move to two aspects of the problem of legitimacy, or the degree to which institutions are valued for themselves, and considered right and proper. The relations between legitimacy and the effectiveness of the system (the latter primarily a function of economic development) will be followed by a discussion of the sources of cleavage in a society and the ways in which various resolutions of historically crucial issues result either in disruptive forms of cleavage or in cross-cutting affiliations which reduce conflict to a manageable level. Finally, the bearing of these various factors upon the future of democracy will be assessed.

No detailed examination of the political history of individual countries will be undertaken in accordance with the generic definition, since the relative degree or social content of democracy in different countries is not the real problem of this paper. Certain problems of method in the handling of relationships between complex characteristics of total societies do merit brief discussion, however.

An extremely high correlation between aspects of social structure, such as income, education, religion, on the one hand, and democracy, on the other, is not to be anticipated even on theoretical grounds, because to the extent that the political sub-system of the society operates autonomously, a particular political form may persist under conditions normally adverse to the *emergence* of that form. Or, a political form may develop because of a syndrome of fairly unique historical factors, even though major social characteristics favor another form. Germany is an example of a nation in which the structural changes—growing industrialization, urbanization, wealth, and education—all favored the establishment of a democratic system, but in which a series of adverse historical events prevented democracy from securing legitimacy in the eyes of many important segments of society, and thus weakened German democracy's ability to withstand crisis.

The high correlations which appear in the data to be presented between democracy and other institutional characteristics of societies must not be overly stressed, since unique events may account for *either* the persistence *or* the failure of democracy in any particular society. Max Weber argued strongly that differences in national patterns often reflect key historical events which set one process in motion in one country, and a second process in another. To illustrate his point, he used the analogy of a dice game in which each time the dice came up with a certain number they were increasingly loaded in the direction of coming up with that number again.[6] To Weber, an event predisposing a country toward democracy sets a process in motion which increases the likelihood that at the next critical point in the country's history democracy will win out again. This process can only have meaning if we assume that once established, a democratic political system gathers some momentum, and creates some social supports (institutions) to ensure its continued existence. Thus a "premature" democracy which survives will do so by (among other things) facilitating the growth of other conditions conducive to democracy, such as universal literacy, or autonomous private associations. This paper is primarily concerned with explicating the social conditions which serve to *support* a democratic political system, such as education or legitimacy; it will not deal in detail with the kinds of internal mechanisms which serve to *maintain* democratic systems such as the specific rules of the political game.[7]

Comparative generalizations dealing with complex social systems must necessarily deal rather summarily with particular historical features of any one society within the scope of the investigation. In order to test

---

[6] Max Weber, *The Methodology of the Social Sciences* (Glencoe: The Free Press, 1949), pp. 182–185; see also S. M. Lipset, "A Sociologist Looks at History," *Pacific Sociological Review*, Vol. I (Spring 1958), pp. 13–17.

[7] See Morris Janowitz and Dwaine Marvick, *Competitive Pressure and Democratic Consent*, Michigan Governmental Studies, no. 32 (Bureau of Government, Institute of Public Administration, University of Michigan, 1956), and Robert A. Dahl, *A Preface to Democratic Theory* (University of Chicago, 1956), esp. pp. 90–123, for recent systematic efforts to specify some of the internal mechanisms of democracy. See David Easton, "An Approach to the Analysis of Political Systems," *World Politics*, Vol. 9 (1957), pp. 383–400, for discussion of problems of internal analysis of political systems.

these generalizations bearing on the differences between countries which rank high or low in possession of the attributes associated with democracy, it is necessary to establish some empirical measures of the type of political system. Individual deviations from a particular aspect of democracy are not too important, as long as the definitions unambiguously cover the great majority of nations which are located as democratic or undemocratic. The precise dividing line between "more democratic" and "less democratic" is also not a basic problem, since presumably democracy is *not* a quality of a social system which either does or does not exist, but is rather a complex of characteristics which may be ranked in many different ways. For this reason it was decided to divide the countries under consideration into two groups, rather than to attempt to rank them from highest to lowest. Ranking *individual* countries from the most to the least democratic is much more difficult than splitting the countries into two classes, "more" or "less" democratic, although even here borderline cases such as Mexico pose problems.

Efforts to classify all countries raise a number of problems. Most countries which lack an enduring tradition of political democracy lie in the traditionally underdeveloped sections of the world. It is possible that Max Weber was right when he suggested that modern democracy in its clearest forms can only occur under the unique conditions of capitalist industrialization.[8] Some of the complications introduced by the sharp variations in political practices in different parts of the earth can be reduced by dealing with differences among countries within political culture areas. The two best areas for such internal comparison are Latin America as one, and Europe and the English-speaking countries as the other. More limited comparisons may be made among the Asian states, and among the Arab countries.

The main criteria used in this paper to locate European democracies are the uninterrupted continuation of political democracy since World War I, *and* the absence over the past 25 years of a major political movement opposed to the democratic "rules of the game."[9] The somewhat less stringent criterion employed for Latin America is whether a given country has had a history of more or less free elections for most of the post-World War I period. Where in Europe we look for stable democracies, in South America we look for countries which have not had fairly constant dictatorial rule (see Table A–1). No detailed analysis of the political history of either Europe or Latin America has been made

---

[8] See Max Weber, "Zur Lage der burgerlichen Demokratie in Russland," *Archiv für Sozialwissenschaft und Sozialpolitik*, Vol. 22 (1906), pp. 346 ff.

[9] The latter requirement means that no totalitarian movement, either Fascist or Communist, received 20 percent of the vote during this time. Actually all the European nations falling on the democratic side of the continuum had totalitarian movements which secured less than seven percent of the vote.

TABLE A–1

Classification of European, English-Speaking and Latin American Nations by Degree of Stable Democracy

European and English-Speaking Nations		Latin American Nations	
Stable Democracies	Unstable Democracies and Dictatorships	Democracies and Unstable Dictatorships	Stable Dictatorships
Australia	Austria	Argentina	Bolivia
Belgium	Bulgaria	Brazil	Cuba
Canada	Czechoslovakia	Chile	Dominican Republic
Denmark	Finland	Colombia	Ecuador
Ireland	France	Costa Rica	El Salvador
Luxemburg	Germany (West)	Mexico	Guatemala
Netherlands	Greece	Uruguay	Haiti
New Zealand	Hungary		Honduras
Norway	Iceland		Nicaragua
Sweden	Italy		Panama
Switzerland	Poland		Paraguay
United Kingdom	Portugal		Peru
United States	Rumania		Venezuela
	Spain		
	Yugoslavia		

with an eye toward more specific criteria of differentiation; at this point in the examination of the requisites of democracy, election results are sufficient to locate the European countries, and the judgments of experts and impressionistic assessments based on fairly well-known facts of political history will suffice for Latin America.[10]

---

[10] The historian Arthur P. Whitaker, for example, has summarized the judgments of experts on Latin America to be that "the countries which have approximated most closely to the democratic ideal have been . . . Argentina, Brazil, Chile, Colombia, Costa Rica, and Uruguay." See "The Pathology of Democracy in Latin America: A Historian's Point of View," *American Political Science Review*, Vol. 44 (1950), pp. 101–118. To this group I have added Mexico. Mexico has allowed freedom of the press, of assembly, and of organization to opposition parties, although there is good evidence that it does not allow them the opportunity to win elections, since ballots are counted by the incumbents. The existence of opposition groups, contested elections, and adjustments among the various factions of the governing *Partido Revolucionario Institucional* does introduce a considerable element of popular influence in the system.

The interesting effort of Russell Fitzgibbon to secure a "statistical evaluation of Latin American democracy" based on the opinion of various experts is not useful for the purposes of this paper. The judges were asked not only to rank countries as democratic on the basis of purely political criteria, but also to consider the "standard of living" and "educational level." These latter factors may be conditions for democracy, but they are not an aspect of democracy as such. See Russell H. Fitzgibbon, "A Statistical Evaluation of Latin American Democracy," *Western Political Quarterly*, Vol. 9 (1956), pp. 607–619.

ECONOMIC DEVELOPMENT AND DEMOCRACY

Perhaps the most widespread generalization linking political systems to other aspects of society has been that democracy is related to the state of economic development. Concretely, this means that the more well-to-do a nation, the greater the chances that it will sustain democracy. From Aristotle down to the present, men have argued that only in a wealthy society in which relatively few citizens lived in real poverty could a situation exist in which the mass of the population could intelligently participate in politics and could develop the self-restraint necessary to avoid succumbing to the appeals of irresponsible demagogues. A society divided between a large impoverished mass and a small favored elite would result either in oligarchy (dictatorial rule of the small upper stratum) or in tyranny (popularly based dictatorship). And these two political forms can be given modern labels: tyranny's modern face is Communism or Peronism; oligarchy appears today in the form of traditionalist dictatorships such as we find in parts of Latin America, Thailand, Spain, or Portugal.

As a means of concretely testing this hypothesis, various indices of economic development—wealth, industrialization, urbanization, and education—have been defined, and averages (means) have been computed for the countries which have been classified as more or less democratic in the Anglo-Saxon world and Europe and Latin America.

In each case, the average wealth, degree of industrialization and urbanization, and level of education is much higher for the more democratic countries, as the data presented in Table A–2 indicate. If we had combined Latin America and Europe in one table, the differences would have been greater.[11]

---

[11] Lyle W. Shannon has correlated indices of economic development with whether a country is self-governing or not, and his conclusions are substantially the same. Since Shannon does not give details on the countries categorized as self-governing and non-self governing, there is no direct measure of the relation between "democratic" and "self-governing" countries. All the countries examined in this paper, however, were chosen on the assumption that a characterization as "democratic" is meaningless for a non-self-governing country, and therefore, presumably, all of them, whether democratic or dictatorial, would fall within Shannon's "self-governing" category. Shannon shows that underdevelopment is related to lack of self-government; my data indicate that once self-government is attained, development is still related to the character of the political system. See Shannon (ed.), *Underdeveloped Areas* (New York: Harper, 1957), and also his article, "Is Level of Government Related to Capacity for Self-Government?" *American Journal of Economics and Sociology*, Vol. 17 (1958), pp. 367–382. In the latter paper, Shannon constructs a composite index of development, using some of the same indices, such as inhabitants per physician, and derived from the same United Nations sources, as appear in the tables to follow. Shannon's work did not come to my attention until after this paper was prepared, so that the two papers can be considered as separate tests of comparable hypotheses.

The main indices of wealth used here are per capita income, number of persons per motor vehicle and per physician, and the number of radios, telephones, and newspapers per thousand persons. The differences are striking on every score, as Table A–2 indicates in detail. In the more democratic European countries, there are 17 persons per motor vehicle compared to 143 for the less democratic countries. In the less dictatorial Latin American countries there are 99 persons per motor vehicle, as against 274 for the more dictatorial ones.[12] Income differences for the groups are also sharp, dropping from an average per capita income of $695 for the more democratic countries of Europe to $308 for the less democratic ones; the corresponding difference for Latin America is from $171 to $119. The ranges are equally consistent, with the lowest per capita income in each group falling in the "less democratic" category, and the highest in the "more democratic" one.

Industrialization—indices of wealth are clearly related to this, of course—is measured by the percentage of employed males in agriculture, and the per capita commercially produced "energy" being used in the country, measured in terms of tons of coal per person per year. Both of these indices show equally consistent results. The average percentage of employed males working in agriculture and related occupations was 21 in the "more democratic" European countries, and 41 in the "less democratic," 52 in the "less dictatorial" Latin American countries, and 67 in the "more dictatorial." The differences in per capita energy employed in the country are equally large.

The degree of *urbanization* is also related to the existence of democracy.[13] Three different indices of urbanization are available from data

---

[12] It must be remembered that these figures are means, compiled from census figures for the various countries. The data vary widely in accuracy, and there is no way of measuring the validity of compound calculated figures such as those presented here. The consistent direction of all these differences, and their large magnitude, is the main indication of validity.

[13] Urbanization has often been linked to democracy by political theorists. Harold J. Laski asserted that "organized democracy is the product of urban life," and that it was natural therefore that it should have "made its first effective appearance" in the Greek city states, limited as was their definition of "citizen." See his article "Democracy" in the *Encyclopedia of the Social Sciences* (New York: Macmillan, 1937), Vol. V, pp. 76–85. Max Weber held that the city, as a certain type of political community, is a peculiarly Western phenomenon, and traced the emergence of the notion of "citizenship" from social developments closely related to urbanization. For a partial statement of his point of view, see the chapter on "Citizenship," in *General Economic History* (Glencoe: The Free Press, 1950), pp. 315–338. It is significant to note that before 1933 the Nazi electoral strength was greatest in small communities and rural areas. Berlin, the only German city of over two million, never gave the Nazis over 25 percent of the vote in a free election. The modal Nazi, like the modal French Poujadist or Italian neo-Fascist today, was a self-employed resident of a small town or rural district. Though the communists, as a workers' party, are strongest in the working-class neighborhoods of large cities within countries, they have great electoral strength only in the less urbanized European nations, e.g., Greece, Finland, France, Italy.

TABLE A–2

A Comparison of European, English-Speaking and Latin American Countries, Divided into Two Groups, "More Democratic" and "Less Democratic," by Indices of Wealth, Industrialization, Education, and Urbanization[1]

A. Indices of Wealth

Means	Per Capita Income[2] in $	Thousands of Persons per Doctor[3]	Persons per Motor Vehicle[4]	Telephones per 1,000 Persons[5]	Radios per 1,000 Persons[6]	Newspaper Copies per 1,000 Persons[7]
European and English-Speaking Stable Democracies..........	695	.86	17	205	350	341
European and English-Speaking Unstable Democracies and Dictatorships...............	308	1.4	143	58	160	167
Latin American Democracies and Unstable Dictatorships........	171	2.1	99	25	85	102
Latin American Stable Dictatorships.....................	119	4.4	274	10	43	43
Ranges						
European Stable Democracies.....	420–1,453	.7– 1.2	3–62	43–400	160–995	242–570
European Dictatorships.........	128– 482	.6– 4	10–538	7–196	42–307	46–390
Latin American Democracies.....	112– 346	.8– 3.3	31–174	12– 58	38–148	51–233
Latin American Stable Dictatorships.....................	40– 331	1.0–10.8	38–428	1– 24	4–154	4–111

B. Indices of Industrialization

Means	Percentage of Males in Agriculture[8]	Per Capita Energy Consumed[9]
European Stable Democracies..................	21	3.6
European Dictatorships.......................	41	1.4
Latin American Democracies..................	52	.6
Latin American Stable Dictatorships............	67	.25
Ranges		
European Stable Democracies..................	6–46	1.4 –7.8
European Dictatorships.......................	16–60	.27–3.2
Latin American Democracies..................	30–63	.30–0.9
Latin American Stable Dictatorships............	46–87	.02–1.27

C. Indices of Education

Means	Percentage Literate[10]	Primary Education Enrollment per 1,000 Persons[11]	Post-Primary Enrollment per 1,000 Persons[12]	Higher Education Enrollment per 1,000 Persons[13]
European Stable Democracies.......	96	134	44	4.2
European Dictatorships............	85	121	22	3.5
Latin American Democracies.......	74	101	13	2.0
Latin American Dictatorships.......	46	72	8	1.3
Ranges				
European Stable Democracies.......	95–100	96–179	19–83	1.7–17.83
European Dictatorships............	55– 98	61–165	8–37	1.6– 6.1
Latin American Democracies.......	48– 87	75–137	7–27	.7– 4.6
Latin American Dictatorships.......	11– 76	11–149	3–24	.2– 3.1

TABLE A–2 (*Continued*)
D. Indices of Urbanization

Means	Per Cent in Cities over 20,000[14]	Per Cent in Cities over 100,000[15]	Per Cent in Metropolitan Areas[16]
European Stable Democracies...............	43	28	38
European Dictatorships....................	24	16	23
Latin American Democracies..............	28	22	26
Latin American Stable Dictatorships.........	17	12	15
Ranges			
European Stable Democracies...............	28–54	17–51	22–56
European Dictatorships....................	12–44	6–33	7–49
Latin American Democracies..............	11–48	13–37	17–44
Latin American Stable Dictatorships.........	5–36	4–22	7–26

[1] A large part of this table has been compiled from data furnished by International Urban Research, University of California, Berkeley, California.

[2] United Nations, Statistical Office, *National and Per Capita Income in Seventy Countries*, 1949, Statistical Papers, Series E, No. 1, New York, 1950, pp. 14–16.

[3] United Nations, *A Preliminary Report on the World Social Situation, 1952*, Table 11, pp. 46–48.

[4] United Nations, *Statistical Yearbook, 1956*, Table 139, pp. 333–338.

[5] *Ibid.*, Table 149, p. 387.

[6] *Ibid.*, Table 189, p. 641. The population bases for these figures are for different years than those used in reporting the numbers of telephones and radios, but for purposes of group comparisons, the differences are not important.

[7] United Nations, *A Preliminary Report . . .* , *op. cit.*, Appendix B, pp. 86–89.

[8] United Nations, *Demographic Yearbook, 1956*, Table 12, pp. 350–370.

[9] United Nations, *Statistical Yearbook, 1956*, Table 127, pp. 308–310. Figures refer to commercially produced energy, in equivalent numbers of metric tons of coal.

[10] United Nations, *A Preliminary Report . . .* , *op. cit.*, Appendix A, pp. 79–86. A number of countries are listed as more than 95 percent literate.

[11] *Ibid.*, pp. 86–100. Figures refer to persons enrolled at the earlier year of the primary range, per 1,000 total population, for years ranging from 1946 to 1950. The first primary year varies from five to eight in various countries. The less developed countries have more persons in that age range per 1,000 population than the more developed countries, but this biases the figures presented in the direction of increasing the percentage of the total population in school for the less developed countries, although fewer of the children in that age group attend school. The bias from this source thus reinforces the positive relationship between education and democracy.

[12] *Ibid.*, pp. 86–100.

[13] UNESCO, *World Survey of Education*, Paris, 1955. Figures are the enrollment in higher education per 1,000 population. The years to which the figures apply vary between 1949 and 1952, and the definition of higher education varies for different countries.

[14] Obtained from International Urban Research, University of California, Berkeley, California.

[15] *Ibid.*

[16] *Ibid.*

compiled by International Urban Research (Berkeley, California), the percentage of the population in places of 20,000 and over, the percentage in communities of 100,000 and over, and also the percentage residing in standard metropolitan areas. On all three of these indices of urbanization, the more democratic countries score higher than the less democratic, for both of the political culture areas under investigation.

Many have suggested that the better educated the population of a country, the better the chances for democracy, and the comparative data available support this proposition. The "more democratic" countries of Europe are almost entirely literate: the lowest has a rate of 96 percent, while the "less democratic" nations have an average literacy rate of 85 percent. In Latin America, the difference is between an average rate of 74 percent for the "less dictatorial" countries and 46 percent of the "more dictatorial."[14] The educational enrollment per thousand total population at three different levels, primary, post-primary, and higher educational, is equally consistently related to the degree of democracy. The tremendous disparity is shown by the extreme cases of Haiti and the United States. Haiti has fewer children (11 per thousand) attending school in the primary grades than the United States has attending colleges (almost 18 per thousand).

The relationship between education and democracy is worth more extensive treatment since an entire philosophy of democratic government has seen in increased education the spread of the basic requirement of democracy.[15] As Bryce wrote with special reference to Latin America, "education, if it does not make men good citizens, makes it at least easier for them to become so."[16] Education presumably broadens men's outlooks, enables them to understand the need for norms of tolerance, restrains them from adhering to extremist and monistic doctrines, and increases their capacity to make rational electoral choices.

The evidence bearing on the contribution of education to democracy is even more direct and strong in connection with individual behavior *within* countries, than it is in cross-national correlations. Data gathered by public opinion research agencies which have questioned people in different countries with regard to their belief in various democratic norms of tolerance for opposition, to their attitudes toward ethnic or racial minorities, and with regard to their belief in multi-party as against one-party systems have found that *the most important single factor differentiating those giving democratic responses from others has been education.* The higher one's education, the more likely one is to believe in democratic values and support democratic practices.[17] All the relevant studies indicate that education is far more significant than income or occupation.

---

[14] The pattern indicated by a comparison of the averages for each group of countries is sustained by the ranges (the high and low extremes) for each index. Most of the ranges overlap, that is, some countries which are in the low category with regard to politics are higher on any given index than some which are high on the scale of democracy. It is noteworthy that in both Europe and Latin America, the nations which are lowest on any of the indices presented in the table are also in the "less democratic" category. Conversely, almost all countries which rank at the top of any of the indices are in the "more democratic" class.

[15] See John Dewey, *Democracy and Education* (New York, 1916).

[16] Quoted in Arthur P. Whitaker, *op. cit.,* p. 112; see also Karl Mannheim, *Freedom, Power and Democratic Planning* (New York, 1950).

[17] See C. H. Smith, "Liberalism and Level of Information," *Journal of Educational Psychology,* Vol. 39 (1948), pp. 65–82; Martin A. Trow, *Right Wing Radicalism and Political Intolerance,* Ph.D. dissertation, Columbia University, 1957, p. 17; Samuel Stouffer, *Communism, Conformity and Civil Liberties* (New York, 1955), pp. 138–9; K. Kido and M. Suyi, "Report on Social Stratification and Mobility in Tokyo, . . . Mobility in Tokyo, III: The Structure of Social Consciousness," *Japanese Sociological Review* (January 1954), pp. 74–100.

These findings should lead us to anticipate a far higher correlation between national levels of education and political practice than in fact we do find. Germany and France have been among the best educated nations of Europe, but this by itself clearly did not stabilize their democracies. It may be, however, that education has served to inhibit other anti-democratic forces. Post-Nazi data from Germany indicate clearly that higher education is linked to rejection of strong-man and one-party government.[18]

If we cannot say that a "high" level of education is a sufficient condition for democracy, the available evidence does suggest that it comes close to being a necessary condition in the modern world. Thus if we turn to Latin America, where widespread illiteracy still exists in many countries, we find that of all the nations in which more than half the population is illiterate, only one, Brazil, can be included in the "more democratic" group.

There is some evidence from other economically impoverished culture areas that literacy is related to democracy. The one member of the Arab League which has maintained democratic institutions since World War II, Lebanon, is by far the best educated (over 80 percent literacy) of the Arab countries. In the rest of Asia east of the Arab world, only two states, the Philippines and Japan, have maintained democratic regimes without the presence of large anti-democratic parties since 1945. And these two countries, although lower than any European state in per capita income, are among the world's leaders in educational attainment. The Philippines actually ranks second to the United States in its proportion of people attending high school and university, while Japan has a higher level of educational attainment than any European state.[19]

Although the various indices have been presented separately, it seems clear that the factors of industrialization, urbanization, wealth, and educa-

---

[18] Dewey has suggested that the character of the educational system will influence its effect on democracy, and this may shed some light on the sources of instability in Germany. The purpose of German education, according to Dewey, writing in 1916, was "disciplinary training rather than . . . personal development." The main aim was to produce "absorption of the aims and meaning of existing institutions," and "thoroughgoing subordination" to them. This point raises issues which cannot be entered into here, but indicates the complex character of the relationship between democracy and closely related factors, such as education. See Dewey, *Democracy and Education, op. cit.*, pp. 108–110. It suggests caution, too, in drawing optimistic inferences about the prospects of democratic developments in Russia, based on the great expansion of education now taking place there.

[19] Ceylon, which shares with the Philippines and Japan the distinction of being the only democratic countries in South and Far Asia in which the Communists are unimportant electorally, also shares with them the distinction of being the only countries in this area in which a *majority* of the population is literate. It should be noted, however, that Ceylon does have a fairly large Trotskyist party, now the official opposition; and while its educational level is high for Asia, it is much lower than either Japan or the Philippines.

tion, are so closely interrelated as to form one common factor.[20] And the factors subsumed under economic development carry with it the political correlate of democracy.[21]

Before moving to a discussion of the inner connections between the development complex and democracy, mention may be made of a study of the Middle East, which, in its essential conclusions, substantiates these empirical relationships for another culture area. A survey of six Middle Eastern countries (Turkey, Lebanon, Egypt, Syria, Jordan, and Iran), conducted by the Columbia University Bureau of Applied Social Research in 1950–51, found high associations between urbanization, literacy, voting rates, media consumption and production, and education.[22] Simple and multiple correlations between the four basic variables were computed for all countries for which United Nations statistics were available, in this case 54. The multiple correlations, regarding each as the dependent variable in turn, are as follows:[23]

Dependent Variable	Multiple Correlation Coefficient
Urbanization	0.61
Literacy	0.91
Media Participation	0.84
Political Participation	0.82

In the Middle East, Turkey and Lebanon score higher on most of these indices than do the other four countries analyzed, and Lerner points out that the "great post-war events in Egypt, Syria, Jordan and Iran have been the violent struggles for the control of power—struggles

[20] A factor analysis carried out by Leo Schnore, based on data from 75 countries, demonstrates this. (To be published.)

[21] This statement is a "statistical" statement, which necessarily means that there will be many exceptions to the correlation. Thus we know that poorer people are more likely to vote for the Democratic or Labor parties in the U.S. and England. The fact that a large minority of the lower strata vote for the more conservative party in these countries does not challenge the proposition that stratification position is the main determinant of party choice, given the multivariate causal process involved in the behavior of people or nations. Clearly social science will never be able to account for (predict) all behavior.

[22] The study is reported in Daniel Lerner, *The Passing of Traditional Society* (Glencoe: The Free Press, 1958). These correlations are derived from census data; the main sections of the survey dealt with reactions to and opinions about the mass media, with inferences as to the personality types appropriate to modern and to traditional society.

[23] *Ibid.*, p. 63. The index of political participation was the percent voting in the last five elections. These results cannot be considered as independent verification of the relationships presented in this paper, since the data and variables are basically the same (as they are also in the work by Lyle Shannon, *op. cit.*), but the identical results using three entirely different methods, the phi coefficient, multiple correlations, and means and ranges, show decisively that the relationships cannot be attributed to artifacts of the computations. It should also be noted that the three analyses were made without knowledge of each other.

notably absent in Turkey and Lebanon, where the control of power has been decided by elections."[24]

One of Lerner's contributions is to point to the consequences, for overall stability, of disproportionate development in one direction or another, and the need for coordinated changes in all of these variables. Thus, he compares urbanization and literacy in Egypt and Turkey, and concludes that although Egypt is far more urbanized than Turkey, it is not really "modernized," and does not even have an adequate base for modernization, because literacy has not kept abreast. In Turkey, all of the several indices of modernization have kept pace with each other, with rising voting participation (36 percent in 1950), rising literacy, urbanization, etc. In Egypt, by contrast, the cities are full of "homeless illiterates," who provide a ready audience for political mobilization in support of extremist ideologies. On Lerner's scale, following the assumption of the functional interdependence of "modernization" factors, Egypt should be twice as literate as Turkey, since it is twice as urbanized. The fact that it is only half as literate explains, for Lerner, the "imbalances" which "tend to become circular and to accelerate social disorganization," political as well as economic.[25]

Lerner introduces one important theoretical addition, the suggestion that these key variables in the modernization process may be viewed as historical phases, with democracy a part of later developments, the "crowning institution of the participant society," one of his terms for a modern industrial society. His view on the relations between these variables, seen as stages, is worth quoting at some length:

The secular evolution of a participant society appears to involve a regular sequence of three phases. Urbanization comes first, for cities alone have developed the complex of skills and resources which characterize the modern industrial economy. Within this urban matrix develop both of the attributes which distinguish the next two phases—literacy and media growth. There is a close reciprocal relationship between these, for the literate develop the media which in turn spread literacy. But, literacy performs the key function

---

[24] *Ibid.*, pp. 84–85.

[25] *Ibid.*, pp. 87–89. Other theories of underdeveloped areas have also stressed the circular character of the forces sustaining a given level of economic and social development; and in a sense this paper may be regarded as an effort to extend the analysis of the complex of institutions constituting a "modernized" society to the political sphere. Leo Schnore's unpublished monograph, *Economic Development and Urbanization, An Ecological Approach*, relates technological, demographic and organizational (including literacy and per capita income) variables as an interdependent complex. Harvey Leibenstein's recent volume, *Economic Backwardness and Economic Growth* (New York, 1957), views "underdevelopment" within the framework of a "quasi-equilibrium" economic theory, as a complex of associated and mutually supportive aspects of a society, and includes cultural and political characteristics—illiteracy, the lack of a middle class, a crude communications system—as part of the complex. (See pp. 39–41.)

in the second phase. The capacity to read, at first acquired by relatively few people, equips them to perform the varied tasks required in the modernizing society. Not until the third phase, when the elaborate technology of industrial development is fairly well advanced, does a society begin to produce newspapers, radio networks, and motion pictures on a massive scale. This in turn, accelerates the spread of literacy. Out of this interaction develop those institutions of participation (e.g., voting) which we find in all advanced modern societies.[26]

Lerner's thesis concerning the functional interdependence of these elements of modernization is by no means established by his data, but the material presented in this paper offers an opportunity for research along these lines. Deviant cases, such as Egypt, where "lagging" literacy is associated with serious strains and potential upheaval, may also be found in Europe and in Latin America, and their analysis, a task not attempted here, will clarify further the basic dynamics of modernization, and the problem of social stability in the midst of institutional change.

A number of processes underlie these correlations, observed in many areas of the world, in addition to the effect, already discussed, of a high level of education and literacy in creating or sustaining belief in democratic norms. Perhaps most important is the relationship between modernization and the form of the "class struggle." For the lower strata, economic development, which means increased income, greater economic security, and higher education, permit those in this status to develop longer time perspectives and more complex and gradualist views of politics. A belief in secular reformist gradualism can only be the ideology of a relatively well-to-do lower class.[27] Increased wealth and education also serve democracy by increasing the extent to which the lower strata are exposed to cross pressures which will reduce the intensity of their commitment to given ideologies and make them less receptive to support-

---

[26] *Ibid.*, p. 60. Lerner also focuses upon certain personality requirements of a "modern" society which may also be related to the personality requirements of democracy. According to him, the physical and social mobility of modern society requires a mobile personality, capable of adaptation to rapid change. Development of a "mobile sensibility so adaptive to change that rearrangement of the self-system is its distinctive mode" has been the work of the 20th century. Its main feature is *empathy*, denoting the "general capacity to see oneself in the other fellow's situation, whether favorably or unfavorably." (p. 49 ff.). Whether this psychological characteristic results in a predisposition toward democracy (implying a willingness to accept the viewpoint of others) or is rather associated with the anti-democratic tendencies of a "mass society" type of personality (implying the lack of any solid personal values rooted in rewarding participation) is an open question. Possibly empathy, a more or less "cosmopolitan" outlook, is a general personality characteristic of modern societies, with other special conditions determining whether or not it has the social consequence of tolerance and democratic attitudes, or rootlessness and anomie.

[27] See S. M. Lipset, "Socialism—East and West—Left and Right," *Confluence*, Vol. 7 (Summer 1958), pp. 173–192.

ing extremist ones. The operation of this process will be discussed in more detail in the second part of the paper, but essentially it functions through enlarging their involvement in an integrated national culture as distinct from an isolated lower class one, and hence increasing their exposure to middle-class values. Marx argued that the proletariat were a revolutionary force because they have nothing to lose but their chains and can win the whole world. But Tocqueville in analyzing the reasons why the lower strata in America supported the system paraphrased and transposed Marx before Marx ever made this analysis, by pointing out that "only those who have nothing to lose ever revolt."[28]

Increased wealth is not only related causally to the development of democracy by changing the social conditions of the workers, but it also affects the political role of the middle class through changing the shape of the stratification structure so that it shifts from an elongated pyramid, with a large lower-class base, to a diamond with a growing middle-class. A large middle class plays a mitigating role in moderating conflict since it is able to reward moderate and democratic parties and penalize extremist groups.

National income is also related to the political values and style of the upper class. The poorer a country, and the lower the absolute standard of living of the lower classes, the greater the pressure on the upper strata to treat the lower classes as beyond the pale of human society, as vulgar, as innately inferior, as a lower caste. The sharp difference in the style of living between those at the top and those at the bottom makes this psychologically necessary. Consequently, the upper strata also tend to regard political rights for the lower strata, particularly the right to share in power, as essentially absurd and immoral. The upper strata not only resist democracy themselves, but their often arrogant political behavior serves to intensify extremist reactions on the part of the lower classes.

The general income level of a nation will also affect its receptivity to democratic political tolerance norms. The values which imply that it does not matter greatly which side rules, that error can be tolerated even in the governing party, can best develop where (a) the government has little power to affect the crucial life chances of most powerful groups, or (b) there is enough wealth in the country so that it actually does not make too much difference if some redistribution does take place. If loss of office is seen as meaning serious loss for major power groups, then they will be readier to resort to more drastic measures in seeking to retain or secure office. The wealth level will also affect the extent to which given countries can develop "universalistic" norms among its

---

[28] Alexis de Tocqueville, *Democracy in America*, Vol. I (New York: Alfred A. Knopf, Vintage edition, 1945), p. 258.

civil servants and politicians (selection based on competence; performance without favoritism). The poorer the country, the greater the emphasis which is placed on nepotism, i.e., support of kin and friends. The weakness of the universalistic norms reduces the opportunity to develop efficient bureaucracy, a condition for a modern democratic state.[29]

Less directly linked but seemingly still associated with greater wealth is the presence of intermediary organizations and institutions which can act as sources of countervailing power, and recruiters of participants in the political process in the manner discussed by Tocqueville and other exponents of what has come to be known as the theory of the "mass society."[30] They have argued that a society without a multitude of organizations relatively independent of the central state power has a high dictatorial as well as a revolutionary potential. Such organizations serve a number of functions necessary to democracy: they are a source of countervailing power, inhibiting the state or any single major source of private power from dominating all political resources; they are a source of new opinions; they can be the means of communicating ideas, particularly opposition ideas, to a large section of the citizenry; they serve to train men in the skills of politics; and they help increase the level of interest and participation in politics. Although there are no reliable data which bear on the relationship between national patterns of voluntary organizations and national political systems, evidence from studies of individual behavior within a number of different countries demonstrates that, independently of other factors, men who belong to associations are more likely to hold democratic opinions on questions concerning tolerance and party systems, and are more likely to participate in the political process— to be active or to vote. Since we also know that, within countries, the more well-to-do and the better educated one is, the more likely he is to belong to voluntary organizations, it seems likely that the propensity to form such groups is a function of level of income and opportunities for leisure within given nations.[31]

[29] For a discussion of this problem in a new state, see David Apter, *The Gold Coast in Transition* (Princeton University Press, 1955), esp. chapters 9 and 13. Apter shows the importance of efficient bureaucracy, and the acceptance of bureaucratic values and behavior patterns, for the existence of a democratic political order.

[30] See Emil Lederer, *The State of the Masses* (New York, 1940); Hannah Arendt, *Origins of Totalitarianism* (New York, 1950); Max Horkheimer, *Eclipse of Reason* (New York, 1947); Karl Mannheim, *Man and Society in an Age of Reconstruction* (New York, 1940); Philip Selznick, *The Organizational Weapon* (New York, 1952); José Ortega y Gasset, *The Revolt of the Masses* (New York, 1932).

[31] See Edward Banfield, *The Moral Basis of a Backward Society* (Glencoe: The Free Press, 1958), for an excellent description of the way in which abysmal poverty serves to reduce community organization in southern Italy. The data which do exist from polling surveys conducted in the United States, Germany, France, Great Britain, and Sweden show that somewhere between 40 and 50 percent of the adults in these countries belong to voluntary associations, without lower rates of membership for the less stable democracies, France and Germany, than among

It is obvious that democracy and the conditions related to stable democracy discussed here are essentially located in the countries of northwest Europe and their English-speaking offspring in America and Australasia. It has been argued by Max Weber among others that the factors making for democracy in this area are a historically unique concatenation of elements, part of the complex which also produced capitalism in this area. The basic argument runs that capitalist economic development (facilitated and most developed in Protestant areas) created the burgher class whose existence was both a catalyst and a necessary condition for democracy. The emphasis within Protestantism on individual responsibility furthered the emergence of democratic values. The greater initial strength of the middle classes in these countries resulted in an alignment between burghers and throne, an alignment which preserved the monarchy, and thus facilitated the legitimation of democracy among the conservative strata. Thus we have an interrelated cluster of economic development, Protestantism, monarchy, gradual political change, legitimacy, and democracy.[32] Men may argue as to whether any aspect of this cluster is primary, but the cluster of factors and forces hangs together.

---

the more stable ones, the United States, Great Britain, and Sweden. These results seemingly challenge the general proposition, although no definite conclusion can be made, since most of the studies employed non-comparable categories. This point bears further research in many countries. For the data on these countries see the following studies: for France, Arnold Rose, *Theory and Method in the Social Sciences* (Minneapolis, University of Minnesota Press, 1954), p. 74; and O. R. Gallagher, "Voluntary Associations in France," *Social Forces*, Vol. 36 (Dec. 1957), pp. 154–56; for Germany, Erich Reigrotzki, *Soziale Verflechtungen in der Bundesrepublik* (Tubingen: J. C. B. Mohr, 1956), p. 164; for the U.S., Charles R. Wright and Herbert H. Hyman, "Voluntary Association Memberships of American Adults: Evidence from National Sample Surveys," *American Sociological Review*, Vol. 23 (Jun 1958), p. 287, and J. C. Scott, Jr., "Membership and Participation in Voluntary Associations," *id.*, Vol. 22 (1957), pp. 315–26; Herbert Maccoby, "The Differential Political Activity of Participants in a Voluntary Association," *id.*, Vol. 23 (1958), pp. 524–33; for Great Britain see "Mass Observation," *Puzzled People* (London: Victor Gollanz, 1947), p. 119; and Thomas Bottomore, "Social Stratification in Voluntary Organizations," in David Glass, ed., *Social Mobility in Britain* (Glencoe: The Free Press, 1954), p. 354; for Sweden see Gunnar Heckscher, "Pluralist Democracy: The Swedish Experience," *Social Research*, Vol. 15 (December 1948), pp. 417–61.

[32] In introducing historical events as part of the analysis of factors *external* to the political system, which are part of the causal nexus in which democracy is involved, I am following in good sociological and even functionalist tradition. As Radcliffe-Brown has well put it: ". . . one 'explanation' of a social system will be its history, where we know it—the detailed account of how it came to be what it is and where it is. Another 'explanation' of the same system is obtained by showing . . . that it is a special exemplification of laws of social psychology or social functioning. The two kinds of explanation do not conflict but supplement one another." A. R. Radcliffe-Brown, "On the Concept of Function in Social Science," *American Anthropologist*, New Series, Vol. 37 (1935), p. 401; see also Max Weber, *The Methodology of the Social Sciences* (Glencoe: The Free Press, 1949), pp. 164–88, for a detailed discussion of the role of historical analysis in sociological research.

appendix

B

Party leaders and followers—
Differences and similarities*[1]

HERBERT MCCLOSKY, PAUL J. HOFFMAN,
and ROSEMARY O'HARA

American political parties are often regarded as "brokerage" organizations, weak in principle, devoid of ideology, and inclined to differ chiefly over unimportant questions. In contrast to the "ideological" parties of Europe—which supposedly appeal to their followers through sharply defined, coherent, and logically related doctrines—the American parties are thought to fit their convictions to the changing demands of the political contest.[2] According to this view, each set of American party leaders is satisfied to play Tweedledee to the other's Tweedledum.

PRESSURES TOWARD UNIFORMITY AND CLEAVAGE

Although these "conclusions" are mainly derived from *a priori* analysis or from casual observations of "anecdotal" data (little systematic effort

* This appeared under the title "Issue Conflict and Consensus among Party Leaders and Followers" in *American Political Science Review*, Vol. 54 (June 1960), pp. 406–27. Reprinted by permission of the American Political Science Association.

[1] This article is the first of a series reporting the findings of a national field study of political belief and affiliation among American party leaders and followers. The study was carried out through the Laboratory for Research in Social Relations at the University of Minnesota under grants made to the senior author by the Committee on Political Behavior of the Social Science Research Council, and supplementary grants from the Graduate School Research Fund. The manuscript was prepared at the Survey Research Center, University of California, Berkeley, under a Fellowship in Legal and Political Philosophy awarded to the senior author by the Rockefeller Foundation.

[2] Maurice Duverger, *Political Parties, Their Organization and Activity in the Modern State* (New York, 1955), p. 102.

having been made so far to verify or refute them), they are often taken as confirmed—largely, one imagines, because they are compatible with certain conspicuous features of American politics. Among these features is the entrenchment of a two-party system which, by affording both parties a genuine opportunity to win elections, tempts them to appeal to as many diverse elements in the electorate as are needed to put together a majority.[3] Since both parties want to attract support from the centrist and moderate segments of the electorate, their views on basic issues will, it is thought, tend to converge. Like giant business enterprises competing for the same market, they will be led to offer commodities that are in many respects identical.[4] It is one thing for a small party in a multi-party system to preserve its ideological purity, quite another for a mass party in a two-party system to do so. The one has little hope of becoming a majority, and can most easily survive by remaining identified with the narrow audience from which it draws its chief supporters; the other can succeed only by accommodating the conflicting claims of many diverse groups—only, in short, by blunting ideological distinctions.[5]

Constraints against enlarging intellectual differences also spring from the loosely confederated nature of the American party system, and from each national party's need to adjust its policies to the competing interests of the locality, the state, and the nation.[6] Many party units are more concerned with local than with national elections, and prefer not to be handicapped by clear-cut national programs. Every ambitious politician, moreover, hopes to achieve a *modux vivendi* tailored to the particular and often idiosyncratic complex of forces prevailing in his constituency, an objective rarely compatible with doctrinal popularity.[7] Often, too, local politics are largely nonpartisan or are partisan in ways that scarcely affect the great national issues around which ideologies might be expected to form.[8] The development and enforcement of a sharply delineated ideology is also hindered by the absence in either party of a firmly established, authoritative, and continuing organizational center em-

---

[3] The analysis of these and related tendencies associated with the American party system is ably set forth in Pendleton Herring, *The Politics of Democracy* (New York, 1940), p. 102 and *passim.* Also, James M. Burns, *Congress on Trial: The Legislative Process and the Administrative State* (New York, 1949), p. 34.

[4] See especially E. E. Schattschneider, *Party Government* (New York, 1942), p. 92 and *passim;* and V. O. Key, *Politics, Parties, and Pressure Groups,* 4th ed. (New York, 1958), ch. 8; Howard R. Penniman, *Sait's American Parties and Elections,* 5th ed. (New York, 1952), p. 162.

[5] William Goodman, *The Two-Party System in the United States* (New Jersey, 1956), p. 43.

[6] Duverger, *op. cit.,* pp. 187, 418.

[7] Pendleton Herring, *op. cit.,* p. 133.

[8] *American State Legislatures,* ed. Belle Zeller (New York, 1954); but see also Malcolm E. Jewell, "Party Voting in American State Legislatures," *American Political Science Review,* Vol. 49 (Sept. 1955), pp. 773–791.

powered to decide questions of doctrine and discipline.[9] Party affiliation is loosely defined, responsibility is weak or non-existent, and organs for indoctrinating or communicating with party members are at best rudimentary.

Cultural and historical differences may also contribute to the weaker ideological emphasis among American, as compared with European, parties. Many of the great historical cleavages that have divided European nations for centuries—monarchism v. republicanism; clericalism v. anticlericalism; democracy v. autocracy, etc.—have never taken root in this country. Apart from the slavery (and subsequently the race) issue, the United States has not experienced the intense class or caste conflict often found abroad, and contests of the capitalism v. socialism variety have never achieved an important role in American politics. In addition, never having known a titled nobility, we have largely been freed from the conflicts found elsewhere between the classes of inherited and acquired privilege.

Consider, too, the progress made in the United States toward neutralizing the forces which ordinarily lead to sharp social, and hence intellectual and political, differentiation. The class and status structure of American society has attained a rate of mobility equalling or exceeding that of any other long-established society. Popular education, and other facilities for the creation of common attitudes, have been developed on a scale unequalled elsewhere. Improvements in transportation and communication and rapid shifts in population and industry have weakened even sectionalism as a source of political cleavage. Rural-urban differences continue to exist, of course, but they too have been diminishing in force and have become less salient for American politics than the differences prevailing, for example, between a French peasant proprietor and a Parisian *boulevardier*.[10] In short, a great many Americans have been subjected in their public lives to identical stimuli—a condition unlikely to generate strong, competing ideologies.

The research reported here was designed not to refute these observations but to test the accuracy of the claim that they are sufficient to prevent differences in outlook from taking root in the American party system. We believed that the homogenizing tendencies referred to are strongly offset by contrary influences, and that voters are preponderantly led to support the party whose opinions they share. We further thought that the competition for office, though giving rise to similarities between the parties, also impels them to diverge from each other in order to sharpen their respective appeals. For this and other reasons, we expected to find that the leaders of the two parties, instead of ignoring differences

---

[9] Report of the Committee on Political Parties, American Political Science Association, *Toward A More Responsible Two-Party System* (New York, 1950), *passim*.

[10] Data bearing on these generalizations will be presented in companion articles which specifically deal with sectional and rural-urban influences on issue outlook.

alleged to exist within the electorate, would differ on issues more sharply than their followers would. We believed further that even in a brokerage system the parties would serve as independent reference groups, developing norms, values, and self-images to which their supporters could readily respond.[11] Their influence, we felt, would frequently exceed that of ethnic, occupational, residential, and other reference groups. In sum, we proceeded on the belief that the parties are not simply spokesmen for other interest groups, but are in their own right agencies for formulating, transmitting, and anchoring political opinions, that they attract adherents who in general share those opinions, and that through a feedback process of mutual reinforcement between the organization and its typical supporters, the parties develop integrated and stable political tendencies. Other hypotheses will be specified as we present and analyze our findings.

PROCEDURES

The questions considered in this paper were part of a large field study made in 1957–1958 on the nature, sources, and correlates of political affiliation, activity, and belief in the American party system (hereafter referred to as the PAB study). Pilot studies on Minnesota samples had led us to suspect that many "settled" notions about party affiliation and belief in America would not stand up under careful empirical scrutiny; further, we felt that little progress would be made in the exploration of this subject until a comprehensive portrait of party membership in America had been drawn. Accordingly, a nationwide study was launched to acquire a detailed description of party leaders and supporters, gathering data on their backgrounds, political experiences, personality characteristics, values, motivations, social and political attitudes, outlooks on key issues, and related matters.

For our samples of party "leaders" we turned to the Democratic and Republican national conventions, largely because they are the leading and most representative of the party organs, their delegates coming from every part of the United States and from every level of party and government activity. Our samples ranged from governors, senators, and national committeemen at the one end to precinct workers and local officials at the other. In the absence of comprehensive information about the characteristics of the party élites in America, no one can say how closely the convention delegates mirror the total party leadership. We felt it fair to assume, nevertheless, that the delegates represented as faithful a cross section of American party leadership as could be had without an extraordinary expenditure of money and labor. Using convention delegates

---

[11] *Cf.* James W. Prothro, Ernest Q. Campbell, and Charles M. Grigg, "Two Party Voting in the South: Class vs. Party Identification," *American Political Science Review,* Vol. 52 (March, 1958), pp. 131–139. Also, Peter H. Odegard and E. Allen Helms, *American Politics: A Study in Political Dynamics* (New York, 1947 ed.), pp. 809–821.

as our universe of leaders also held some obvious advantages for research, since the composition of this universe (by name, address, party, state, sex, place of residence, and party or public office) can usually be ascertained from the convention calls. Of the 6,848 delegates and alternates available to be sampled, 3,193 actually participated; 3,020 (1,788 Democrats and 1,232 Republicans) completed and returned questionnaires that were usable in all respects.[12] The proportion of returns was roughly equivalent for both sets of party leaders.

The rank and file sample, which we wanted both for its intrinsic value and for its utility as a control group, was obtained by special arrangement with the American Institute of Public Opinion. In January 1958, Gallup interviewers personally distributed our questionnaire to 2,917 adult voters in two successive national cross-section surveys. Some 1,610 questionnaires were filled out and returned, of which 1,484 were completely usable. This sample closely matched the national population on such characteristics as sex, age, region, size of city, and party affiliation, and, though it somewhat oversampled the upper educational levels, we considered it sufficiently large and representative for most of our purposes. Of the 1,484 respondents, 821 were Democratic supporters (629 "pure" Democrats, plus 192 whom we classified as "independent" Democrats) and 623 were Republican supporters (479 "pure" Republicans, plus 144 "independent" Republicans). Forty respondents could not be identified as adherents of either party.

The lengthy questionnaire developed for the study was designed to be self-administered. It contained, in addition to questions on the respondents' personal backgrounds, a number of queries on their political history and experience, their attitudes toward the party system and toward such related matters as party organization, discipline and responsibility, their self-images with regard to social class and liberalism-conservatism, their reference group identifications, and their views on party leadership and ideology. The largest part of the questionnaire consisted of 390 scale items, randomly arranged, which when sorted and scored fell into 47 scales for measuring the personality, attitude, and value characteristics of each of the respondents. We had validated and used all but three of these scales in earlier studies.

The questions most relevant for the present article were those which asked each respondent to express his attitudes toward twenty-four important national issues, and to state whether he believed support for each issue should be "increased," "decreased," or "remain as is." The list of

---

[12] This gratifyingly large number of returns of so lengthy and detailed a questionnaire was attained through a number of follow-up mailings and special letters. These and other procedures designed to check the adequacy of the sample will be fully described in the volume containing the report of the overall study. The difference in the number of returns from the two parties was largely a result of the greater number of Democratic delegates to begin with.

issues and the responses of each sample will be found in Tables B–2–A through B–2–E, where for convenience of analysis, the issues have been grouped under five broad headings: Public Ownership, Government Regulation of the Economy, Equalitarianism and Human Welfare, Tax Policy, and Foreign Policy.

In tabulating the results, we first scored each individual on each issue and then computed aggregate scores for all the members of a given sample. To begin with, percentages were used to show the proportion who favored increasing, decreasing, or retaining the existing level of support on each issue. But as it was clumsy to handle three figures for each issue, we constructed a single index or "ratio of support" which would simultaneously take account of all three scores. The index was built by assigning a weight of 1.0 to each "increase" response in the sample, of 0 to each "decrease" response, and of .50 to each "remain as is" (or "same") response. Thus the ratio-of-support score shown for any given sample is in effect a mean score with a possible range of 0 to 1.0, in which support for an issue increases as the scores approach 1.0 and decreases as they approach 0. In general, the scores can be taken to approximate the following over-all positions: .0 to .25—strongly wish to reduce support; .26 to .45—wish to reduce support; .46 to .55—satisfied with the *status quo*; .56 to .75—wish to increase support; and .76 to 1.00—strongly wish to increase support. Note that the differences in degree suggested by these categories refer not to the *strength of feeling* exhibited by individuals toward an issue but rather to the *numbers* of people in a sample who hold points of view favoring or opposing that issue.

Because they include "same" and "no code" as well as "increase" and "decrease" responses, our ratios of support sometimes flatten the differences between groups. Had we employed only the percentage scores for the "increase" or "decrease" responses, the differences between samples would in many instances have seemed larger. Nevertheless, the ratio of support offers so many advantages that we have employed it as our principal measure. For one thing, as the equivalent of a mean score, it takes into account all scores, omitting no respondent from the tabulation. For the same reason it enables us to assess the amount of dispersion or homogeneity exhibited by any sample and makes it easy to calculate significances of difference.[13] Reliance upon a single, uniform

---

[13] The measure of dispersion used for this purpose was the standard deviation, which was computed by using the scores of 0, .50 and 1.00 as intervals in the calculations. To avoid having to calculate separate significances of difference for each of the comparisons we wanted to observe, we simply made the assumption—erring on the side of caution—that the maximum variance of .50 had occurred in each instance. The magnitude of the significance of difference is, in other words, often greater than we have reported. The significance test used in this procedure was the critical ratio. Unless otherwise indicated, all the differences reported are statistically significant at or beyond the .01 level.

statistic also allows us to make ready comparisons not only *between* but *within* samples, and to determine quickly how large the differences actually are. By observing whether a ratio of support is above or below .50 we can see at once whether a particular group predominantly favors or opposes the issue in question, and how strongly it does so. The use of ratio scores also makes it possible to compare issues as well as groups, e.g., to see whether one issue is more preferred than another.

For further information on the meaning of the issue responses, we also compared samples on a number of related scales and items. Tabulating and statistical operations were carried out to control for demographic influences like education, occupation, age, and sectionalism; to ascertain homogeneity of opinion within the several samples; to rank the issues according to the magnitude of the differences between samples; to compare members' positions on issues against official platform statements; and to determine whether leaders and followers are able to name the issues which actually divide the parties. Some of the findings yielded by these operations will be considered here, while others, for reasons of space, will have to be reserved for future publications.

A word of caution before we turn to the findings. The respondents were offered only the twenty-four issues that impressed us in February, 1957, as most significant and enduring. However, they may not all be as salient today as they seemed at that time. Nor, within the limitations of a single questionnaire, could we explore every issue that informed observers might have considered important. Some presumably vital issues such as states rights, political centralization, and expansion of government functions could not be stated explicitly enough within our format to be tested properly. These are issues that are so generalized as to encompass many other specific issues, and so highly charged as to awaken a profusion of symbolic and emotive associations.

The form of our issue questions may also be open to criticism, for space limitations prevented our subjects from indicating how strongly they felt and how much they knew about each of the issues. This deficiency, however, may be less important than it appears, since for the groups we most wanted to compare (e.g., Democratic v. Republican leaders), the degree of political knowledge and intensity is likely to be rather similar. The difficulty is greater when comparing leaders with followers, but is somewhat offset by controlling for education and socio-economic status. Although some subtleties of interpretation are bound to be lost because these variables have been omitted, we are satisfied that our issue questions in their present form furnish a useful measure for assessing group (as distinguished from *individual*) opinion.

Finally, one may wonder about the value of opinions stated on a questionnaire compared with the worth of views formally expressed by an organization or implicit in the actions of its leaders. Advantages can

TABLE B–1
Average Differences in the Ratio-of-Support Scores among Party Leaders and Followers for Five Categories of Issues

Category of Issues	Dem. Leaders v. Rep. Leaders	Dem. Followers v. Rep. Followers	Dem. Leaders v. Dem. Followers	Rep. Leaders v. Rep. Followers	Dem. Leaders v. Rep. Followers	Rep. Leaders v. Dem. Followers
a. Public Ownership of Resources..................	.28	.04	.06	.18	.10	.22
b. Government Regulation of the Economy...................	.22	.06	.08	.10	.12	.16
c. Equalitarianism, Human Welfare..................	.22	.05	.08	.21	.06	.25
d. Tax Policy...............	.20	.06	.06	.20	.04	.26
e. Foreign Policy.............	.15	.02	.05	.08	.07	.10
Average Differences in Ratio Scores for All Categories	.21	.04	.07	.15	.08	.20

Sample sizes: Democratic leaders, 1,788; Republican leaders, 1,232; Democratic followers, 821; Republican followers, 623.

be cited on both sides. The beliefs expressed in official party statements or in legislative roll calls, it might be claimed, represent, the *operating* beliefs of the organization by virtue of having been tested in the market-place or in the competition of legislative struggle. Positions taken on issues on which a party stakes its future may be more valid evidence of what the party truly believes than are the opinions expressed by individual members under conditions of maximum safety. On the other hand, the responses to the issue and attitude questions in the PAB study represent the anonymous, private opinions of party leaders and followers, uncomplicated by any need to make political capital, to proselytize, to conciliate critics, or to find grounds for embarrassing the opposition at the next election. Hence they may for some purposes represent the most accurate possible reflection of the "actual" state of party opinion. The controversy over the value of the two approaches is to some extent spurious, however, for they offer different perspectives on the same thing. In addition, considerable correspondence exists between the party positions evident in congressional roll calls and the privately expressed opinions of the party leaders in our study.[14]

[14] See, for example, the congressional roll-call results reported by Julius Turner, *Party and Constituency: Pressures on Congress*, the Johns Hopkins University Studies in Historical and Political Science Series, LXIX, #1 (1951). The complexities affecting the determination of party votes in Congress are thoroughly explored in David B. Truman, *The Congressional Party: A Case Study* (New York, 1959).

FINDINGS: COMPARISONS BETWEEN LEADERS

No more conclusive findings emerge from our study of party issues than those growing out of the comparisons between the two sets of party leaders. Despite the brokerage tendency of the American parties, their active members are obviously separated by large and important differences. The differences, moreover, conform with the popular image in which the Democratic party is seen as the more "progressive" or "radical," the Republican as the more "moderate" or "conservative" of the two.[15] In addition, the disagreements are remarkably consistent, a function not of chance but of systematic points of view, whereby the responses to any one of the issues could reasonably have been predicted from knowledge of the responses to the other issues.

Examination of Tables B–2–A through B–2–E and B–3 shows that the

TABLE B–2–A
Comparisons of Party Leaders and Followers on "Public Ownership" Issues, by Percentages and Ratios of Support

Issues	Leaders		Followers	
	Dem. N = 1,788	Rep. N = 1,232	Dem. N = 821	Rep. N = 623
		(%'s down)		
Public Ownership of Natural Resources:				
% favoring: Increase	57.5	12.9	35.3	31.1
Decrease	18.6	51.9	15.0	19.9
Same, n.c.*	23.8	35.2	49.7	49.0
Support Ratio	.69	.30	.60	.56
Public Control of Atomic Energy:				
% favoring: Increase	73.2	45.0	64.2	59.4
Decrease	7.2	15.3	7.1	10.0
Same, n.c.	19.6	39.7	28.7	30.6
Support Ratio	.83	.65	.79	.75
Mean Support Ratios for the "Public Ownership" Category	.76	.48	.70	.66

* n.c. = no code.

[15] Conservatism is here used not in the classical but in the more popular sense, in which it refers to negative attitudes toward government ownership, intervention, and regulation of the economy; resistance to measures for promoting equalitarianism and social welfare through government action; identification with property, wealth, and business enterprise; etc.

leaders differ significantly on 23 of the 24 issues listed and that they are separated on 15 of these issues by .18 or more ratio points—in short, by differences that are in absolute magnitude very large. The two samples are furthest apart in their attitudes toward public ownership and are especially divided on the question of government ownership of natural

TABLE B–2–B

Comparison of Party Leaders and Followers on "Government Regulation of the Economy" Issues, by Percentages and Ratios of Support

	Leaders		Followers	
	Dem.	*Rep.*	*Dem.*	*Rep.*
	N = 1,788	*N = 1,232*	*N = 821*	*N = 623*
Issues		(%'s down)		
Level of Farm Price Supports:				
% favoring: Increase	43.4	6.7	39.0	23.0
Decrease	28.1	67.4	27.6	40.3
Same, n.c.	28.5	25.8	33.4	36.7
Support Ratio	.58	.20	.56	.41
Government Regulation of Business:				
% favoring: Increase	20.2	0.6	18.6	7.4
Decrease	38.5	84.1	33.4	46.2
Same, n.c.	41.3	15.3	48.0	46.4
Support Ratio	.41	.08	.43	.31
Regulation of Public Utilities:				
% favoring: Increase	59.0	17.9	39.3	26.0
Decrease	6.4	17.6	11.1	12.0
Same, n.c.	34.6	64.5	49.6	62.0
Support Ratio	.76	.50	.64	.57
Enforcement of Anti-Monopoly Laws:				
% favoring: Increase	78.0	44.9	53.2	51.0
Decrease	2.9	9.0	7.9	6.6
Same, n.c.	19.1	46.1	38.9	42.4
Support Ratio	.88	.68	.73	.72
Regulation of Trade Unions:				
% favoring: Increase	59.3	86.4	46.6	57.8
Decrease	12.4	4.5	8.9	10.6
Same, n.c.	28.3	9.2	44.5	31.6
Support Ratio	.73	.91	.69	.74
Level of Tariffs:				
% favoring: Increase	13.0	19.2	16.6	15.2
Decrease	43.0	26.3	25.3	21.3
Same, n.c.	43.9	54.5	58.1	63.4
Support Ratio	.35	.46	.46	.47
Restrictions on Credit:				
% favoring: Increase	24.8	20.6	26.1	25.7
Decrease	39.3	20.6	22.2	23.8
Same, n.c.	35.9	58.8	51.8	50.5
Support Ratio	.43	.50	.52	.51
Mean Support Ratios for "Government Regulation of the Economy" Category	.59	.48	.58	.53

TABLE B–2–C
Comparison of Party Leaders and Followers on "Equalitarian and Human Welfare"
Issues, by Percentages and Ratios of Support

	Leaders		Followers	
	Dem.	Rep.	Dem.	Rep.
	N = 1,788	N = 1,232	N = 821	N = 623
Issues		(%'s down)		
Federal Aid to Education:				
% favoring: Increase	66.2	22.3	74.9	64.8
Decrease	13.4	43.2	5.6	8.3
Same, n.c.	20.4	34.5	19.5	26.8
Support Ratio	.76	.40	.85	.78
Slum Clearance and Public Housing:				
% favoring: Increase	78.4	40.1	79.5	72.5
Decrease	5.6	21.6	5.8	7.9
Same, n.c.	16.0	38.3	14.6	19.6
Support Ratio	.86	.59	.87	.82
Social Security Benefits:				
% favoring: Increase	60.0	22.5	69.4	57.0
Decrease	3.9	13.1	3.0	3.8
Same, n.c.	36.1	64.4	27.5	39.2
Support Ratio	.78	.55	.83	.77
MinimumWages:				
% favoring: Increase	50.0	15.5	59.0	43.5
Decrease	4.7	12.5	2.9	5.0
Same, n.c.	45.2	72.0	38.1	51.5
Support Ratio	.73	.52	.78	.69
Enforcement of Integration:				
% favoring: Increase	43.8	25.5	41.9	40.8
Decrease	26.6	31.7	27.4	23.6
Same, n.c.	29.5	42.8	30.7	35.6
Support Ratio	.59	.47	.57	.59
Immigration into United States:				
% favoring: Increase	36.1	18.4	10.4	8.0
Decrease	27.0	29.9	52.0	44.6
Same, n.c.	36.9	51.7	37.6	47.4
Support Ratio	.54	.44	.29	.32
Mean Support Ratios for "Equalitarian and HumanWelfare" Category	.71	.50	.70	.66

seen in the responses to the issues listed under Government Regulation of the Economy, Equalitarianism and Human Welfare, Tax Policy. Democratic leaders are far more eager than Republican leaders to strengthen enforcement of antimonopoly laws and to increase regulation of public utilities and business. Indeed, the solidarity of Republican opposition to the regulation of business is rather overwhelming: 84 percent want to decrease such regulation and fewer than .01 percent say they want to increase it. Although the Democrats, on balance, also feel that government controls on business should not be expanded further, the differences between the two samples on this issue are nevertheless substantial.

The two sets of leaders are also far apart on the farm issue, the Democrats preferring slightly to increase farm supports, the Republicans wanting strongly to reduce them. The Republican ratio score of .20 on this issue is among the lowest in the entire set of scores. The magnitude of these scores somewhat surprised us, for while opposition to agricultural subsidies is consistent with Republican dislike for state intervention, we had expected the leaders to conform more closely to the familiar image of the Republican as the more "rural" of the two parties.[17] It appears, however, that the party's connection with business is far more compelling than its association with agriculture. The Republican desire to reduce government expenditures and to promote independence from "government handouts" prevails on the farm question as it does on other issues, while the Democratic preference for a more regulated economy in which government intervenes to reduce economic risk and to stabilize prosperity is equally evident on the other side. Party attitudes on this issue appear to be determined as much by ideological tendencies as by deliberate calculation of the political advantages to be gained by favoring or opposing subsidies to farmers. Comparison of our findings with Turner's earlier data on farm votes in Congress[18] suggests, in addition, that the sharp party difference on the farm issue is neither a recent development nor a mere product of the personal philosophy of the present Secretary of Agriculture.

Having implied that agricultural policies partly result from principle, we must note that on three other issues in this category (trade unions, credit, and tariffs), principle seems to be overweighed by old-fashioned economic considerations. In spite of their distaste for government interference in economic affairs, the Republicans almost unanimously favor greater regulation of trade unions and they are more strongly disposed

---

[17] The friendlier attitude toward farmers among Democratic leaders than Republican leaders is borne out in the responses to several other questions used in the study. For example, the Republican leaders list farmers as having "too much power" far more frequently than do the Democratic leaders. Equally, the Democrats are significantly more inclined to regard farmers as having "too little power."

[18] Turner, *op. cit.*, p. 64.

than the Democrats toward government intervention to restrict credit and to raise tariffs. Of course, party cleavages over the credit and tariff issues have a long history,[19] which may by now have endowed them with ideological force beyond immediate economic considerations.[20] The preponderant Democratic preference for greater regulation of trade unions is doubtless a response to recent "exposures" of corrupt labor practices, though it may also signify that the party's perspective toward the trade unions is shifting somewhat.

The closer Republican identification with business, free enterprise, and economic conservatism in general, and the friendlier Democratic attitude toward labor and toward government regulation of the economy, are easily observed in the data from other parts of our questionnaire. Republican leaders score very much higher than Democratic leaders on, for example, such scales as economic conservatism, independence of government, and business attitudes. On a question asking respondents to indicate the groups from which they would be most and least likely to take advice, 41 percent of the Democratic leaders but only 3.8 percent of the Republican leaders list trade unions as groups from which they would seek advice. Trade unions are scored in the "least likely" category by 25 percent of the Democrats and 63 percent of the Republicans. Similarly, more than 94 percent of the Republican leaders, but 56 percent of the Democratic leaders, name trade unions as groups that have "too much power." These differences, it should be noted, cannot be accounted for by reference to the greater number of trade union members among the Democratic party leadership, for in the 1956 conventions only 14 percent of the Democrats belonged to trade unions, and while an even smaller percentage (4 percent) of the Republicans were trade unionists, this disparity is hardly great enough to explain the large differences in outlook. The key to the explanation has to be sought in the symbolic and reference group identifications of the two parties, and in their underlying values.

Nowhere do we see this more clearly than in the responses to the Equalitarian and Human Welfare issues. The mean difference in the ratio scores for the category as a whole is .22, a very large difference and one that results from differences in the expected direction on all six issues that make up the category. On four of these issues—federal aid to education, slum clearance and public housing, social security, and minimum wages—the leaders of the two parties are widely separated,

---

[19] See John B. Johnson, Jr., *The Extent and Consistency of Party Voting in the United States Senate*, Ph.D. thesis, University of Chicago, 1943. By applying the Rice Index-of-Likeness to Senate votes, Johnson finds the tariff to have been the most partisan issue before the Congress in the years 1880–1940.

[20] Corinne Silverman, "The Legislator's View of the Legislative Process," *Public Opinion Quarterly*, Vol. 18 (1954–1955), p. 180.

the differences in their ratio scores ranging from .36 to .21. The percentages showing the proportions who favor increased support for these issues are even more striking. In every instance the Democratic percentages are considerably higher: 66 v. 22 percent (education); 78 v. 40 percent (slum clearance and housing); 60 v. 23 percent (social security); and 50 v. 16 percent (minimum wages). The Democratic leaders also are better disposed than the Republican leaders toward immigration: twice as many of them (36 percent v. 18 percent) favor a change in policy to permit more immigrants to enter. The over-all inclination of both party élites, however, is to accept the present levels of immigration, the Democratic ratio score falling slightly above, and the Republican slightly below, the midpoint.

More surprising are the differences on the segregation issue, for, despite strong Southern influence, the Democratic leaders express significantly more support for enforcing integration than the Republicans do. Moreover, the difference between the two parties rises from .12 for the national samples as a whole to a difference of .18 when the southern leaders are excluded. In his study of Congress, Turner found that the Republicans gave more support to Negro rights than the Democrats did.[21] The reversal of this finding in our data does not necessarily mean that a change has occurred since Turner made his study, but only that the votes of the congressional parties do not always reflect the private feelings of the national party leadership. Then, too, Southern influence is disproportionately stronger in the Democratic congressional party than in the national Democratic organization as a whole, and disproportionately weaker in the Republican congressional party than in the Republican organization as a whole.

Examination of the actual magnitude of the ratio scores in this category reveals that the Republicans want not so much to abrogate existing social welfare or equalitarian measures as to keep them from being broadened. The Democrats, by comparison, are shown to be the party of social equality and reform, more willing than their opponents to employ legislation for the benefit of the underprivileged. Support for these inferences and for the greater liberalism of the Democrats can be found elsewhere in our data as well. Analysis of the scale results show Republican leaders scoring higher than Democratic leaders on such measures as chauvinism, élitism, conservatism, and right-wing values, and lower on tolerance, procedural rights, and faith in democracy. No differences worth noting, however, were found for ethnocentrism, faith in freedom, or the California F scale. The Democrats had a slightly higher average score on the left-wing scale, but the number of leaders in either party who scored high on this measure was fairly small.

---

[21] Turner, *op. cit.*, p. 54.

The self-images and reference group identifications of the two parties also should be noted in this connection. For example, many more Democratic than Republican leaders call themselves liberal and state that they would be most likely to take advice from liberal reform organizations, the Farmers' Union, and (as we have seen) from the trade unions; only a small number consider themselves conservative or would seek advice from conservative reform organizations, the National Association of Manufacturers, or the Farm Bureau Federation. The Republicans have in almost all instances the reverse identifications. only a handful regard themselves as liberal or would seek counsel from liberal organizations, while more than 42 percent call themselves conservative and would look to the NAM or to conservative reform organizations for advice. Almost two-thirds of the Republicans (compared with 29 percent of the Democrats) regard the Chamber of Commerce as an important source of advice. Businessmen are listed as having "too much power" by 42 percent of the Democrats but by only 9 percent of the Republicans. The Democrats are also significantly more inclined than the Republicans to consider Catholics, Jews, and the foreign born as having "too little power." While self-descriptions and reference group identifications often correspond poorly with actual beliefs—among the general population they scarcely correspond at all, in fact—we are dealing, in the case of the leaders, with a politically informed and highly articulate set of people who have little difficulty connecting the beliefs they hold and the groups that promote or obstruct those beliefs.

Our fourth category, Tax Policy, divides the parties almost as severely as do the other categories. The mean difference for the category as a whole is .20, and it would doubtless have been larger but for the universal unpopularity of proposals to increase taxes on small and middle income groups. Table B–2–D shows that the differences between the parties on the tax issues follow the patterns previously observed and that tax policy is for the Democrats a device for redistributing income and promoting social equality. Neither party, however, is keen about raising taxes for *any* group: even the Democrats have little enthusiasm for new taxes on upper income groups or on business and corporate enterprises. The Republican leaders are overwhelmingly opposed to increased taxes for *any* group, rich *or* poor. This can be seen in their low ratio scores on the tax issues, which range from only .15 to .24. But while they are far more eager than the Democratic leaders to cut taxes on corporate and private wealth, they are less willing to reduce taxes on the lower income groups. These differences, it should be remarked, are not primarily a function of differences in the income of the two samples. Although there are more people with high incomes among the Republican leaders, the disproportion between the two samples is not nearly great enough to account for the dissimilarities in their tax views.

Of the five categories considered, Foreign Policy shows the smallest average difference, but even on these issues the divergence between Democratic and Republican leader attitudes is significant. Except for defense spending the Democrats turn out to be more internationalist than the Republicans, as evidenced in their greater commitment to the United Nations and to American participation in international military alliances like NATO. Twice as many Democrats as Republicans want the United States to rely more heavily upon such organizations, while many more Republicans want to reduce our international involvements. Both parties are predominantly in favor of cutting back foreign aid—a somewhat surprising finding in light of Democratic public pronouncements on this subject—but more Republicans feel strongly on the subject. Our data thus furnish little support for the claim that the parties hold the same views on foreign policy or that their seeming differences are merely a response to the demands of political competition.[22]

Nevertheless, it would be incorrect to conclude that one party believes in internationalism and the other in isolationism. The differences are far too small to warrant any such inference. Traces of isolationism, to be sure, remain stronger in the Republican party than in the Democratic party—an observation buttressed by the finding that twice as many Republicans as Democrats score high on the isolationism scale. The pattern of Republican responses on both the issue and scale items signifies, however, that the leaders of that party generally accept the degree of "internationalism" now in effect, but shrink from extending it further. Consider too, the similarities in the leaders' scores on defense spending, for despite their greater leaning toward isolationism, the Republicans are no more inclined than the Democrats to leave the country defenseless.[23]

In treating issues in the Elmira election study of 1948, Berelson, Lazars-

---

[22] *Cf.* Turner, *op. cit.*, p. 56, in which he found differences on foreign policy difficult to assess in Congress, partly because of its tie with the executive branch; see also, George Belknap and Angus Campbell, "Political Party Identification and Attitudes toward Foreign Policy," *Public Opinion Quarterly,* Vol. 15 (Winter, 1951–52), pp. 608–19.

[23] The issue of defense spending has been kept separate from the other foreign policy issues because the magnitude of the scores for some of the leaders and all of the followers were obviously inflated by the launching of Sputnik I in November, 1957. The Sputnik incident occurred between the first and second wave of the leader survey and produced an increase in the number favoring defense spending of 40 percent for the Democrats and 33 percent for the Republicans. While this is a fascinating testimonial to the influence sometimes exercised by events on public opinion, its effect in this case was to distort scores in such a way as to make the leader and follower samples non-comparable. With proper caution, however, comparisons can be made between the Democratic and Republican leaders since both samples were affected in roughly the same way by Sputnik. For a similar reason we can also compare the Democratic followers with the Republican followers. Comparisons between leaders and followers on this issue cannot, however, be justified from our data.

feld, and McPhee[24] found it helpful to distinguish between "style" and "position" issues. "Style" issues principally yield symbolic, psychological, or subjective gratifications, and have relatively intangible consequences; "position" issues reflect direct, personal and material interests, and have more objective consequences. According to the Elmira report, "position" issues (or what politicians might call "bread and butter" issues) divide voters more sharply than style issues. Most of the issues tested in the present study would have to be classified as position issues, but five of them—United Nations, international alliances, foreign aid, immigration, and segregation—could be classified as style issues. Four others—natural resources, atomic energy, education, and slum clearance—contain both symbolic and material elements and can best be described as "mixed."

Although the classification is crude, the findings it yields are generally consistent with the claims of the Elmira study. On the fourteen position issues—taxes, trade unions, tariffs, minimum wages, farm prices, social security, credit restrictions, and the regulation of business, public utilities and monopolies—Democratic and Republican leaders show an average ratio score difference of .21. On the style issues the two parties differ by .13—a significantly smaller difference. Largest of all, however, are the differences for the "mixed" issues, which average more than .30. This result should occasion little surprise, for when ideology and interest are *both* at work, partisanship is likely to be intensified. Several considerations could account for the superiority of position over style issues as causes of political cleavage: they are "bread and butter" issues, and are thus more often subject to pressure by organized interest groups; they have immediate and tangible consequences, which may lead politicians to pay greater attention to them than they do to issues whose payoff is more uncertain; and, finally, they are not so likely to be part of the common core of values upon which the community structure rests.

Comparison of the magnitude of the differences between groups can be seen in Table B–3, where we have ranked the issues, high to low, according to the size of the difference between the groups being compared. By presenting a rank-order of differences for the two leader groups, for the two follower groups, and for the leaders and followers of each party, this table makes it possible to observe not only which issues most and least divide the several party groups, but whether they divide the leaders and followers in the same way.

Notice that the issues commonly thought to be most divisive do not always evoke the greatest cleavage between the parties. Immigration, tariffs, civil rights, monopoly control, and credit regulation fall toward the lower end of the rank order, while farm supports, federal aid to

[24] Bernard R. Berelson, Paul F. Lazarsfeld, and William N. McPhee, *Voting* (Chicago, 1954), ch. 9.

education, slum clearance, social security, minimum wages, public housing, and issues dealing with the regulation and taxation of business fall
toward the upper end. Though by no means uniformly, the older, more
traditional issues appear to have been superseded as sources of controversy
by issues that have come into prominence chiefly during the New Deal
and Fair Deal.

COMPARISONS BETWEEN FOLLOWERS

So far we have addressed ourselves to the differences between Democratic and Republican *leaders*. In each of the tables presented, however,
data are included from which the two sets of party *followers* may also
be compared.

The observation most clearly warranted from these data is that the
rank and file members of the two parties are far less divided than their
leaders. Not only do they diverge significantly on fewer issues—seven
as compared with 23 for the leaders samples—but the magnitudes of
the differences in their ratio scores are substantially smaller for every
one of the 24 issues. No difference is larger than .14, and on the majority
of the issues the disparity is smaller than .05. Insofar as they differ at
all, however, the followers tend to divide in a pattern similar to that
shown by the leaders, the correlation between their rank orders being
.72. All the issues on which the followers significantly disagree are of
the "bread and butter" variety, the more symbolic issues being so re-
motely experienced and so vaguely grasped that rank and file voters are
often unable to identify them with either party. Policies affecting farm
prices, business regulation, taxes, or minimum wages, by contrast, are
quickly felt by the groups to whom they are addressed and are therefore
more capable of arousing partisan identifications. It should also be noted
that while the average differences are small for all five categories, they
are smallest of all for foreign policy—the most removed and least well
understood group of issues in the entire array.[25]

Democratic and Republican followers were also compared on a number
of scales and reference group questions. The results, while generally
consistent with the differences between the leaders, show the followers
to be far more united than their leaders on these measures as well. Even

---

[25] For comparative data on party affiliation and issue outlooks among rank and
file voters, see Angus Campbell, Philip E. Converse, Warren E. Miller, and Donald
E. Stokes, *The American Voter* (in press), especially chs. 8 and 9 dealing with
issues and ideology. The text of this important report on the 1956 election study
carried out by the Michigan Survey Research Center unfortunately reached us
too late to be used to full advantage in the present analysis. The findings of
the Michigan and the PAB studies, relative to the role of issues and ideology
among the general population, corroborate and supplement each other to a very
great degree.

on business attitudes, independence of government, and economic conservatism, the differences are small and barely significant. No differences were found on such scales as tolerance, faith in democracy, procedural rights, conservatism-liberalism (classical), the California F scale and isolationism. The average Democrat is slightly more willing than the average Republican to label himself a liberal or to seek advice from liberal organizations; the contrary is true when it comes to adopting conservative identifications. Only in the differential trust they express toward business and labor are the two sets of followers widely separated.

These findings give little support to the claim that the "natural divisions" of the electorate are being smothered by party leaders.[26] Not only do the leaders disagree more sharply than their respective followers, but the level of consensus among the electorate (with or without regard to party) is fairly high. Inspection of the "increase" and "decrease" percentage scores (Tables B–2–A through B–2–E) shows that substantial differences of opinion exist among the electorate on only five of the 24 issues (credit restrictions, farm supports, segregation, and corporate and business taxes). Of course, voters may divide more sharply on issues at election time, since campaigns intensify party feeling and may also intensify opinions on issues. Available data from election studies allow no unequivocal conclusion on this point,[27] but even the party-linked differences found among voters during elections may largely be echoes of the opinions announced by the candidates—transient sentiments developed for the occasion and quickly forgotten.

LEADER CONFLICT AND FOLLOWER CONSENSUS: EXPLANATIONS

Considering the nature of the differences between the leader and follower samples, the interesting question is not why the parties fail to represent the "natural division" in the electorate (for that question rests on an unwarranted assumption) but why the party élites disagree at all, and why they divide so much more sharply than their followers?

Despite the great pressures toward uniformity we have noted in American society, many forces also divide the population culturally, economi-

---

[26] Cf. Stephen K. Bailey, *The Condition of Our National Parties* (monograph), Fund for the Republic, 1959.

[27] The data reported by the Elmira study of 1948 show the supporters of the two parties to be largely in agreement on issues. See Berelson, *et al., Voting,* pp. 186, 190, 194, 211. The findings of the 1956 Michigan Survey suggest strongly that most voters, even at election time, do not know much about issues and are unable to link the parties with particular issues. Campbell and his associates conclude, for example, that "many people fail to appreciate that an issue exists; others are insufficiently involved to pay attention to recognized issues; and still others fail to make connections between issue positions and party policy." *The American Voter,* ch. 8.

cally, and politically. The United States is, after all, a miscellany of ethnic and religious strains set down in a geographically large and diverse country. Many of these groups brought old conflicts and ideologies with them, and some have tried to act out in the new world the hopes and frustrations nurtured in the old. Then, too, despite rapid social mobility, social classes have by no means been eliminated. No special political insight is needed to perceive that the two parties characteristically draw from different strata of the society, the Republicans from the managerial, proprietary, and to some extent professional classes, the Democrats from labor, minorities, low income groups, and a large proportion of the intellectuals.[28] Partly because the leaders of the two parties tend to over-respond to the modal values of the groups with which they are principally identified, they gradually grow further apart on the key questions which separate their respective supporters.[29] The Republican emphasis on business ideology in both a cause and a consequence of its managerial and proprietary support; the greater Democratic emphasis on social justice, and on economic and social levelling, is both the occasion and the product of the support the party enjoys among intellectuals and the lower strata. These interrelationships are strengthened, moreover, by the tendency for a party's dominant supporters to gain a disproportionate number of positions in its leadership ranks.[30]

The differences which typically separate Democratic from Republican leaders seem also to reflect a deep-seated ideological cleavage often found among Western parties. One side of this cleavage is marked by a strong belief in the power of collective action to promote social justice, equality, humanitarianism, and economic planning, while preserving freedom; the other is distinguished by faith in the wisdom of the natural competitive process and in the supreme virtue of individualism, "character," self-reliance, frugality, and independence from government. To this cleavage is added another frequent source of political division, namely, a difference in attitude toward change between "radicals" and "moderates," between those who prefer to move quickly or slowly, to reform or to conserve. These differences in social philosophy and posture do not always coincide with the divisions in the social structure, and their elements do not, in all contexts, combine in the same way. But, however crudely, the American parties do tend to embody these competing points of view and to serve as reference groups for those who hold them.

---

[28] For an analysis of the connection between intellectuals and liberal politics, see Seymour M. Lipset, *Political Man* (New York, 1960), ch. 10; also Paul F. Lazarsfeld and Wagner Thielens, Jr., *The Academic Mind* (Glencoe, 1958), chs. 1 and 2.

[29] Samuel P. Huntington, "A Revised Theory of American Party Politics," *American Political Science Review*, Vol. 44 (1950), p. 676.

[30] PAB data supporting this generalization will be presented in a future publication.

Party cleavage in America was no doubt intensified by the advent of the New Deal, and by its immense electoral and intellectual success. Not only did it weld into a firm alliance the diverse forces that were to be crucial to all subsequent Democratic majorities, but it also made explicit the doctrines of the "welfare state" with which the party was henceforth to be inseparably identified. Because of the novelty of its program and its apparently radical threat to the familiar patterns of American political and economic life, it probably deepened the fervor of its Republican adversaries and drove into the opposition the staunchest defenders of business ideology. The conflict was further sharpened by the decline of left-wing politics after the war, and by the transfer of loyalties of former and potential radicals to the Democratic party. Once launched, the cleavage has been sustained by the tendency for each party to attract into its active ranks a disproportionate number of voters who recognize and share its point of view.

Why, however, are the leaders so much more sharply divided than their followers? The reasons are not hard to understand and are consistent with several of the hypotheses that underlay the present study.

(1) Consider, to begin with, that the leaders come from the more articulate segments of society and, on the average, are politically more aware than their followers and far better informed about issues.[31] For them, political issues and opinions are the everyday currency of party competition, not esoteric matters that surpass understanding. With their greater awareness and responsibility, and their greater need to defend their party's stands, they have more interest in developing a consistent set of attitudes—perhaps even an ideology. The followers of each party, often ignorant of the issues and their consequences, find it difficult to distinguish their beliefs from those of the opposition and have little reason to be concerned with the consistency of their attitudes. Furthermore, the American parties make only a feeble effort to educate the rank and file politically, and since no central source exists for the authoritative pronouncement of party policy,[32] the followers often do not know what their leaders believe or on what issues the parties chiefly divide. In short, if we mean by ideology a coherent body of informed social doctrine, it is possessed mainly by the articulate leadership, rarely by the masses.

(2) Differences in the degree of partisan involvement parallel the differences in knowledge and have similar consequences. The leaders, of course, have more party spirit than the followers and, as the election studies make plain, the stronger the partisanship, the larger the differences on issues. The leaders are more highly motivated not only to belong

---

[31] For the effects of education on issue familiarity, see Campbell *et al.*, *The American Voter*, ch. 8.

[32] E. E. Schattschneider, *op. cit.; Toward A More Responsible Two-Party System, passim.*

to a party appropriate to their beliefs, but to accept its doctrines and to learn how it differs from the opposition party. Since politics is more salient for leaders than for followers, they develop a greater stake in the outcome of the political contest and are more eager to discover the intellectual grounds by which they hope to make victory possible. Through a process of circular reinforcement, those for whom politics is most important are likely to become the most zealous participants, succeeding to the posts that deal in the formation of opinion. Ideology serves the instrumental purpose, in addition, of justifying the heavy investment that party leaders make in political activity. While politics offers many rewards, it also makes great demands on the time, money, and energies of its practitioners—sacrifices which they can more easily justify if they believe they are serving worthwhile social goals. The followers, in contrast, are intellectually far less involved, have less personal stake in the outcome of the competition, have little need to be concerned with the "correctness" of their views on public questions, and have even less reason to learn in precisely what ways their opinions differ from their opponents'. Hence, the party élites recruit members from a population stratified in some measure by ideology, while the rank and file renews itself by more random recruitment and is thus more likely to mirror the opinions of a cross section of the population.

(3) Part of the explanation for the greater consensus among followers than leaders resides in the nature and size of the two types of groups. Whereas the leader groups are comparatively small and selective, each of the follower groups number in the millions and, by their very size and unwieldiness, are predisposed to duplicate the characteristics of the population as a whole. Even if the Republicans draw disproportionately from the business-managerial classes and the Democrats from the trade union classes and the Democrats from the trade union movement, neither interest group has enough influence to shape distinctively the aggregate opinions of so large a mass of supporters. Size also affects the nature and frequency of interaction within the two types of groups. Because they comprise a smaller, more selectively chosen, organized, and articulate élite, the leaders are apt to associate with people of their own political persuasion more frequently and consistently than the followers do. They are not only less cross-pressured than the rank and file but they are also subjected to strong party group efforts to induce them to conform. Because their political values are continually renewed through frequent communication with people of like opinions, and because they acquire intense reference group identifications, they develop an extraordinary ability to resist the force of the opposition's arguments. While the followers, too, are thrown together and shielded to some extent, they are likely to mingle more freely with people of hostile political persuasions, to receive fewer partisan communications, and to hold views that are

only intermittently and inconsistently reinforced. Since, by comparison with the leaders, they possess little interest in or information about politics, they can more easily embrace "deviant" attitudes without discomfort and without challenge from their associates. Nor are they likely to be strongly rewarded, for troubling to have "correct" opinions. The followers, in short, are less often and less effectively indoctrinated than their leaders. The group processes described here would function even more powerfully in small, sectarian, tightly organized parties of the European type, but they are also present in the American party system, where they yield similar though less potent consequences.

(4) Political competition itself operates to divide the leaders more than the followers. If the parties are impelled to present a common face to the electorate, they are also strongly influenced to distinguish themselves from each other.[33] For one thing, they have a more heightened sense of the "national interest" than the followers do, even if they do not all conceive it in the same way. For another, they hope to improve their chances at the polls by offering the electorate a recognizable and attractive commodity. In addition, they seek emotional gratification in the heightened sense of brotherhood brought on by the struggle against an "out-group" whose claim to office seems always, somehow, to border upon usurpation. As with many ingroup-outgroup distinctions, the participants search for moral grounds to justify their antagonisms toward each other, and ideologies help to furnish such grounds. Among the followers, on the other hand, these needs exist, if at all, in much weaker form.

LEADERS VERSUS FOLLOWERS

In comparing each party élite with its own followers we were mainly interested in seeing how closely each body of supporters shared the point of view of its leaders, in order to test the hypothesis that party affiliation, even for the rank and file, is a function of ideological agreement. In predicting that the parties would tend to attract supporters who share their beliefs, we expected, of course, to find exceptions. We knew that many voters pay little attention to the ideological aspects of politics and that, in Gabriel Almond's phrase, a party's more "esoteric doctrines" are not always known to its followers.[34] Nevertheless we were not prepared for the findings turned up by this phase of the inquiry, for the differences between leaders and followers—among the Republicans at least—are beyond anything we had expected. Indeed, the conclusion is

---

[33] See E. E. Schattschneider, *Party Government*, p. 192.

[34] Gabriel Almond, *The Appeals of Communism* (Princeton, 1954), pp. 5-6, and ch. 3.

TABLE B-3
Rank Order of Differences in the Support-Ratio Scores of Party Leaders and Followers*

Dem. v. Rep. Leaders	Diff. between Scores†	Dem. v. Rep. Followers	Diff. between Scores	Dem. Leaders v. Followers	Diff. between Scores	Rep. Leaders v. Followers	Diff. between Scores
Natural Resources	+.39	Farm Supports	+.14	Immigration	+.25	Fed. Aid to Edu.	−.39
Farm Supports	+.38	Gov't. Reg. of Business	+.12	Anti-Monopoly	+.15	Taxes-Large Income	−.32
Fed. Aid to Edu.	+.37	Taxes-Large Income	+.10	Taxes-Large Income	+.15	Taxes-Corp.	−.28
Taxes-Corp.	+.33	Minimum Wages	+.09	Taxes-Business	−.13	Taxes-Business	−.27
Reg.-Business	+.33	Taxes-Business	+.09	Reg. Pub. Util.	+.12	Natural Resources	−.25
Taxes-Large Inc.	+.28	Reg. Pub. Util.	+.07	Tariffs	−.11	Pub. Housing	−.23
Pub. Housing	+.27	Taxes-Corp.	+.07	Restrict. Credit	−.09	Reg. Business	−.22
Reg. Pub. Util.	+.26	Social Security	+.07	Natural Resources	+.09	Social Security	−.22
Social Security	+.23	Fed. Aid to Edu.	+.06	Fed. Aid to Edu.	−.08	Farm Supports	−.22
Taxes-Business	+.22	Reg. Trade Unions	−.05	Foreign Aid	+.08	Minimum Wages	−.18
Minimum Wages	+.21	Natural Resources	+.05	Reliance on U.N.	+.07	Reg. Trade Unions	+.17
Reliance on U.N.	+.21	Public Housing	+.05	Minimum Wages	−.05	Immigration	+.13
Anti-monopoly	+.20	Taxes-Small Income	−.04	Social Security	−.05	Reliance on U.N.	−.12
Atomic Energy Control	+.18	American Participation, NATO	+.04	Reg. Trade Unions	+.05	Enforce Integration	−.12
Reg. Trade Unions	−.18	Atomic Energy Control	+.04	Atomic Energy Control	+.04	Taxes-Middle Income	−.11
American Participation, NATO	+.13	Immigration	−.03	Farm Supports	+.02	Atomic Energy Control	−.10
Enforce Integration	+.12	Defense Spending	+.02	Reg. Business	−.02	American Participation, NATO	−.10
Tariffs	−.11	Taxes-Middle Income	−.02	Enforce Integration	+.01	Reg. Public Utilities	−.07
Foreign Aid	+.10	Reliance on U.N.	+.02	Taxes-Middle Income	−.01	Anti-Monopoly	−.04
Increase Immigration	+.10	Tariffs	−.01	Taxes-Corporation	−.01	Foreign Aid	−.03
Taxes-Small Income	−.08	Enforce Integration	−.01	Taxes-Small Income	−.01	Taxes-Small Income	+.03
Taxes-Middle Income	+.08	Restriction Credit	+.01	American Participation, NATO	−.01	Restriction Credit	−.01
Restriction Credit	−.07	Foreign Aid	−.01	Public Housing	.00	Tariffs	−.01
Defense Spending	+.03	Anti-Monopoly	.00	Defense Spending	**	Defense Spending	**

N's. Democratic leaders: 1,788; Republican leaders: 1,232; Democratic followers: 821; Republican followers: 623.

* The plus sign means the first group listed in the heading is more favorable to the issue named than the second group; the minus sign means that the second group is the more favorable.

** Leaders and followers cannot be compared on defense spending, for reasons given in footnote 23.

† Size of difference required for differences to be significant at .01 level: Democratic leaders v. Republican—.048; Democratic v. Republican followers—.068; Democratic leaders v. followers—.054; Republican leaders v. followers—.063.

inescapable that the views of the Republican rank and file are, on the whole, much closer to those of the Democratic leaders than to those of the Republican leaders. Although conflicts in outlook also exist between Democratic leaders and followers, they are less frequent or severe.

If we turn once again to the table of rank order differences, we see that the Democratic followers differ significantly from their leaders on twelve of the 23 issues, and that the average difference in the ratio scores of the two samples is .07. Democratic leaders and Republican followers differ significantly on only eleven of the 23 issues, with an average difference between them of only .08. Notice, by contrast, that Republican leaders and followers diverge significantly on 18 of the 23 issues, and show an average difference of .16. To complete the comparison, the Republican leaders and Democratic followers were in disagreement on 19 of the 23 issues, their average difference being .20. As these comparisons make plain, there is substantial consensus on national issues between Democratic leaders and Democratic and Republican followers, while the Republican leaders are separated not only from the Democrats but from their own rank and file members as well.

Examination of the Democratic scores shows the leaders to be slightly more "progressive" than their followers on most of the issues on which differences appear. The leaders are, for example, more favorable to public ownership of natural resources, to regulation of monopolies and public utilities, to a reduction of tariffs, and to a liberalized credit policy. They are more internationalist on the foreign aid and United Nations issues and substantially more sympathetic to the maintenance and expansion of immigration. The results showing the relative radicalism of the two samples are not unequivocal, however, for on several issues—federal aid to education, minimum wages, and taxes on business enterprise and large incomes—the followers take the more radical view. Nor are the differences significant on such issues as atomic energy, slum clearance, segregation, farm price supports, government control of business and trade unions, and taxes on middle and small income groups. In general, the followers turn out more radical chiefly on a few of the bread and butter issues—a reflection, no doubt, of their lower socio-economic status. When we control for occupation, the differences between Democratic leaders and followers on these issues largely disappear.

Consideration of the scores of Republican leaders and followers shows not only that they are widely separated in their outlooks but also that the leaders are uniformly more conservative than their followers. Only on the immigration issue is the trend reversed. The followers hold the more "radical" ideas on the two public ownership issues, on five of the six equalitarian and human welfare issues, on four of the seven regulation-of-the-economy issues, and on four of the five tax policy issues. They are also more willing to place greater reliance upon the U.N.

and upon international military alliances. Observe that the largest differences occur on those issues which have most sharply separated New Deal-Fair Deal spokesmen from the hard core of the Republican opposition—federal aid to education, redistribution of wealth through taxes on business, corporations and the wealthy, public ownership of natural resources, public housing, regulation of business, social security, farm price supports, minimum wages, and trade union regulations.

In short, whereas Republican leaders hold to the tenets of business ideology and remain faithful to the spirit and intellectual mood of leaders like Robert A. Taft, the rank and file Republican supporters have embraced, along with their Democratic brethren, the regulatory and social reform measures of the Roosevelt and Truman administrations. This inference receives further support from the scores on our Party Ideology scale where, on a variety of attitudes and values which characteristically distinguish the leaders of the two parties, the Republican followers fall closer to the Democratic than to the Republican side of the continuum. Thus, in addition to being the preferred party of the more numerous classes, the Democrats also enjoy the advantages over their opponents of holding views that are more widely shared throughout the country.

Assuming the findings are valid, we were obviously wrong to expect that party differentiation among followers would depend heavily upon ideological considerations.[35] Evidently, party attachment is so much a function of other factors (e.g. class and primary group memberships, religious affiliation, place of residence, mass media, etc.) that many voters can maintain their party loyalties comfortably even while holding views that contradict the beliefs of their own leaders.

Still, we are not entitled to conclude that issue outlook has no effect on the party affiliation of ordinary members. It is conceivable, for example, that the Republican party has come to be the minority party partly because the opinions of its spokesmen are uncongenial to a majority of the voters. We have no way of knowing from our data—collected at only a single point in time—how many "normally" Republican voters, if any, have defected to the Democrats or fled into independency because they disapprove of Republican beliefs. At the present stage of the analysis, we have no grounds for going beyond the proposition that political affiliation without conformity on issues is possible on a wide scale. In future analyses we shall attempt to learn more about the nature of the relationship between belief and party affiliation by stratifying voters according to the frequency with which they conform to the beliefs of their party leaders. We hope, in this way, to discover whether those who conform least are also less firm in their party loyalties.

---

[35] See the discussion bearing on this conclusion in Campbell *et al., op. cit.,* chs. 8 and 9. Also, Avery Leiserson, *Parties and Politics, An Institutional and Behavioral Approach* (New York, 1958), pp. 162–166.

THE HOMOGENEITY OF SUPPORT FOR LEADERS
AND FOLLOWERS

So far we have only considered conflict and agreement *between* groups. We should now turn to the question of consensus *within* groups. To what extent is each of our samples united on fundamental issues?

In order to assess homogeneity of opinion within party groups, standard deviation scores were computed on each issue for each of the four samples. The higher the standard deviation, of course, the greater the disagreement. The range of possible sigma scores is from 0 (signifying that every member of the sample has selected the same response) to .500 (signifying that all responses are equally divided between the "increase" and "decrease" alternatives). If we assume that the three alternative responses had been randomly (and therefore equally) selected, the standard deviations for the four samples would fall by chance alone around .410. Scores at or above this level may be taken to denote extreme dispersion among the members of a sample while scores in the neighborhood of .300 or below suggest that unanimity within the sample is fairly high. By these somewhat arbitrary criteria we can observe immediately (Table B–4) that consensus within groups is greater on most issues than we would expect by chance alone, but that it is extremely high in only a few instances. Although the Republican leaders appear on the average to be the most united and the Democratic leaders the least united of the four groups, the difference between their homogeneity scores (.340 v. .310) is too small to be taken as conclusive. The grounds are somewhat better for rejecting the belief that leaders are more homogeneous in their outlooks than their followers, since the hypothesis holds only for one party and not for the other.

While generalizations about the relative unity of the four samples seem risky, we can speak more confidently about the rank order of agreement *within* samples. In Table B–4 we have ranked the issues according to the degree of consensus exhibited toward them by the members of each of the four party groups. There we see that the leaders of the Republican party are most united on the issues that stem from its connections with business—government regulation of business, taxes (especially on business), regulation of trade unions, and minimum wages. The Democratic leaders are most united on those issues which bear upon the support the party receives from the lower and middle income groups—taxes on small and middle incomes, anti-monopoly, slum clearance, social security, and minimum wages. The Republican leaders divide most severely on federal aid to education, slum clearance, U.N. support, segregation, and public control of atomic energy and natural resources; the Democratic leaders are most divided on farm prices, segregation, credit restrictions, immigration, and the natural resources issue. Among the followers the

TABLE B-4
Consensus within Party Groups: Rank Order of Homogeneity of Support on 24 Issues

Average Rank Order*	Issue	Democratic Leaders Rank Order	Democratic Leaders Sigma	Republican Leaders Rank Order	Republican Leaders Sigma	Democratic Followers Rank Order	Democratic Followers Sigma	Republican Followers Rank Order	Republican Followers Sigma
1	Tax on Small Incomes	1	.220	6	.270	1	.224	1	.250
2	Tax on Middle Incomes	3	.276	4	.248	6	.292	2	.278
3	Social Security Benefits	5	.282	8	.296	2	.266	3	.286
4	Minimum Wages	6	.292	5	.268	4	.276	4	.294
5	Enforcement of Anti-Monopoly	2	.246	13	.321	8	.324	7	.314
6	Regulation of Public Utilities	8	.307	10	.300	10	.336	5.5	.310
7	Slum Clearance	4	.276	23	.386	3	.274	5.5	.310
8	Regulation of Trade Unions	12	.356	3	.240	9	.331	15	.345
9	Government Regulation of Business	17	.376	1	.192	20	.363	8	.315
10	Tax on Business	9	.338	2	.236	19	.362	16	.348
11	Level of Tariffs	10	.350	16	.344	11	.338	9	.316
12	Public Control of Atomic Energy	7	.302	20	.362	7	.312	13	.340
13	Federal Aid to Education	13	.360	24	.394	5	.283	11	.322
14	Foreign Aid	19	.383	12	.317	12.5	.340	12	.340
15	Tax on Large Incomes	11	.356	9	.298	17	.358	22	.379
16	American Participation in Military Alliances, NATO	14	.370	18	.351	14	.350	14	.344
17	Immigration into U.S.	21	.399	17	.345	12.5	.340	10	.318
18	Corporate Income Tax	16	.375	7	.284	21	.371	17	.361
19	Restrictions on Credit	22	.400	14	.324	16	.358	18	.362
20	Defense Spending	15	.371	15	.334	22	.380	21	.366
21	Public Ownership of Natural Resources	20	.393	19	.354	15	.352	19	.362
22	Reliance on U.N.	18	.380	22	.384	18	.359	20	.365
23	Level of Farm Supports	24	.421	11	.306	23	.414	23	.397
24	Enforce Integration	23	.416	21	.382	24	.418	24	.399

* The range of sigma scores is from .192 to .421, out of a possible range of .000 (most united) to .500 (least united). Hence, the lower the rank order the greater the unity on the issue named.

patterns of unity and division are very similar, as attested by the high correlation of .83 between the rank orders of their homogeneity scores. Both Republican and Democratic followers exhibit great cohesion, for example, on taxes on small and middle incomes, social security, slum clearance, and minimum wages. Both divide rather sharply on segregation, farm price supports, defense spending, U.N. support, and taxes on large incomes. The two sets of followers, in short, are alike not only in their opinions on issues but in the degree of unanimity they exhibit toward them.

Inspection of the homogeneity data furnishes additional evidence on the between-group comparisons made earlier. Whereas Democratic and Republican followers divide on issues in approximately the same way, the two sets of leaders differ from each other in this respect also (the correlation between their rank orders on homogeneity is only .28). Democratic leaders and followers tend to unite or divide on the same issues for the most part (r equals .77), but Republican leaders and followers are not parallel in this respect either (r equals .30). The pattern of homogeneity and dispersion among Republican followers is, in fact, much closer to that of the Democratic leaders (r equals .75).

In computing scores for homogeneity we were in part concerned to test the belief that political parties develop greatest internal solidarity on those questions which most separate them from their opponents. According to this hypothesis, external controversy has the effect of uniting the members further by confronting them with a common danger. Whether or not this hypothesis would be borne out in a study of small, sectarian parties we cannot say, but it receives no support from the present study of the American mass parties. Comparisons of the rank order data in Tables B–3 and B–4 show that there is no consistent connection between interparty conflict and intra-party cohesion. The correlations between the rank orders of difference and the rank orders of homogeneity are in every case insignificant.[36]

SUMMARY AND CONCLUSIONS

The research described in this paper—an outgrowth of a nationwide inquiry into the nature and sources of political affiliation, activity, and belief—was principally designed to test a number of hypotheses about the relation of ideology to party membership. Responses from large samples of Democratic and Republican leaders and followers were compared on twenty-four key issues and on a number of attitude questions and scales. Statistical operations were carried out to assess conflict and consen-

---

[36] For an interesting set of comparative data on the relation of internal party cohesion to issue outlook, see Morris Davis and Sidney Verba, "Party Affiliation and International Opinions in Britain and France, 1947–1956," *Public Opinion Quarterly,* Winter 1960–61.

sus among party groups and to estimate the size and significance of differences. From the data yielded by this inquiry, the following inferences
seem most warranted:

1.   Although it has received wide currency, especially among Euro-
peans, the belief that the two American parties are identical in principle
and doctrine has little foundation in fact. Examination of the opinions
of Democratic and Republican leaders shows them to be distinct communities of co-believers who diverge sharply on many important issues.
Their disagreements, furthermore, conform to an image familiar to many
observers and are generally consistent with differences turned up by
studies of Congressional roll calls. The unpopularity of many of the positions held by Republican leaders suggests also that the parties submit
to the demands of their constituents less slavishly than is commonly
supposed.

2.   Republican and Democratic leaders stand furthest apart on the
issues that grow out of their group identification and support—out of
the managerial, proprietary, and high-status connections of the one, and
the labor, minority, low-status, and intellectual connections of the other.
The opinions of each party élite are linked less by chance than by membership in a common ideological domain. Democratic leaders typically
display the stronger urge to elevate the lowborn, the uneducated, the
deprived minorities, and the poor in general; they are also more disposed
to employ the nation's collective power to advance humanitarian and
social welfare goals (e.g., social security, immigration, racial integration,
a higher minimum wage, and public education). They are more critical
of wealth and big business and more eager to bring them under regulation.
Theirs is the greater faith in the wisdom of using legislation for redistributing the national product and for furnishing social services on a
wide scale. Of the two groups of leaders, the Democrats are the more
"progressively" oriented toward social reform and experimentation. The
Republican leaders, while not uniformly differentiated from their opponents, subscribe in greater measure to the symbols and practices of indi-
vidualism, *laissez-faire*, and national independence. They prefer to overcome humanity's misfortunes by relying upon personal effort, private
incentives, frugality, hard work, responsibility, self-denial (for both men
and government), and the strengthening rather than the diminution of
the economic and status distinctions that are the "natural" rewards of
the differences in human character and fortunes. Were it not for the
hackneyed nature of the designation and the danger of forcing traits
into a mold they fit only imperfectly, we might be tempted to describe
the Republicans as the chief upholders of what Max Weber has called
the "Protestant Ethic."[37] Not that the Democrats are insensible to the

---

[37] Max Weber, *Protestant Ethic and the Spirit of Capitalism* (London, 1948),
ch. V.

"virtues" of the Protestant-capitalistic ethos, but they embrace them less firmly or uniformly. The differences between the two élites have probably been intensified by the rise of the New Deal and by the shift of former radicals into the Democratic party following the decline of socialist and other left-wing movements during and after the war.

3. Whereas the leaders of the two parties converge strongly, their followers differ only moderately in their attitudes toward issues. The hypothesis that party beliefs unite adherents and bring them into the party ranks may hold for the more active members of a mass party but not for its rank and file supporters. Republican followers, in fact, disagree far more with their own leaders than with the leaders of the Democratic party. Little support was found for the belief that deep cleavages exist among the electorate but are ignored by the leaders. One might, indeed more accurately assert the contrary, to wit: that the natural cleavages between the leaders are largely ignored by the voters. However, we cannot presently conclude that ideology exerts no influence over the habits of party support, for the followers do differ significantly and in the predicted directions on some issues. Furthermore, we do not know how many followers may previously have been led by doctrinal considerations to shift their party allegiances.

4. Except for their desire to ingratiate themselves with as many voters as possible, the leaders of the two parties have more reason than their followers to hold sharply opposing views on the important political questions of the day. Compared with the great mass of supporters, they are articulate, informed, highly partisan, and involved; they comprise a smaller and more tightly knit group which is closer to the well-springs of party opinion, more accessible for indoctrination, more easily rewarded or punished for conformity or deviation, and far more affected, politically and psychologically, by engagement in the party struggle for office. If the leaders of the two parties are not always candid about their disagreements, the reason may well be that they sense the great measure of consensus to be found among the electorate.

5. Finding that party leaders hold contrary beliefs does not prove that they *act* upon those beliefs or that the two parties are, in practice, governed by different outlooks. In a subsequent paper we shall consider these questions more directly by comparing platform and other official party pronouncements with the private opinions revealed in this study. Until further inquiries are conducted, however, it seems reasonable to assume that the views held privately by party leaders can never be entirely suppressed but are bound to crop out in hundreds of large and small ways—in campaign speeches, discussions at party meetings, private communications to friends and sympathizers, statements to the press by party officials and candidates, legislative debates, and public discussions on innumerable national, state, and local questions. If, in other words,

the opinions of party leaders are as we have described them, there is every chance that they are expressed and acted upon to some extent. Whether this makes our parties "ideological" depends, of course, on how narrowly we define that term. Some may prefer to reserve that designation for parties that are more obviously preoccupied with doctrine, more intent upon the achievement of a systematic political program, and more willing to enforce a common set of beliefs upon their members and spokesmen.

6. The parties are internally united on some issues, divided on others. In general, Republican leaders achieve greatest homogeneity on issues that grow out of their party's identification with business, Democratic leaders on issues that reflect their connection with liberal and lower-income groups. We find no support for the hypothesis that the parties achieve greatest internal consensus on the issues which principally divide them from their opponents.

In a sequel to this paper we shall offer data on the demographic correlates of issue support, which show that most of the differences presented here exist independently of factors like education, occupation, age, religion, and sectionalism. Controlling for these influences furnishes much additional information and many new insights but does not upset our present conclusions in any important respect. Thus, the parties must be considered not merely as spokesmen for other interest groups but as reference groups in their own right, helping to formulate, to sustain, and to speak for a recognizable point of view.

chapter

5

The context of discovery

The knowledge of forms and requirements of concepts, generalizations, and testing procedures are of little value without substance,[1] but where do we get the substance? In large part we get the substance from the literature, i.e., the generalizations that other people have discovered and tested.[2] If our knowledge of why political systems persist or change and why people behave as they do in a variety of situations is to advance beyond what others have discovered in the past, however, we must be as conscious of discovery as we are of testing.

Unfortunately, little time or space is devoted to a discussion of discovery in any field. It is either viewed as the result of a happy accident occurring to properly skilled people who are able to recognize it as a discovery or as the culmination of a tenaciously pursued goal by someone who has most of the knowledge in his field at his fingertips. The discovery of an idea is not expected to happen to a beginner. But a major discovery involves shaking the theoretical constraints in a field, something that is very difficult to do after someone has been trained to accept and use them all of his student and professional life. We feel, therefore, that the context of discovery merits some discussion and consideration for those who have not yet internalized the theoretical constraints and, consequently, need not shake them before making a discovery.

Many of the "truths" in every field are in fact myths that have gained general acceptance because they have been repeated so many times. The scholar must rigorously train himself not to disregard surprising findings that contradict these myths. He must take that surprising finding and worry it until he can subsume it under accepted generalizations or con-

---

[1] One can also say that a knowledge of the facts of substance is of little value without an appropriate knowledge of form and requirements.

[2] We will describe many of these generalizations in later chapters.

struct new patterns which explain it as well as many of the observations accounted for by the old generalizations. The beginner, on the other hand, has less background for deciding what is or is not a surprising finding and, at least in the case of political science, may be equally burdened with the political myths of his society. If he can surmount these hurdles, he will worry less about going against the grain of professional knowledge. We are saying, therefore, that while the beginner must labor under the burden of inadequate knowledge and skills, he is not without the advantage of freedom from professional truths in his pursuit of new ideas. With this advantage in mind, we will categorize types of discovery and describe some of the techniques that can be used as vehicles for discovery.

The nature of discovery

You may be thinking that there is nothing new under the sun, that every well-known discovery, e.g., Darwin's theory of evolution, has been based on someone else's ideas. When people say this, they are confusing the continuing presence of most sense datum with the way that people see that sense datum. One of the basic assumptions is that our visual experiences are the same, but variations in the ways we organize these experiences cause us to say that we see different things. Figures 5–1 and 5–2 illustrate this organizational aspect of seeing.[3] The figures all

FIGURE 5–1	FIGURE 5–2
Perceptual Variation: 1	Perceptual Variation: 2

Source: Norwood Russell Hanson, *Patterns of Discovery* (Cambridge, England: Cambridge University Press, 1958).

appear to be birds in Figure 5–1 until we "see" that the "bird" in the lower right-hand corner of Figure 5–1 is "seen" as an antelope in Figure 5–2.

While retaining the part of the assumption that deals with the variation in the organization of our seeing, some recent research findings suggest

---

[3] Figures 5–1 and 5–2 are taken with permission from Norwood Russell Hanson, *Patterns of Discovery* (Cambridge, England: Cambridge University Press, 1958), pp. 13–14.

that we should include some variation in the visual experience aspect. Estimates that perhaps 20 to 25 percent of us have physiologically based perceptual handicaps have been made. While the work on identifying the basic types and the physiological characteristics of these handicaps is not well developed, we can point to the example of people seeing things backwards as an example. In the severest cases, not only do words appear backwards, but a car that is seen by others as coming from the side road on the right may be seen by most of us as coming from the side road on the left. We will begin, then, with the assumption that there is some variation in our visual experiences and greater variation in the patterns that give these experiences organization and coherence.

This may seem like a digression from the main subject of this chapter, but we are trying to suggest that what may be new under the sun is the discovery of a new pattern that organizes our sense experiences in a way different from that accepted by others. Therefore, your problem, like ours, is to try to "look" at the same data in a different way—not for the sake of being different, but in the hope that this different way will produce a better explanation for the behavior that we are observing than the pattern that was previously accepted.

Strategies for discovery

One general search strategy is to read extensively in other areas, looking for patterns and models whose application to your problem will allow you to see the problem in ways different from the known patterns. Some, for example, have worked in economics, particularly in the economic theories of different types of markets—competitive, oligopolistic, and monopolistic—looking for models to apply to democracies, authoritarian regimes, and totalitarian regimes. As you read in different disciplines, you should continuously ask yourself the following two questions: Can I restate my problem this way? Can I relate this to some aspect of my problem?

One danger involved in transferring a concept or a theory from one discipline to another is that the concepts, assumptions, and hypotheses are not precisely the same when we apply them to our own problem by specifying new empirical indicators. The use of the human organism as an analogy for the political system is frequently criticized for this.[4] When thinking of a political system as a human organism with processes and functions designed to maintain the system, many have failed to note the difference between the relatively closed nature of the human organism and the open nature of the political system. In other words, we have to be careful not to transfer the excess and perhaps inconsistent baggage

---

[4] See our discussion of functionalism in Chapter 7 for an analogy of this type.

of assumptions and concept meanings when we transfer models and patterns to our problem area.

One, need not go into another discipline, of course; we may find a new way of looking at the same observations by examining a subfield in political science that is new. Transferring patterns across fields within the same discipline may produce some of the same problems encountered, in transferring across disciplines. The empirical indicators will usually have to be changed, and the consistency of the concepts and the new indicators will have to be checked.[5]

Within this general interdisciplinary strategy, one can develop a number of competencies or skills in the use of techniques and research designs that have been created primarily for the purpose of discovery rather than hypothesis testing. Of these, we will describe concept development, case studies, simulation, and small group studies.

Vehicles to discovery

Theoretical concept development in political science consists primarily of identifying from among the concepts already defined or used one that interests the researcher and that can be expanded and refined in definition. In its modified state, the concept is then related to other concepts. The approaches described in Chapters 8 and 9 present the outcomes of this process. Conflict, for example, has been defined and classified, and the different types of conflict are related to decision-making procedures, group consensus and cohesion, perception, change, revolution, communication, power, influence, and role conflict. The variety of conceptual and empirical studies in the literature suggests that it may be possible to develop a more general definition of the concept of choice behavior, to develop a classification of different types of choice situations, and to relate choice to a number of other concepts. The same can be said for participation and political mobility.

Concept development may take the form of the construction of a typology such as those suggested in Chapter 2 relating to the characteristics of political systems.[6] In most cases, a typology will be developed out of the logical construction of two or more classificatory concepts. At this stage, the concern is to spell out all of the logically possible combinations. For example, in Aristotle's typology of political systems (see Chapter 2) there are six logically possible outcomes based on the two classification principles: number of rulers (one, few, many) and

---

[5] Even with a small chance of success, we are recommending that the beginner skip around in his reading and thinking in the hope that he will happen across a new idea for organizing our observations.

[6] For an extended discussion of typological construction, see John C. McKinney, *Constructive Typology and Social Theory* (New York: Appleton-Century-Crofts, 1966).

interest of the rulers (all or the rulers). Whether a typology is fruitful will depend on a number of considerations, including (1) whether there are real-world examples of the combinations, (2) whether the typology is simple enough to provide for utility and at the same time complex enough to capture meaningful aspects of a situation, and (3) whether it leads to the discovery of significant generalizations.

Constructing new typologies consists primarily of trying to identify the characteristics of the thing that will be related to the distinctive patterns of behavior that we are ultimately interested in predicting and explaining. The common typology of democratic, authoritarian, and totalitarian political systems is based on selecting characteristics which will assign nations to each of these types. The characteristic names are common to all three, but have distinctive values associated with the different types. Regularity of elections might be used as one of the characteristics. An admittedly simplistic specification of values for this characteristic would be to say that a nation (1) with regular periodic elections is democratic, (2) with some irregularity of elections is authoritarian, and (3) with infrequent nonregular elections is totalitarian. As we indicated in Chapter 3, a good typology is both exhaustive and mutually exclusive; each nation can be assigned to one type, and no nation can be assigned to more than one type. To develop such typologies one takes the object, process, situation, or behavior of interest, and from descriptive sources tries to identify distinctive "clusters." Although there is no necessary relationship to theory building, many people think about behaviors that might be associated with each of their clusters.

Another less impressionistic way of identifying types is to compare possible subsets of nations, people, groups, or behaviors with the generalizations or aggregate (macro) data for all nations, people, groups, or behaviors. Beginning with the aggregate generalization that international conflict is not correlated with internal conflict, we might ask if there is a subset of nations for which there appears to be an association. That is, the correlation for the total population might be very low, but for a subset of nations the correlation could be high. To find if this is the case, a measure of association is computed for all, or what the researcher believes are the most likely, subsets. If he finds that there are some combinations which have significantly different associations from the macro association, he will look at these combinations for similarities that they do not share with the other nations. He might find, for example, that they are similar with respect to ideology, size, homogeneity of political culture, or level of economic development. From this finding, he would construct a typology that grouped nations in terms of their values on these characteristics and name the types.

The maximum number of types is limited by the total number of objects, processes, people, nations, groups, or behaviors in the population.

In the example above, more than 140 types are possible, but such a typology is not likely to be very helpful since it does not simplify the problem. Also, the number of types may be limited by the amount of variation that has been conceptualized for the behavior that we ultimately want to associate with these types. If we want to predict the degree of political mobility in a group and we have defined the values of the concept as being low, medium, and high, a typology consisting of six types would be useless. There are not six variations in the behavior we want to predict. Therefore, the number of types in a typology should in part be determined by the number of values of the behavior that you would like to associate with the types.

A case study can lead to the development of new concepts and typologies as well as suggesting new hypotheses. A case study is an extensive description and intensive examination of a single case, whether that case be a single action, a decision, an individual, an organization, or a system. Case studies will most frequently stress the uniqueness of the case in question, and the complexity and richness of supporting data can be quite extensive. This is, in fact, the prime virtue of the case approach. It allows the investigator to immerse himself in the abundance and variety of the case materials. Typically, a person decides to do a case study when he asks such questions as: How and why did we get into Vietnam? How and why is the model cities program in my town being criticized by the people that it is supposed to help? Even though the individual may really be interested in more general questions, such as what the consequences are of federal aid to the local level compared to state and local aid in the community, there may be so little research on this question that he is driven by necessity to consider a case study.

Before discussing the discovery aspects of case studies, we should indicate that they are not appropriate for rejecting statistical hypotheses. Why not? Let us take an example of the hypothesized relationship between low economic development and authoritarian political regimes. Suppose that one case chosen for investigation revealed an authoritarian regime with high economic development. Would this invalidate the hypothesis? The obvious answer is that it would not, because the hypothesis was framed as a statistical relationship.[7] Therefore, a single case which does not fit cannot invalidate the hypothesis. What if we did find an authoritarian regime and low economic development both present in the case? Are we any better off? Again, the answer is clearly no, for we have no way of knowing from the single case if authoritarian regimes are absent when economic development is high. The logical form of a "one-shot" case study is diagrammed in Figure 5–3. In effect, a case

---

[7] If our hypothesis had been presented as a universal relationship, i.e., *all* authoritarian systems have low levels of economic development, one case which does not support it would be sufficient to reject the hypothesis.

FIGURE 5–3
The Logical Form of a "One-Shot" Case Study

Presumed Causal (Independent) *Factor*	*Presumed Effect (Dependent)* *Factor*
x ——————————————→ y	
Economic development (high or low)	Democracy (present or absent)

study of this design allows for *no* inferences about the relationships between x and y, either in terms of association or in terms of causation. This is so for three reasons:

1. Given the static nature of the "one-shot" case study, we do not even know for sure that changes in x are accompanied by changes in y within the case under question.[8]
2. As mentioned above, we do not have a comparison with what happens when x is not present.
3. We do not have any control over possible confounding third factors, such as other events which might produce both economic development and democracy. This is the problem of "spuriousness."

It seems clear from this discussion that a case study would be an inappropriate way to gather data which had the potential for invalidating the hypotheses in question. However, exploratory research is just as important as hypothesis testing in social science. Case studies may be a fruitful source for the generation of ideas. Of particular use may be the examination of purposefully selected cases.

What are the uses of case studies? Generally, the uses are in the areas of hypothesis generation and illustration. As an example of hypothesis generation, we have the classical study of the German Social Democratic political party by Robert Michels.[9] According to his observation, the party, which had a radical democratic ideology, was actually an undemocratic (oligarchical) organization. This observation of a single case, plus other selected evidence, led Michels to formulate his famous "iron law of oligarchy"—"who says organization, says oligarchy."[10]

In addition, deviant cases may provide the stimulus for hypothesis generation or theory modification. Following Michels, the sociologists Seymour Martin Lipset, Martin Trow, and James Coleman[11] observed that although many trade unions appeared to conform to the "iron law," there was at least one prominent exception: the International Typographical Workers Union. An examination of this case led to a series of hypothe-

---

[8] Of course, examining a case over time can alleviate this problem by allowing for the observation of changes in x and y.

[9] *Political Parties* (New York: Free Press, 1962).

[10] *Ibid.*, p. 15.

[11] *Union Democracy* (Garden City, N.Y.: Doubleday & Co., 1962).

ses about the conditions under which Michels' arguments were not valid or should be modified.

Finally, a particularly well-chosen case may *illustrate* a line of argument very well. As an example, a case study of the 1964 presidential election provides an excellent illustration of what happens in American politics when a party nominates a candidate who is perceived by the electorate as "too extreme" to be elected.[12]

There are really two discovery processes involved in a case study. First, as you describe the behavior and event sequence over time, you may notice that certain recurring patterns of behavior or uniformities occur. You are trying to develop a pattern that relates discrete events and behaviors in the case study. At this point, you have no idea if this pattern is common to all cases of this type or representative of the majority of cases. You probably cannot even describe a total population of such cases. Then you are involved in the second discovery process. You try to restate your pattern of discrete events in more general terms so that you or someone else can go on to other case studies to check your more generally formulated hypotheses.

To illustrate this, consider a case study of a 10-year industrial development of a particular town and its effects on the numbers and types of people that join organized interest groups to participate in a variety of community issues. As you gather all documentary evidence, together with interviews with city officials, members of community interest groups, and those residents of the community that do not participate; you discover that the executives of the Jay, Brown, and Kerry companies frequently are found as leaders in interest groups like the Chamber of Commerce. The executives of the Zero Electronics Company and the TeeVee Tape Corporation, however, are usually leaders and participants in the Library Guild, the Historical Society, and school groups. Those not employed by these companies rarely participate in any interest groups. This is your first discovery, and it is stated in a fairly particularistic manner: note the company name and interest group identifications.

At this point you may wonder if variations in industrial development are associated with variations in political participation. Looking back at the company names and determining their products suggests that you might substitute heavy and light industry for the two sets of company names, respectively. Considering now the interest group names, you may notice that the interest groups to which the heavy industry leaders belong are primarily business groups. The other interest groups might be called community conservation groups. Now that you have generalized your concepts, you can formulate the statement that is your second discovery:

---

[12] For a discussion, see Philip E. Converse *et al.*, "Electoral Myth and Reality: The 1964 Election," *American Political Science Review*, Vol. 59 (June 1965), pp. 321–36.

there will be greater participation of executives in business groups in towns undergoing rapid growth in heavy industry, while towns experiencing light industrial growth will have greater participation of executives in community conservation groups. Also, towns with no or little growth of either type will have fewer people participating in any type of interest group.[13]

One problem with case studies is that you may be examining a case study by someone else who did not have your interests in mind. Because the writer did not mention that everyone not employed by one of the new industries has an income at or below the poverty level does not mean that it cannot be so. If you are going through several case studies, you can encounter another problem. Different interests of different writers can mean that one will describe the income level of those people not employed by either type of company while the other writers will not mention income levels in their studies of other towns. You cannot conclude that the income levels in the other towns are average, low, or high. Therefore, you need to check and gather additional information about some of the case studies before you make statements about the presence or significance of factors not discussed by everyone.

A related problem of consistency frequently encountered within a single case study is that the writer notes certain things being present or absent at one time period without mentioning it again in his discussion of other time periods. Does this mean these factors stayed the same or were no longer present in other time periods? We do not know; for the writer merely may have failed to specify and systematically use his criteria for including and excluding information throughout his whole case study. In other words, he did a sloppy job. If you are going to write your own case study, you will want to be more systematic in making sure that the factors you consider at one point are also considered at other points in your discussion. It sometimes happens that you discover or notice other factors at later time periods that you missed earlier. If this is the case, you should go back to check the relevance of these factors in the remaining time periods to ensure consistency.

Similar to case studies, but allowing more control and manipulative capacity, simulation and small group research designs are particularly well suited to exploratory research. Simulation is a technique for representing certain aspects of real-world behavior and processes.[14] Assuming you are interested in finding out about the relations, if any, between certain attitudes of foreign policy leaders and their crisis decision-making

---

[13] Recall that the case study neither confirms nor explains the first or the second discovery. Rather, it has generated these hypotheses that now have to be tested, using different data.

[14] We will describe only human simulations here, because computer and man-computer simulations require more technical knowledge.

behavior, you might wonder if people with ethnocentric (antiforeign) attitudes are more likely to stereotype their enemies in this decision situation than people with few or no ethnocentric attitudes. You have no access to foreign policy leaders, but you do have some descriptive case studies. In these case studies are descriptions of the kind of information that researchers believe precipitate crisis decision situations. For example, there may be discussions about responses to information about troop movements or the shipment of nuclear weapons to a nearby country from a country that is perceived to be an enemy, and about the characteristics of the people occupying the political positions in crisis decision situations.

Equipped with this information, you ask people to take part in your simulation. You will administer a standard questionnaire to them to get information about their ethnocentric attitudes before assigning them randomly to two or more fictitious nations as foreign policy decision makers.[15] Each individual will be given a short background paper (scenario) giving him the historical background of his domestic and international behavior and the situation to date, together with the directions or rules specifying the options that you want to give each person.[16] In this example you could specify that they can do nothing, trade, sever diplomatic relations, ally themselves with any nation, move their troops and weapons anywhere they choose, and go to war. Then you will distribute information to one or several individuals that they will perceive as threatening, surprising, and demanding an immediate response.[17] Their response to this event is communicated to individuals in other nations. The interaction between nations can continue until you or they decide that it shall terminate. You will want to record their actions as they take place. Simulations can run for only part of a day or for a few hours a week for several weeks. If the simulation is to run for the longer

---

[15] You may suspect that a group of very ethnocentric persons will behave differently than will some of these individuals in a mixed group or in a group of individuals that have few antiforeign attitudes. In this case, you can assign individuals so as to make possible a comparison of these three types of group contexts.

[16] Many commercial simulation manuals are available now for teaching and research purposes in almost every substantive area of political science. See Harold Guetzkow and C. H. Cherryholmes, *Inter-Nation Simulation Kit,* Participant's and Director's Manuals (Chicago: Science Research Associates, Inc., 1966); M. G. Weinbaum and L. H. Gold, *Presidential Election: A Simulation with Readings* (New York (Holt, Rinehart & Winston, 1969); W. A. Gamson, *SIMSOC: Simulated Society,* Participant's and Director's Manuals (New York: Free Press, 1969), and various issues of *Simulation and Games: An International Journal of Theory, Design and Research.*

[17] A dilemma of simulation research is to provide a situation which is realistic enough to provoke a response and at the same time is not so realistic as to constitute a threat to the individuals which might cause unanticipated and undesirable consequences.

period of time, it is more interesting to the participants if you put in new information, e.g., telling one nation's decision makers that they have lost an election and another group of people will take over.

When you have completed the runs, you will go back over their behavior to see if you can associate different patterns of action and reaction with variations in antiforeign attitudes held by them. These patterns that you identify are then formulated as hypotheses to be tested on real-world data. The simulation can only provide a test of hypotheses for the individuals involved in the simulation and then only if certain procedures are followed. The simulation results cannot be used as a basis for inferences about all crisis decision situations. Simulation, however, does allow you to look for the relationships between a reasonably small set of variables and may help you to identify questions demanding further research.

An example of this latter type of payoff is to think of what you would predict about a situation in which people in one nation received a number of different threats of varying magnitude from a variety of other nations. Would their behavior in a multithreatening situation be the same as in a situation in which they perceived only one threat from one nation? It is sometimes said that you cannot simulate aspects of the real world unless you know a lot about that behavior. We would say that you have to know something about it, but where you have no idea, you can try varying that factor to see if other behaviors vary with it. The hypothesis that might be formulated could be that multiple threats are associated with behaviors that are less likely when there is no threat or a single threat.

A small group research design usually has a more elaborate set of procedures and correspondingly better control of factors extraneous to the hypotheses being generated than a simulation. In the example of the simulation extending over several weeks, there are no controls for international events taking place in the real world that might affect the ways that some individuals behave in the simulation. In small group research designs, efforts are more systematically directed toward preventing the contamination of the results by uncontrolled variables.

The type of question that suggests a small group research design is, on the one hand, more general and, on the other hand, more particularistic than the type of question that suggests a simulation. It is more general in that the researcher might want to discover hypotheses relating ethnocentric attitudes to crisis decision making wherever it occurs, rather than to foreign policy decision-making behavior; and more particularistic in that the restrictions on the situation are typically so many that there are few real-world situations that approximate it. The main purpose or justification for choosing a small group research design is that one needs to begin simply and complicate life only if he is forced to by the finding that the hypothesis generated in this exceedingly simple situation must be rejected in more complex situations.

Probably the simplest but still acceptable design is one in which you observe the individuals in a group, treat them in some fashion, and observe them after the treatment for changes in behavior. The changes, if any, in this group are compared with a matched group which was observed before and after but did not receive the treatment. This design will not control for the effects of two observations on the individuals' behavior, but it will give you an idea for formulating a hypothesis about the effects of the treatment variable on their behavior, the dependent variable. The ethnocentric standard questionnaire could be given to the individuals in both groups; both groups would be matched on the basis of characteristics that you think would be relevant to the treatment variable, e.g., level of education. Only one group would receive a bogus newspaper containing both positive and negative articles about politicians, some of whom have foreign-sounding names. The second group would be given a regular newspaper. After reading the newspapers, both groups of individuals would be asked to write down all the information they could remember from what they read. We would expect that those with more ethnocentric attitudes would remember more about those politicians with whom they share issue agreement who do not have foreign names than they would about those politicians who have foreign names. The hypothesis suggested by these results would be that antiforeign attitudes affect memory retention of information about politicians.[18] As with the simulation, you would not have tested the hypothesis; instead, you would have generated a hypothesis for testing when you could get the relevant data.

SUMMARY AND CONCLUSIONS

We have described ways that you might approach finding an idea. Some of the vehicles for discovery are more appropriate for certain types of problems than others, just as some techniques are more appropriate for hypothesis testing than discovery. Appropriateness varies with accessibility to the people in which you have an interest; the amount of available factual information and literature; the desired specificity or generality of the discovery; and the availability of resources, skills, money, and time.

All of these different techniques will not help someone make discoveries if he is not paying attention and systematically observant. Ideas about a problem do not occur to people who do not work with it. The process of discovery can be frustrating generally, and ultimately a failure in producing consistently predictive and explanatory results; but it can also culminate in a very exciting state when everything falls together

---

[18] We are assuming "all things being equal" again.

in a way that you have not seen before. Once you discover the new pattern, it appears to be so obvious that you wonder how it could have escaped you before; mathematicians call such a problem a trivial problem after they have solved it. This fit may be illusionary and momentary, but it is without exception exciting.[19] It is on this note that we move on to what some believe is the most exciting activity of all—theory building.

---

[19] In fact, we think that it is so exciting that this book was written to convince the reader that he need not spend all of his time being spoon-fed the ideas and research findings of others. With a minimum of analytical practice to serve as a guide for deciding what has to be done with a discovery before it can be accepted as having predictive or explanatory capacity with a low risk, the beginner can mix his receipt of ideas and information from others with his active participation in and contribution to the process of learning and accumulating knowledge about political behavior.

chapter
6

Theory and explanation

Those familiar with the logical-deductive method from geometry or the organization of published scientific research may wonder why we have waited until now to discuss empirically testable theory. Shouldn't you have been directed to a theory to organize your knowledge about a given problem, to separate data which is relevant to the research question(s) from that which is not, and to deduce (explain) the relationship(s) between these concepts?[1]

First, the answer depends upon whether the research question at hand is a question arising in a well-plowed and seeded field or whether the field is still lying fallow. That is, is the state of the theory in the research area well specified and developed or is it ambiguous, underdeveloped, or contradictory? If you find that it is the latter, after exploring the relevant literature, you are facing a construction job of the first order and, in our minds, one of the most exciting and creative tasks of the political scientist or anyone who wants to estimate an answer to a question.

We will offer an illustrative example here, the consideration of revolutionary behavior associated with the transformation of democratic systems. Ideas generated by thinking about the breaking down of a political system may bring us back to a reconsideration of what maintains a stable system. We will pretend for the moment that there are no well-developed theories of revolutionary behavior,[2] but that we now feel that we want to develop such a theory to aid us in (1) generating predictive hypotheses relating the withdrawal of support (decreasing legitimacy), violence, revolutionary behavior, and the transformation of democratic systems, and (2) explaining or accounting for these relationships. One reason for deciding to construct a theory is that the interest generated from tackling

---

[1] These are the generally accepted functions of empirical or systematic theory.

[2] Unfortunately, this pretense is closer to reality than we would like it to be.

the first hypothesis may spur you to invest additional time to look for other factors that may be related to the behavior that you wish to predict and explain. Secondly, we, and most social scientists, feel uneasy about one or two factor explanations of what we identify as complex behavior. Changes in other types of behavior also may be related to change in democratic systems. This is of particular importance if the cost of change when it does not occur or predicting its nonoccurrence when it usually occurs is high for us. Presumably, the active revolutionary would be more concerned about prediction errors than the individual who has a more passing academic interest in the question.

Having suggested several bases for motivating us to take on a theory-building task, the next step is to ask: What do I do now? Since theory construction involves relating a number of ideas to each other in a variety of ways, i.e., trying several possibilities on for size to see which fits best, most of us will want to go to the available theory and research for sources of ideas about units that are likely to be relevant and to identify the patterns and relationships that have been discovered and tested.[3]

Thus far, we have three concepts—withdrawal of support, the incidence of revolutionary behavior, and system change. The research areas that we choose to explore are determined partly by chance (e.g., getting lost in the library and finding yourself looking at titles on aggressive behavior) and partly because of the initial reasons for our interest in the relationship between these variables. Do we look at the literature on campus upheavals, conflict behavior, revolution, revolutionary movements, alienation, anomie, political instability or disequilibrium, disintegration, attitude change, aggression? Which or all? Our search criteria are of some importance, because an idea may occur to any of us at any time but a full-blown theory clearly does not.

Perhaps we are intrinsically interested in the campus setting for the problem because we are participants, observers, or because we have an affective response to the behavior—we like it or we don't like it. We may have read or heard that the classical revolutions which brought about system changes, such as the Russian, were preceded by alienation of the intellectuals and violence, or that Ho Chi Minh and Mao Tse-tung began their long roads to leadership from study groups when they were university students. These subjective interests will usually determine the areas we choose to examine first. From here, however, new ideas about additional variables and relationships suggested by the first materials read, together with footnote citations and ideas generated by discussing the problem with others, will suggest additional ideas.

---

[3] If we are unbelievably lucky we may find an available theory that is clearly applicable to our problem with little or no modification.

Whatever the interests affecting our choices of areas to study, we will find from reading in these areas that researchers have typed conflict behavior and the various ways it develops and what happens to it after it has developed. One of these paths of conflict development appears to fit rather well with some of the research findings about revolutionary behavior. At the same time, we discover that attitude change, aggressive behavior, and anomie have been studied extensively in psychology, sociology, and political science; while violence has received a great deal of attention in the writings of scholars on international relations and internal war.

Without going further, it is only too obvious that we are considering several ideas, both macro and micro, that may be contradictory. We know that we have to be careful, because we are mixing units and levels in ways that may lead us into certain fallacies. At the same time we do not want premature closure before having explored several ideas.[4] At this point the researcher tries to keep one eye looking for inconsistencies, inferential fallacies, and other errors of reasoning as he sorts through the ideas obtained directly from or suggested by the several areas that he has explored.

This is the process where imagination or creativity and serendipity are significant for combining ideas with research findings. But how can intuition, unexpected good fortune, and previously supported research findings produce empirically testable theory? We can attempt to do it by reworking the ideas and their interrelationships until they form a theory of the proper scientific form so that the theory can be evaluated for its predictive and explanatory capacities. That is, the theory builder knows what the final structure and form of the theory must be and what it must be able to do. Since we want to predict and explain how alienation and revolutionary behavior relate to system change, we must then consider the requirements of empirically testable theory before working and reworking our ideas.

Unfortunately, one can find in the social science literature numerous examples of the use of the term "theory" other than the use we will specify here. Sometimes it is equated with the term "hypothesis," as in the statement: "My theory of revolution is that the alienation of intellectuals will be associated with a revolution." "Theory" is also used instead of the more accurate term "conceptual or theoretical framework," in which the concepts for a theory are developed but are not related to one another in assumption or hypothesis statements. As indicated in Chapter 3, concepts have no power to explain or predict anything; only

---

[4] Sometimes we have the opposite difficulty; we continue to search the literature long after it is apparent that we have culled all the ideas relevant to our problem. In other words, we hold on to the hope that someone else has already solved our problem in the face of evidence to the contrary.

generalizations can be used to explain or predict. Therefore, although conceptual analysis is theory-relevant and a very important activity, it is not the same as theory building. Third, "theory" may be incorrectly used as a synonym for a classification system or typology. While a typology or classification of behaviors, events, or political systems (such as a typology of revolutions) may be helpful to the construction of a theory, and some elements of a theory may be implied by a classification system, a classification system also lacks the assumption and hypothesis statements necessary to an empirical theory.

"Theory" and "model" are frequently used interchangeably, particularly when the theorist is working with mathematical models. Some political scientists are more concerned than others about differentiating these last two. Many bases are used for distinguishing the two, but probably two distinctions are the most commonly accepted.[5] One views models as a pretheory stage. Models are used to discover theory and, therefore, never include laws. They are a skeletal representation of variable interrelationships which ultimately may be incorporated in a theory. Only the testable hypotheses—the relationships between operationalized units or the empirical indicators of concepts—that are expected to predict in the real world are included in the model. Consequently, a model can only predict; it cannot explain. A second view is that a model is made up of interrelated empirical relationships that are implied by a theory. The model represents the parameters or boundaries of applicability and generalizations predicted by the theory. The distinction, then, between these two views is based on whether a model is a pretheory or a posttheory stage of theory building.

In our view, concepts, conceptual or theoretical frameworks, classification systems or typologies, models, and theories are terms used to communicate what one is attempting and can be expected to do in his work. If you keep in mind the different characteristics of these terms and look past the use of the particular term by the writer, you should be able to tell when you can or cannot expect prediction and explanation from a particular work, even though the writer may not always use the customary terminology.

THE CHARACTERISTICS OF EMPIRICALLY TESTABLE THEORY

An empirically testable theory is a set of generalizations which are structurally integrated or connected, i.e., bear a distinctive set of relationships to one another. The pattern of organization of these generalizations

---

[5] May Brodbeck, "Models, Meaning, and Theories," in May Brodbeck (ed.), *Readings in the Philosophy of the Social Sciences* (New York: Macmillan Co., 1968), pp. 579–600.

is hierarchical and deductive; predictive generalizations are deduced from other consistent generalizations.

From the beginning, it should be understood that a theory is never realistic or unrealistic, true or false, because as a whole it is always an abstraction from reality. In other words, we cannot deal directly with facts without some intervening conception of the ordering of such facts.[6] Just as a painting of a landscape does not include every blade of grass or a photograph omits movement, smell, and the feel of objects, so is a theory a simplification of the real world. For this reason, we speak of empirically testable theory rather than empirical theory. If it were not a means of ordering and simplifying the real world of our problem, we would have no reason to build or use theory.

Therefore, the choices that we make in the abstracting process are clearly not objective choices, although they should be explicitly stated choices. This means that the old distinction between normative and empirical theory, which is based on the belief that empirical theory is objective while normative theory is subjective, does not hold. Since both types of theory involve subjective choices, the main distinction must be based on the use and, thus, the evaluative criteria for rejecting or accepting the assertions and implications, of a theory. We will describe the purposes and criteria for evaluating empirically testable theory later in this chapter when we discuss prediction and explanation.

The basic components of a theory are units (concepts), both primitive and defined. Primitive units are those that are purposely left undefined to avoid circularities or tautologies in our theory. The mathematician, for example, defines a set as a collection of elements but does not define elements. In other words, he does not want to define his concepts in terms of one another.[7] An empirically testable theory must contain some units which are operationally defined by stating their empirical indicators to link the theory to the real world. Therefore, a theory that does not contain such units is not an empirically testable theory, the author's promises to the contrary.[8]

Assumption statements (axioms, premises, laws, empirical generalizations) interrelate some of these units. Assumptions are given or taken to be valid statements even though they may never have been tested

---

[6] We are expressing a value preference for a more nominalist-instrumentalist position. To contrast the consequences for theory building and evaluation of taking a realist position, see Alan Ryan, *The Philosophy of the Social Science* (New York: Pantheon Books, 1970), particularly chaps. 4 and 5.

[7] There are very few examples of theories in the social sciences explicitly making use of primitive terms.

[8] Another researcher can develop an auxiliary theory including the operationally defined concepts to link it to the real world, and thus make it an empirically testable theory.

as hypotheses elsewhere. Nevertheless, they must be stated unambiguously and in testable form. The statement that all men are rational or act in self-interest is unacceptable in a theory of revolutionary behavior because it is not in testable form. There is no way of showing that any of the hypotheses will be consistent with such a statement; in fact, contradictory behavior could be predicted from it, since we do not know what it means to say that all men act in their self-interest. If the assumption statements are laws, we are going to be much more confident about the predictive and explanatory capacities of the theory, and the theory is more clearly a scientific theory. If they do not have the status of laws but are in testable form, our theory might more accurately be described as a scientific theory in the making.

The third component of an empirically testable theory might be called hypotheses, propositions, predictions, laws, or empirical generalizations. These statements interrelate two or more units and are derivable from the assumption statements. They predict sets or classes of real-world behaviors. These statements must also be in testable form and differ from the assumption statements only in terms of what is done with them rather than in their structural or formal characteristics. The assumption statements are not tested as assumptions; the hypotheses statements are tested or are in principle testable when the researcher can gain access to the relevant data.

Complex empirically testable theories will have statements interrelating statements of varying levels of generality or discreteness. The chain of statements linking the assumptions to the hypotheses may be quite long. Such a theory is often presented in symbolic or mathematical form, for the implications and the consistency of the theory can much more easily be determined in this rather than verbal form.

Inventories of propositions are not theories. A generalization subsumes discrete facts, while a theory provides the logical and empirical grounds for organizing generalizations in specific areas. Inventories of propositions lack the linkage statements necessary to the logical organization of a theory.

Looking at the deductive form of the more complex theories will often lead the student, and other political scientists as well, to conclude that theory is only for the "great minds." On the contrary, the theorist is following custom in organizing and presenting it in this form; he did not discover it in this order. The reader does not realize the many states of working and reworking that the theorist went through in the process of refining it.

Although it is common to consider the theorist and the practitioner as being quite different from each other, they are only distinguishable by the explicitness of their theory. The theorist consciously and explicitly looks at his theory to make sure that it meets the requirements for scientific theory we have outlined above, while the practitioner's theory remains at the implicit level, unscrutinized. Although a great deal is also made of the distinction between inductive and deductive theories and theorists, the differences are more formal than real. Most simply, inductive theory is derived from data and is considered to be a building-up project while deductive theory, beginning with axioms, predicts to the data. The distinction is generally exaggerated into the dichotomy of "I theorize after I see" and "I see after I theorize." Since all of us do both, the distinction appears to be more descriptive if it refers to the way the theory is written and organized for publication. The two combine in the actual doing of any research project and refer only to which stages of research are carried on and presented more systematically.

The deductive theorist does not create a theory isolated from the real world; he has read a vast amount, noticed certain patterns or relationships obtained in testing different hypotheses, and—perhaps without systematically checking all of his notions about how they might be linked—he begins constructing a deductive theory. The point at which it will be linked systematically to the data is when the hypotheses are operationalized and tested. Nor does the inductive theorist look at data with a blank mind; he has some ideas developed that point him in the direction of looking for certain kinds of things in the data. This may lead him to discoveries, but these frequently turn out to be the implications of ideas that he had not yet systematically developed. He tends to use more sophisticated techniques for aggregating the data into a formulation of assumption statements and hypothesis statements than do some of the deductive theorists. However, if one looks at theory building, testing, and modification as an ongoing research process, then the distinctions blur even more; for at whatever point the individual cuts into the process—formulating assumptions or gathering data for the purpose of formulating assumptions—he eventually gets swept through the inductive and deductive processes involved in both the formalized notions of theory.

We also frequently distinguish between universal deterministic theory and probabilistic theory. A universal deterministic theory is one in which the relationships between units in the assumptions and hypotheses are assumed and predicted to occur everywhere at all times and under all conditions. We can illustrate such a theory with a simplified example. Suppose that the theory concerns the relationship between industrialization and revolution. Let us assume the following:[9]

1. Rapid industrialization leads to the breakdown of traditional social relationships in a society.

---

[9] This example is a simplified version of the argument of William Kornhauser, *The Politics of Mass Society* (Glencoe, Ill.: Free Press, 1959). Needless to say, Kornhauser does not argue for the universality of these generalizations.

2. The breakdown of traditional social relationships leads to the alienation of large numbers of the population of a society.
3. The presence of large numbers of alienated people in a population
leads to the creation of large, extremist political groups in the society.
4. The presence of large, extremist political groups in a society leads
to revolution in that society.

Now if we assume that these generalizations are universal, then we can
deduce the following hypothesis: rapid industrialization will lead to
revolution.

Such deductive theories have great power, but they also have limitations. One is that we may not believe that the universal assumptions
are empirically valid. Thus, we may suspect that alienation does not
inevitably lead to extremist politics. Nevertheless, some theorists build
such systems, saying, in effect, do not judge me by the apparent absurdity
of my axioms, but rather on the utility of my (perhaps) nontrivial deduc-
tions.[10] It is possible that they may get high predictive power, but we
will discuss in the next section the limitations such assumptions have
on their potential explanatory power.

A probabilistic theory is limited with respect to certainty, scope, time,
and conditions. In other words, the domains of the theories differ. This
is important to notice, because the domain of a theory tells us when
and where to expect the theory to predict and/or explain. Since the
universal deterministic theory has no boundaries, it is the most general
type of theory. One usually finds that the more general the theory,
the fewer the parameters or boundaries, and the less predictive the theory
will be. While everyone prefers to construct as general a theory as possible, while also keeping it parsimonious and maintaining an acceptable
predictive and explanatory capacity, frequently these have to be juggled
to get a minimum acceptable performance on all four criteria.

As long as the empirical theory is not probabilistic, deducing predictive
generalizations from assumptions appears to be rather cut-and-dried once
you get the hang of it. Unfortunately, one can encounter difficulties
in the deduction process in a complex probabilistic theory. These are
worth looking at, however, since many social scientists believe that this is
the most appropriate type of theory for their problems. The usual inabil-
ity to manipulate variables experimentally and the human tendency to be
habitual but not absolutely predictable does indeed suggest that universal
determinist theories are not the most appropriate.

The probabilities included in a theory may be of one of two types,
depending on the definitional choices of the theorist. There are either

---

[10] The substance of the argument may be found in Milton Friedman, "The
Methodology of Positive Economics," in Brodbeck, *op. cit.*, pp. 508–28. The classic
example of this type of theorizing in political science is Anthony Downs, *An
Economic Theory of Democracy* (New York: Harper & Row, 1957).

a priori probabilities attached to events or probabilities assigned to events derived from their actual frequency of occurrence. In the latter case, the likelihood of the occurrence of an event might be determined by the times it has occurred divided by the number of times it could have occurred. Most often political scientists use the frequency definition of probability. Those constructing probability theories usually follow the model provided by mathematicians. We can show the calculations in a simple hypothetical example if we are willing to assume "all other things being equal."

Normally, the presentation of a theory begins with a discussion and definition of concepts. This definition of concepts would most desirably include a justification and listing of the empirical indicators for those concepts which are not primitive concepts. The theorist might include, for example, bombing, fire-setting, throwing rocks and bottles, riots, demonstrations, and shooting as empirical indicators of revolutionary behavior. Alienation might be indicated by a decreasing number of people voting in elections, declining contributions sent to political candidates, and increasing numbers of people failing to pay their income tax. Industrialization could be defined as increasing numbers employed in nonfarming occupations, increasing electrical energy consumed, and increasing specialization; while traditional social relationships are extended family living arrangements and the presence of ethnic, religious, and/or sex determinants of interaction. Political extremist groups are those groups of people identified as being "extremist" by the government leaders. Since we have discussed the requirements of scientific concepts to be used here in our previous description of concepts in Chapter 3, we will not repeat this material.

At this point, we are ready to present a hypothetical example of a probabilistic theory. We will build on the previous example of the deductive theory. Let us begin by assuming the following:

1. Rapid industrialization *tends* to lead to the breakdown of traditional social relationships in a society.
2. The breakdown of traditional social relationships *tends* to lead to the alienation of large numbers of the population in a society.
3. The presence of large numbers of alienated people in a population *tends* to lead to the creation of large, extremist political groups in the society.
4. The presence of large, extremist political groups in a society *tends* to lead to revolution in that society.

The difference between this set of generalizations and the ones previously given is in the certainty of the outcome: we are now dealing with "tendency statements" or statistical generalizations.[11] Thus, the conclusion

---

[11] We are following general social science usage here in calling these statistical statements although they do not include exact probabilities.

must be: Rapid industrialization tends to lead to revolution.[12] This conclusion, however, will be more or less certain depending on the strength of the statistical relationships between the variables intervening between industrialization and revolution: the breakdown of traditional social relationships, alienation, and political extremism.

Statistical or probabilistic theories can be made much more precise by attaching exact probabilities to the statements. For example, let us begin with assumption 4 and convert it to a more precise statement:

4a. The probability that revolution will occur in a society is:

$$0.7 : P(R_e) = 0.7$$

where P equals probability and R_e equals revolution in nations with large numbers of extremist political groups.

Now suppose that we know the frequency of societies having large numbers of political extremists. Let that frequency be equal to:

$$0.2 : F(S_e) = 0.2$$

where F stands for frequency and S_e for societies with large numbers of extremist political groups. Now if we are considering 100 societies, 20 percent of which have large numbers of extremist groups, we then can deduce that the probability of revolution among the 100 societies is:[13]

$$P(R_e) \times F(S_e) = 0.7 \times 0.2 = 0.14$$

That is, we may expect that 14 nations will experience revolution.

In this example, the probability theory is both inductive and deductive in form, where the "laws" are frequency probability statements derived from a ratio of past occurrences to possible occurrences and the hypotheses are deduced from these "laws." Before using an empirically testable theory such as the one described above, you should remember that probability theory is not based on and does not predict a single particular event. Rather it predicts a set of events or outcomes. That is, in the long run, the average percentage should run close to the predicted prob-

---

[12] Assuming that the events described in our assumption statements are independent of one another, the event specified in the conclusion may not be very likely.

[13] In probability theory, the likelihood of joint events is the product of the probabilities of the individual events given the fact that the two events are independent of each other, i.e., that the outcome of one event does not affect the occurrence of the other. In this case, the two events are: (1) the probability of revolution with large numbers of extremist political groups, and (2) the frequency with which extremist political groups occur in societies.

ability, although any one incidence of violence might not be close to the predicted figure.

Our human tendency to use probability theory for a particular event anyway cannot be construed as saying more than that the situation we are considering is similar or equivalent to the types of situation subsumed by the theory. Therefore, it fits or can be subsumed by that theory. Intuitively, we will feel more confident about predicting or speculating about the consequences of an American revolution if we know the probabilities of decreasing support, revolutionary behavior, and system change occurring together, but we must continually remind ourselves that this situation could be one of the members of the set of revolutions that behaves differently. Of course, the researcher will ultimately examine the deviant cases to see if he can find anything about them in common that is different from the other cases, so he can specify the conditions under which we can expect the deviation to occur. In the end, this will increase the predictive and explanatory capacities of our theory.

EVALUATING EMPIRICALLY TESTABLE THEORY

Now that we have developed a simple theory, how good is it? How can we evaluate it? First, we have to decide if we want to predict, explain, or control behavior with it. If we are primarily interested in prediction, then the hypothesis will have to be tested in at least a representative sample of nations and hold up to continued testing. If we also want to explain the behavior, then, in addition to the testing of the hypotheses, we have to determine its explanatory capacity.

Although the literature indicates several meanings and usages for the term "explanation," we believe that there is enough agreement to set forth some common principles regarding the adequacy of scientific explanation. First, scientific explanation should be distinguished from subjective evaluation. Subjective evaluation has been called the "aha" experience. This is not to suggest that a psychological feeling of satisfaction on the part of an individual might not accompany a sound scientific explanation, but it is to argue that it is not a sufficient condition and that the theory may be sound even if we do not understand it. We may have high degrees of satisfaction with explanations which simply do not meet other criteria; for example, when the child "understands" that the money under his pillow comes from the tooth fairy.

A second area of agreement is that explanations are sound, in part, because of the context in which they appear—they comport with other things that we know to be true or expect to be true. This is the theoretical component of explanation. It is here, however, that agreement on the nature of explanation probably breaks down, and we begin to present a particular point of view—namely, that scientific explanation is not "discipline-specific"[14] and that it generally results from the application of the following steps:

1. A statement of a fact or event to be explained.
2. The establishment of the empirical validity of a set of "relevant" initial conditions or set of factors which are linked to:
3. A generalization or a set of generalizations, empirically validated, which allow, through the application of logic, the deduction of the occurrence of the event to be explained.[15]

There are, therefore, both logical and empirical criteria which sound explanations must satisfy.

Perhaps an example will clarify the nature of this type of explanation. Suppose that we have the following initial conditions:

1. Initial conditions: (*a*) X-land is a nation; (*b*) X-land has a high number of extremist political groups.

Then we add the following generalization (which we are considering valid in this example):

2. Empirical generalization: All nations with high numbers of extremist groups have revolutions.

From these, we can then deduce the following:

3. Event to be explained: Therefore, a revolution happened in X-land.

The form of this explanation is that once we know the relevant initial conditions and the empirical generalizations, the conclusion is entailed in these premises. That is, the conclusion is a deductive consequence of the initial conditions and the generalizations. Note that if we knew the relevant initial conditions and the generalizations before the event, we could have predicted the occurrence of the event.[16]

This presentation of the ideal kind of explanation must now be jolted by a few of the realities of life. First, the ideal form, called "deductive nomological"[17] explanation, depends upon universal generalizations for

---

[14] For a variety of points of view on this question, see Part 5, "Explanation, Prediction, and Imperfect Knowledge," in Brodbeck, *op. cit.*, pp. 337–455. On the controversy in political science, see the "Symposium on Scientific Explanation in Political Science," *American Political Science Review*, Vol. 63 (December 1969), 1233–62.

[15] Alan C. Isaak, *Scope and Methods of Political Science* (Homewood, Ill.: Dorsey Press, 1969), pp. 101–105.

[16] Also, note that that deductive model of explanation corresponds to deductive theory.

[17] Carl Hempel, "Deductive Nomological vs. Statistical Explanation," in Herbert Feigl and Grover Maxwell (eds.), *Minnesota Studies in the Philosophy of Science*, Vol. III (Minneapolis: University of Minnesota Press, 1962).

the capacity to deduce specific, single events. Probability theory, however, can only be used to deduce collective events. Consequently, although the form of a probabilistic explanation is the same as that of a deductive nomological explanation, the probabilistic explanation differs with regard to its generalizations and conclusions. In probabilistic explanation the generalizations are statistical, and therefore the conclusions we can draw differ. Suppose that the initial conditions of a probabilistic explanation were the same as the previous example:

1. Initial conditions: (*a*) X-land is a nation; (*b*) X-land has a high number of extremist political groups.

Now add the following statistical generalization:

2. Empirical generalization: Nations with high numbers of extremist political groups have a 0.6 probability of experiencing revolutions.

Now we *cannot* reach the specific conclusion:

3. Event to be explained: Therefore, X-land experienced a revolution.

We cannot conclude that X-land experienced a revolution because X-land might have been one of the societies which did not have a revolution. Thus, the conclusion does not deductively follow, because the claim of the generalization is only that 60 percent of the nations with high numbers of extremist political groups will have revolutions. The specific, individual event of revolution in X-land cannot be deduced.[18]

Statistical or probabilistic generalizations can be used, however, to explain (and predict) the occurrence of "collective" events, i.e., sets or classes of similar events. An example may clarify this statement. Suppose that the following initial condition obtained:

1. Initial condition: 30 percent of 100 nations experienced rapid industrialization.

Add this statistical generalization:

2. Empirical generalization: The probability of nations experiencing rapid industrialization having revolutions is 0.6.

From the initial condition and the generalization, we may deduce the following:

3. Event to be explained: Therefore, 18 nations experienced revolution.

---

[18] This event is "individual" insofar as it refers to revolution within a single nation; at a different level of analysis, revolutions are obviously "collective" events.

In effect, we have explained why revolution is probable for rapidly industrializing countries.[19]

To check the explanatory capacity of a theory, we must evaluate its predictive capacity, its internal consistency, and the proportion of assumption statements which have the status of laws. Clearly, if the assumptions are implicit, i.e., not stated or very ambiguously stated, the theory may have predictive capacity, but there is no way to determine its explanatory capacity. A theory which generates contradictory hypotheses also must be reworked before its explanatory capacity can be determined. If you find contradictory hypotheses, you should try to divide the theory in two or more separate theories to eliminate the inconsistencies. Testing would then allow you to eliminate the theories whose hypotheses are repeatedly rejected in testing.[20] Sometimes it is difficult to figure out how to subdivide the contradictory elements of a theory, because such a theory usually has many assumptions or hypothesis statements which are not interconnected or only ambiguously connected with one another. In this case, the problem is that a string of generalizations are unrelated to one another and therefore lack coherent order. A helpful rule of thumb is that the more interconnected the statements of a theory are, the less likely that one will find ambiguous contradictions.

If a theory adequately explains behavior patterns, then it must predict them. The converse is not true. A theory may predict, but not explain. Suppose that we want to explain the frequency of campus violence. Let's say that we frequently observe a tree falling outside the classroom window before violence occurs on campus. If we are interested entirely in successful prediction and having alienation scores allows us to predict violence 60 percent of the time while our observation of the tree falling allows us to predict violence 70 percent of the time, our choice is obvious, and we may be quite satisfied not to go further. If we become curious about why this strange sequence of events occurs, we may be driven to go further. Yet we may hesitate to argue that our generalization linking the falling of trees to campus violence is pointing us to an adequate explanation for the frequency of occurrence, since we cannot think of a theory or set of laws that subsumes an association between falling trees and student violence. Investigating further, we may find that a tree is generally cut down to use as fuel for a bonfire attended by people that later commit violent acts or that the lumber is used by such people

---

[19] Note that, as in the case of deductive theory and deductive explanation, probability explanations correspond to probability theories.

[20] We do not wish to imply here that only one correct theory can exist; there may be several adequate theories from which to choose. They may vary in their predictive and explanatory capacities and in their complexity. Generally, one chooses the simplest or most parsimonious theory that has adequate predictive and explanatory capacities for his purposes.

to make primitive weapons in the absence of rocks, bricks, or guns. The important point to draw from this example is to observe that while we might be tempted to disregard a generalization linking the frequency of trees falling to the frequency of campus violence because it appears ridiculous, we do not reject it out of hand. We also do not accept it as an adequate explanation when we have no theory under which we could subsume falling trees as a cause or as associated with student violence. Instead, we search for more complete observations and to discover a new law or a set of laws which would subsume this association. If we do not find one, we have to set the problem aside for someone else to consider.

If we want to evaluate theory for the purpose of controlling behavior, we have to at least be able to predict that behavior. A measure of control capacity might be noting the success-failure ratio in maintaining or eliminating a behavior after manipulating the situational characteristics of the individuals to approximate the values of the variables subsumed by the theory's predictive statements. If we wanted to decrease the number of revolutions predicted by our simple theory, we might jail or shoot all people who are members of extremist groups. In this case, the controller would probably discover that the theory's simplification had misled him, because it assumed that the initial conditions would be maintained. Instead, the initial conditions might be changed by the introduction of a new variable, sanctions, to include an even larger number of extremist political groups, with the government now lacking the resources to jail or shoot that many people under these new conditions. If we further complicated our theory by assuming that a lack of resources would lead to a lack of control, we might be led to predict an increase in the probability of revolution occurring when sanctions are introduced or increased in severity and scope.

SUMMARY AND CONCLUSIONS

We turn to empirically testable theory whenever we want to predict, explain, and/or control sets of political behaviors or events. When a theory contains interconnected assumptions and hypotheses which have been repeatedly tested as hypotheses and not rejected, the theory is said to have the capacity to predict *and* explain. When the hypotheses alone are not rejected by repeated testing, the theory has predictive capacity. For individuals to be able to control behaviors and events, however, it would appear that the theory they use must not only have predictive and explanatory capacities. To have a capacity to control, the theory should also have a large domain with respect to time and space including those factors affecting the predicted and assumed relationships when a "controller" is introduced into the situation.

Lest our discussion imply that theories will be immutable truths once they pass the logical and empirical tests, we should emphasize that theory is an imperfect and changing tool. Theoretical revolutions do occur in different subject areas, involving radical shifts in how we think things fit together and what we think those things are. Thus, if we have learned anything from the history of science, it is that history is a graveyard of scientific theories once considered useful. Theory development, therefore, is an ongoing and changing enterprise calling for creative imagination and the willingness to sometimes break the bounds of existing theoretical constraints.

chapter

7

Analyzing and evaluating research and public policy statements

We said in the beginning that this first part of the book was written to suggest criteria or a set of decision rules for independently evaluating and analyzing political behavior and statements made about that behavior in books, by politicians, professors, journalists, or friends. This is only one set of decisions rules that could be choosen for estimating the risks we are taking when we reject, accept, or make no decision. Other decision rules frequently used are the authoritativeness of sources, the fit between beliefs and the statements of others, and the trust felt toward the individuals taking action or making statements.

Making authoritativeness the decision rule implies accepting statements made by those believed to be expert without regard for the empirical validity or logical consistency of their statements—if it's printed in a book or a newspaper, that is a sufficient basis for accepting it. The second decision rule involves accepting anything that fits the beliefs one already holds about the problem and rejecting those that contradict these beliefs; this decision rule also omits the empirical criteria. Using the third decision rule, we might accept the President's statements, because he is of our party, group, ideology, or we feel that he is sincere. Again, the decision would be made with no reference to the logical and empirical validity of the statements. This is also what people do when they reject statements made by someone they do not like, e.g., a Communist Party member.

The acceptance of one decision rule over another is, of course, a value or subjective judgment. We have chosen the more complex empirical and logical criteria because we believe that we will be able to analyze systematically and to predict and explain more accurately in the long run than we could if we chose one of the others. If your choices, at least on some occasions,[1] are the same as ours, the following set of questions summarizing previous material may help to break complex problems down into answerable questions.

Questions useful for evaluating the validity of political statements

1. What are the units (concepts) selected? How are they defined? Consistently? Are their empirical indicators (variables) listed and justified? What other units and empirical indicators might have been selected? Why? (Chapter 3)
2. What are the explicit and implicit assumptions? Are the explicit assumptions in testable form? Have they been tested elsewhere as hypotheses? With what results? (Chapter 6)
3. What are the hypotheses? Are they in testable form? Deterministic? Probabilistic? Do any of the hypotheses contradict other hypotheses that are derived or may be derived? (Chapters 4 and 6)
4. What data, if any, was gathered? Sample? Population? Case study? How is it analyzed? (Chapters 4 and 5)
5. What hypotheses are accepted or rejected? Modified? How? What new hypotheses are suggested? (Chapters 4 and 5)
6. Are all the components listed in the previous questions logically consistent? (Chapter 6)
7. Are the findings or conclusions valid? Are there micro-macro or macro-micro fallacies of reasoning? (Chapters 4 and 6)
8. What risks are you running if you tentatively accept or reject the findings or conclusions, given the answers you have given to the above questions and your estimates of predictive and explanatory capacity? Which components need to be changed in what ways to decrease your risks? (Chapter 6)
9. Are the normative conclusions or recommendations, if any, consistent with the empirical generalizations? (Chapter 1)[2]

Not all of these questions are applicable to every book, article, newspaper report, lecture, or public speech. In many cases only some of these questions will be relevant to what the author has written, but the remaining sets of questions can be used to guide your further development of the problem by suggesting what still remains to be done. Thus, these

---

[1] Such an occasion might involve incurring substantial costs if one makes an incorrect prediction.

[2] This is an expanded list of a set of questions found in Joann P. Paine, "Some Frames of Reference—B," in Stephen Wasby, *Political Science: the Discipline and its Dimensions* (New York: Scribner's, 1970), pp. 119–20.

questions are not intended for razing purposes only; construction or reconstruction efforts are at least as important.

To show how the decision rules can be used on both academic and nonacademic materials, we have selected and reprinted, following this chapter, an article by James C. Davies, "The J-Curve of Rising and Declining Satisfactions as a Cause of Some Great Revolutions and a Contained Rebellion,"[3] and President Nixon's speech on United States–Chinese relations. After reading the Davies article you may wish to compare the results of your application of the decision rules with ours.

ANALYZING STATEMENTS ABOUT POLITICAL BEHAVIOR IN ACADEMIC MATERIALS

The first reading of a study such as Davies' article on the causes of revolution should be aimed at identifying the behavior that the author is trying to predict, explain, or recommend. Davies wants to predict the pattern of events leading to revolutions or rebellions. Specifically, he states that:

. . . revolution is most likely to take place when a prolonged period of rising expectations and rising gratifications is followed by a short period of sharp reversal, during which the gap between expectations and gratifications quickly widens and becomes intolerable . . . this is an assertion about the state of mind of individual people in a society who are likely to revolt. It says their state of mind, their mood, is one of high tension and rather generalized hostility. . . .[4]

Using both his introductory words and his descriptions of the French Revolution, the American Civil War, the Nazi revolution and the American black rebellion, we can sketch out the pattern of events diagrammed in Figure 7–1.

Briefly sketching out what the author is trying to predict, explain, or recommend makes the identification of the basic units or concepts easier. The next question is one of definition and consistency. What, for example, is a J-curve, synergic unification, a revolutionary mind, or needs satisfaction? Reading through the article more carefully this time, we find that only the J-curve, revolution, and rebellion are defined (pp. 158, 160, and 158, respectively). An example of synergic unification is presented, (p. 159), but needs satisfaction and frustration are discussed as psychological concepts and are left undefined (p. 160). Without definitions, we cannot check for consistency in the use of concepts.

---

[3] *Violence in America: Historical and Comparative Perspectives*, Vol. 2, A Report to the National Commission on the Causes and Prevention of Violence, June 1969, pp. 547–76.

[4] Compare this with the discussion of Aristotle's and Crane Brinton's ideas in Chapter 2.

FIGURE 7-1
Davies' Pattern of Revolutionary Development

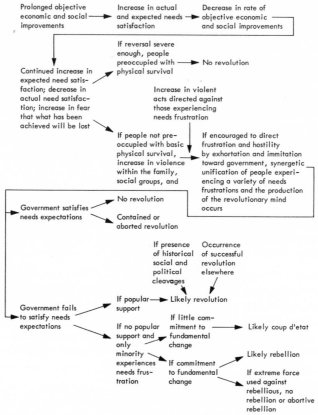

The cases of revolution and rebellion suggest that "rural uprisings, industrial strikes, lost wars, unemployment, and cost of living" might be used as crude indicators of satisfaction and frustration. More specifically, the basic units of frustration and satisfaction are income and educational level (pp. 162–88). The author is assuming, of course, that *expected* needs satisfaction is directly related to these indicators: satisfaction increases as ratio of income to schooling increases and vice versa, while frustration increases as the difference between the two population groups increases. The inconsistency, however, is that income and level of education statistics would be more likely to indicate the actual need satisfaction than the expected need satisfaction line in Figure C–1 of his article. Secondly, if the converse is true, i.e., satisfaction increases with the decrease in the difference between two population groups, what accounts for the increase of violent acts against nonwhites?

This is all that can be done in terms of measurement when the desired data are not available, but having to reason backwards from crude indicators to the definitions of most of the concepts should not be necessary and generally is impossible. Thus, with crude indicators we cannot guess the definitions of concepts such as revolutionary mind, hostility, or fear, and without concept definitions the empirical indicators cannot be identified and justified.

There is also some problem here with language. Concepts like "revolutionary mind" can be confusing when applied to groups. Most social scientists agree that such a concept is a shorthand way of saying that you are talking about attitudes of individuals. Applied to a group, it means that the attitudes of the individuals belonging to the group have been aggregated and the most common or average set is used to type or label the group.

Among other concepts that might have been included is the heterogeneity of the society. As suggested in Davies' description of the French Revolution, the larger the number of different social, ethnic, religious, racial, economic, and political groups, the larger the number of different preferences and attitudes. If these differences are important to people and the people belong to mutually exclusive groups, it is more likely that an economic and social reversal will lead to frustration.[5] The point of trying to think of other potentially relevant concepts is that they can be used to further refine the theory or that they may be included in contradictory hypotheses. If the hypotheses of the author are not rejected while the contradictory hypotheses that you have constructed are, you have a stronger basis for accepting the hypotheses and the theory from which they were derived.

The assumptions are not explicitly labeled in Davies' article. Instead, we must look for hints by asking what we have to assume in order to expect the behavioral sequence predicted. One assumption that appears necessary is that everyone has a set of hierarchically ordered needs. These most basic needs must be substantially satisfied before the other needs provide stimuli to behavior leading to their satisfaction (p. 161). The author also may be assuming that social and economic development is directly related to expected needs satisfaction, whereas political development is not important. The discussion of the reaction of people to sharp economic and social reverses depends on the assumption that people do not vary greatly in their capacity to tolerate reverses and subsequent frustration. Finally, the author assumes a *direct relationship* between expected need satisfaction or level of aspiration and actual need satisfaction

---

[5] How might you relate size as another concept? A hint for identifying possible concepts is to think of psychological, sociological, economic, biological, cultural, political, and international categories of concepts. The author has probably included concepts from some of these categories. Can you think of ones in the omitted categories that might be relevant?

until actual need satisfaction decreases relative to the previous time period.[6]

We are somewhat unhappy about the state of the assumptions, because even though we can identify some assumptions that appear consistent with the hypotheses, we know that there may be another equally consistent set that we have not identified. Also, we cannot evaluate logical consistency or potential explanatory capacity, because implicit assumptions by definition are not in testable form and cannot be laws.

Although they are not always clearly labeled, the hypotheses are stated in the article. Figure 7–1 can be used to identify the hypotheses.

1. A prolonged objective economic and social development is associated with increases in expected and actual need satisfaction (pp. 163–64, 168, 171–72, 175–76, 179, 182–83, 187).

2. If the reversal in development is severe enough that people become occupied solely with physical survival, they do not become rebellious (p. 180).

3. If the reversal is not so severe and most people are not preoccupied with physical survival, they will become frustrated and hostile (pp. 165, 172, 176, 178–79, 187).

4. If a minority of people experiences needs frustration but most people are apathetic, there may be a coup d'etat, but no revolution (p. 178).

5. If there are economic recovery or governmental reforms, there will probably be no revolution (p. 188).

6. If the government uses brute force to suppress the people, there will probably be no revolution (p. 187).

7. If there is no economic recovery, reform, or severe brutal suppression and the rebellious people represent all major groups in society, they will continue to blame the government for suppressing opportunities and unite, which will lead to a revolution (pp. 165–66, 172, 178).

By and large, these hypotheses are not in testable form.[7] To be in testable form, each of the above hypotheses would have to have a set

---

[6] The suggested categories of concepts can also help you to identify assumptions. What assumptions about genetic differences or personality differences might be consistent with the author's hypotheses? What is the author assuming about the variations in what might be happening in the international system and their effects on the likelihood of revolution occurring? Usually, the author assumes that concepts omitted from his discussion are unrelated to his problem or that their effects cancel each other out to produce a zero effect on his predicted relationships. This is what "all things being equal" means.

[7] To determine whether these hypotheses are in testable form, you should ask yourself questions like: From what the author has told me, would I be able to determine consistently that people I meet are highly frustrated or less frustrated? By what indicators can I determine this? If your answers to these questions are "no" and "I don't know," the author has more than likely failed to state his hypotheses in testable form.

of empirical indicators or procedures for gathering the data substituted for each concept. While the hypotheses are not stated in probabilistic terms, the discussion of them suggests that the author is thinking of them as probabilistic rather than deterministic.

Although the hypotheses are not in testable form, four case studies are presented as being consistent with the theoretical pattern. As the figures show (Figures C–2, C–3, C–4, and C–5), the descriptive data presented in each case study gives only evidence of development, reversal, governmental response, and rebellious behavior. The attitudes, beliefs, and frustrations of the people are inferred from this data. This means that the hypotheses with psychological concepts are at the most half consistent with the case studies. If the author really intends to infer attitudes, beliefs, frustrations, and states of mind from the information presented,[8] he has committed the serious error of failing to keep the sets of indicators for the concepts of economic and social change independent of the indicators for rising expectations and frustrations. If you will look back at the hypotheses, you will see this amounts to saying that the evidence for part of each hypothesis proves that the other part is also present.

As far as generalizing from these case studies, the author clearly states on page 162 that available data on revolutions is not all comparable. Case studies are very valuable for theory and hypothesis development, but they cannot be used to make inferences about other revolutions or rebellions. This suggests, then, what type of data gathering must be done after the hypotheses are restated in testable form.

Davies also briefly discusses other examples of rebellions that he believes fit his pattern. Examples, of course, test nothing, because you do not know how representative they are of the total or a sample of the population. Because he is careful to limit his statements to the cases that he has chosen and does not generalize to all or most revolutions and rebellions, there is no statistical fallacy. There may be an ecological fallacy, however. His uses of aggregate or macro indicators for some of his concepts—such as income, education, unemployment, governmental political acts, and growth rate—appear to lead him to draw conclusions about individual patterns of frustration, violent activity, rising expectations, and intensity from the aggregate patterns. The logical possibility should be noted that at least some of the people experiencing deprivation

---

[8] "The J-Curve is a psychological, not a sociological explanation. The units of analysis are individual human beings." See p. 188. Elsewhere Davis has commented: "Lest we shy away from the gathering of crude data, we should bear in mind that Durkheim developed his remarkable insights into modern society in large part by his analysis on suicide rates. . . . We need not always ask people whether they are greviously frustrated by their government; their actions can tell us as well and sometimes better." See James C. Davies, "Toward A Theory of Revolution," *American Sociological Review,* Vol. 27 (February 1962), pp. 5–19.

may not be the ones experiencing frustration and so forth. Although this result would be inconsistent with his assumptions, it is empirically possible.[9]

Given our analysis so far, we would clearly have to conclude that it would be extremely risky for us to accept or reject his arguments about the cause of revolution. Work on concept definition, empirical indicator identification, assumption development, and testing must be done before we would be willing to bet money one way or another. Most importantly, before we would accept the causal statements, we would require independent measures of the psychological factors. Lest you conclude that the article is worthless, however, you should know that a great deal of scholarly work has spun off from the ideas in it and an earlier article by Davies.[10] Why? Because it has generated a number of ideas that others have taken up and attempted to organize into a set of testable generalizations. This article has turned out to be a good example of the kinds of materials that are deficient in many respects, but nevertheless serve to move us ahead when we know how to use the decision rules to tell us what is wrong and to guide us in correcting them.

ANALYZING STATEMENTS ABOUT POLITICAL BEHAVIOR IN NONACADEMIC MATERIALS

You may be thinking now that the decision rules worked reasonably well in academic research, but still be wondering about their use on everyday or more popular types of materials. There is no doubt that, on the average, popular materials, with their more informal use of the language and their heavier load of normative statements, can be more difficult to analyze. We think that we can show, however, that these decision rules are particularly helpful in estimating the risks in accepting, rejecting, or making no decision by analyzing a presidential speech. We will present the transcript of President Nixon's speech, July 15, 1971, as printed by the *New York Times* the following day.

Transcript of the President's Statement

Good evening.

I have requested this television time tonight to announce a major development in our efforts to build a lasting peace in the world.

As I have pointed out on a number of occasions over the past three years, there can be no stable peace and enduring peace without the participation of the People's Republic of China and its 750 million people. That

---

[9] The proper analysis of data obtained from survey questionnaires might avoid this problem for current or future revolutions.

[10] *Ibid.*

is why I have undertaken initiatives in several areas to open the door for more normal relations between our two countries.

In pursuance of that goal, I sent Dr. Kissinger, my assistant for national security affairs, to Peking during his recent world tour for the purpose of having talks with Premier Chou En-lai.

The announcement I shall now read is being issued simultaneously in Peking and in the United States:

"Premier Chou En-lai and Dr. Henry Kissinger, President Nixon's assistant for national security affairs, held talks in Peking from July 9 to 11, 1971. Knowing of President Nixon's expressed desire to visit the People's Republic of China, Premier Chou En-lai on behalf of the Government of the People's Republic of China has extended an invitation to President Nixon to visit China at an appropriate date before May, 1972.

"President Nixon has accepted the invitation with pleasure.

"The meeting between the leaders of China and the United States is to seek the normalization of relations between the two countries and also to exchange views on questions of concern to the two sides."

In anticipation of the inevitable speculation which will follow this announcement, I want to put our policy in the clearest possible context. Our action in seeking a new relationship with the People's Republic of China will not be at the expense of our old friends.

It is not directed against any other nation. We seek friendly relations with all nations. Any nation can be our friend without being any other nation's enemy.

I have taken this action because of my profound conviction that all nations will gain from a reduction of tensions and a better relationship between the United States and the People's Republic of China.

It is in this spirit that I will undertake what I deeply hope will become a journey for peace, peace not just for our generation but for future generations on this earth we share together.

Thank you and good night.

Because we are going to assume that anyone hearing the President's speech on television would have heard the reporters' analysis or commentary afterwards or that anyone reading the transcript of the speech the next day in the newspapers would more than likely have read an accompanying article discussing the implications of the speech, we will present here an article by Max Frankel[11] so that our analysis can begin with an equivalent amount of shared information.

President Nixon's success in arranging a trip to China evoked the widespread judgment here today that American policy, in Mao Tse-tung's phrase, was taking a great leap forward.

Diplomatically, the leap was deemed so great that it vaulted right over some short-range, though still pressing, problems—notably disengagement

[11] Max Frankel, "Plan to Visit China May Bolster U.S. in Soviet Talks," *New York Times*, July 16, 1971. © 1971 by The New York Times Company. Reprinted by permission.

from Vietnam and China's representation at the United Nations. Those issues will obviously be affected, but by no means cleanly resolved, by the President's move. Mr. Nixon's interest, during his Presidency, has always focused on the long-term relationship with Peking and on the additional benefits that may result from a new anxiety about that relationship in Moscow.

Politically, the leap is so bold that it propels the President far away from the already unhappy conservatives in his own party.

One Long Play

Their dismay, voiced by Senator James Buckley and many others, will be recompensed by the praise but not necessarily the votes of many liberals and moderates. Mr. Nixon must be counting, therefore, on the general value of shaking up the international game with one long and dramatic play.

The leap itself was the product of both long-term calculation and shrewd short-term maneuver.

Even before he reached the White House, Mr. Nixon had made it clear that he had put behind him his once fervent conviction that dealings with Peking would only increase its power and "probably irreparably weaken" its non-Communist neighbors. He concluded that the Chinese Communists had been much more prudent in deed than in word and that their continued isolation would be more dangerous to peace than their gradual involvement in world diplomacy.

Moreover, Mr. Nixon decided that he could succeed in overtures to Peking where the like-minded Administrations of President John F. Kennedy and President Lyndon B. Johnson had failed—partly because he could more easily overcome the political barriers that he and other Republicans had erected against such a policy in the nineteen-fifties.

Since his own election coincided with an end of the tumultuous Cultural Revolution in China, Mr. Nixon soon found an opening for maneuver. He made clear from the start, while easing up on travel and trade restrictions, that he was less interested in such tactical progress as the formality of diplomatic relations or a seat for Peking at the United Nations than he was in a new era of gradual accommodation in the Pacific.

And he was particularly eager to play upon the separate but coincident desire of both Peking and Washington to give the Soviet leaders some pause for thought and reason for moderation in their own diplomacy.

Two passages in Mr. Nixon's announcement of his forthcoming trip betray, but also mask, these calculations.

The first said that the search for a new relationship with Peking "will not be at the expense of our old friends." The nation's old friends on Taiwan, some old friends elsewhere in Asia, and some of Mr. Nixon's old friends in the Republican party have already made it plain that they are not reassured by his travel plans.

The President obviously intends to preserve his treaty commitments to the Nationalist Chinese on Taiwan, to the South Koreans, the Thais and other allies. But he is also helping the Communists in Peking to reinforce their claims to legitimate rule on the mainland and has explicitly promised them the opportunity to extend their influence, by peaceful means, throughout Asia. In effect, he is thus reinforcing the evolving view in Asia that diplomacy in Peking offers at least as much protection as military help from the United States.

The impact on Vietnam is not yet clear. For the immediate future, Mr. Nixon has at least blunted the propaganda offensive of Hanoi by diverting attention to his own advances. He has also won a chance to demonstrate to Hanoi that even its best allies have other, larger fish to fry.

But the President may find that he has further undercut American patience for the war and he may find it even more difficult to resume the massive bombing of North Vietnam that he has threatened in retaliation for possible setbacks on the ground in South Vietnam.

The other noteworthy passage in the President's remarks said that his move "is not directed against any other nation."

This was clearly meant to reassure the Russians that he was not yielding to the simplistic temptation to become the friend of their most worrisome adversary. The Soviet Union remains the only power capable of seriously injuring the United States and nuclear coexistence with it therefore remains the highest priority of any American leader.

Their Goal No Secret

But the President and his aides have made no secret of their desire to play on Moscow's fears of encirclement, if only to promote more agreement with the Soviet leaders. The hope here, as in Peking, is that a new Chinese-American relationship will moderate Soviet policy, with the benefits to the United States to be translated into greater progress in negotiations on an arms-control agreement, on the Middle East, and on Berlin.

Both Peking and Washington worry also about the growing economic and incipient military power of Japan. Mr. Nixon plainly hopes to exploit this Chinese fear by getting Peking to settle for something less than American evacuation for Taiwan and, indeed, convincing it of the value of an American presence in the Pacific.

Unmentioned in Mr. Nixon's announcement, but visible in his face, was his added delight at taking the world by surprise. After the row over the Pentagon papers, the President was plainly pleased by this demonstration that the Government can, when it must, keep a secret.

Figure 7–2 diagrams the sequence of events predicted to lead to "lasting peace in the world" by President Nixon.

Turning to Max Frankel, we can develop some additional consequences of the President's announcement. These are diagrammed in Figure 7–3.

As in most political statements and journalist analyses, we can find no concept definitions or listing of empirical indicators. The main concepts in President Nixon's speech appear to be (1) international meeting of leaders, (2) normalization of international relations, (3) expense of old friends, (4) tensions, (5) nations' gains, and (6) lasting and enduring peace. We can probably think of several possible definitions for each of these concepts. "Normalization of relations" could be formal recognition of the Chinese Communist government, exchange of ambassadors, increased trade relations, tourist exchanges, and/or decrease in accusations directed by China to the United States and by the United States to

FIGURE 7-2
Effect of Normalizing Relations between the People's Republic of China and the United States on Relations with Other Countries

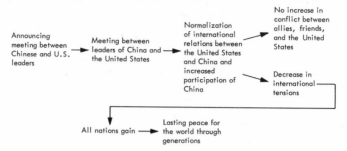

China. "Expense of friends" might be defined as U.S. support for Nationalist China's keeping a seat in the U.N. General Assembly, continued U.S. commitment to and support of governments in conflict with China or allies of China, and/or continuation of the U.S. military presence in Taiwan and other Asian countries. Either psychological or behavioral definitions could be presented for "tensions" as well as "gains for other na-

FIGURE 7-3
Additional Consequences of President Nixon's Speech

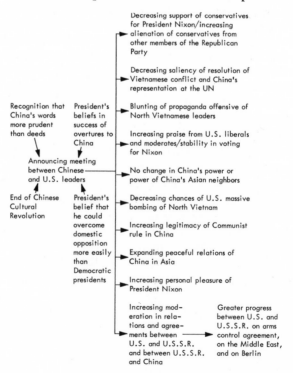

tions." Finally, "lasting peace" can be defined as the absence of international violence, the absence of conflict, the presence of cooperation, or a particular overlapping pattern of conflict that is associated with the absence of deep cleavages. The reader's evaluation of the predictive capacity of the President is likely to vary with the selection of different combinations of choices of definitions.

The assumptions, like the concept definitions, are not explicitly stated. Figures 7–2 and 7–3 both suggest that the President assumes that this policy change will not decrease his chances of reelection.[12] Frankel suggests another assumption; namely, that "diplomacy in Peking offers at least as much protection as military help from the United States." Regarding the link between a meeting of U.S. and Chinese leaders and the normalization of relations between the two countries, President Nixon may be assuming that there will be no translation difficulties leading to a misunderstanding of intentions and that personal meetings can lessen hostility between leaders and subsequently between domestic populations. There may also be an assumption here about possible bargaining payoffs, which would represent gains for both sets of leaders without corresponding or higher costs. In this regard, he may be assuming that there will be no major development (e.g., Chinese weapons development) that would lead the Chinese leaders to figure higher costs than payoffs from such a meeting. However lasting peace is defined, there is clearly an assumption that the U.S.–Chinese conflict is a major obstacle to the realization of that state. It is not clear from the President's statement what weights he attaches to other conflicts in the world or whether he is assuming that increasing U.S.–Chinese cooperation will have a depressing effect on these other conflicts. This last alternative is considered by Frankel. The final assumption that is consistent with what the President said is an "all things being equal" assumption, i.e., the assumption that present relations between all other countries will not change so as to affect his prediction.

Where did these assumptions come from? Some were suggested by Frankel's analysis, while the remaining ones were answers to the question: What do I have to assume about meetings between people, the payoffs of such meetings, and the political, social and economic conditions of the world before I would expect world peace?

Frankel in his predictions of consequences seems to be assuming a variety of conditions:

1. A president's belief in the likelihood of success is necessary before he is likely to make a major change in policy.
2. Conservative Republicans have other alternatives to supporting a Re-

---

[12] Here we are assuming that a major motivation of political leaders is to maintain themselves in office.

publican President, and if they disagree with the President on one important issue, they will decrease their support.

3. This policy issue is so important to most Americans that their attention to and concern with Vietnam and Chinese representation in the United Nations will decrease.

4. This policy will increase support for the United States from other governments.

5. Liberals and moderates are so attached to their party identification that this desired policy change will not result in their changing their voting behavior.

6. A nation that participates more in international relations with other countries will increase its cooperative actions while decreasing its hostile actions. This may be based on the additional assumption that other nations will influence the formerly isolated nation to behave "properly."

7. Increasing moderation will increase the likelihood of agreeing on policy issues.

8. Presidents enjoy surprising people.

The hypotheses essentially consist of linking two or more of the concepts in Figures 7–2 and 7–3, e.g., meetings of leaders will tend to normalize relations between their countries and the normalization of relations tends to decrease international tensions which will increase the likelihood of nations' gains and, lastly, world peace. Without definitions, the hypotheses are not in testable form; therefore, we cannot determine the characteristics of the data on which it would be appropriate to test the hypotheses or logical consistency of the component parts.

The number of possible combinations suggested by the variations in definition, assumption, and hypothesis choices may make one wonder how a political leader can decide anything, much less a major change in policy. However, not deciding only allows someone else to make the decision. The same point can be made with regard to evaluating the predictive and explanatory capacity evidenced by President Nixon's speech.

The speech clearly has so many deficiencies that we would be taking a great risk if we either accepted or rejected his predictions. On the other hand, we may want to make a decision one way or another. In this case, we would make arbitrary choices of definitions, so as to translate the assumptions and hypotheses into testable form. Then we could research the literature for evidence supporting the general propositions (knowing that would not guarantee the predictions in this particular case), storing items of information we garner from newspapers and other sources to undertake an ongoing test of the hypotheses.

If our initial value judgment of the President's change in policy depends on the value we attach to peace, this ongoing test of the hypotheses may lead us to change our value judgment (if we gather disconfirming evidence) or retain it (in the absence of disconfirming evidence). Similarly, our value judgment of revolution or avoiding revolution may be affected by the accumulation of evidence. In both cases, we know that the evidence so gathered is not likely to be representative of a total population. Nevertheless, the knowledge of what we do not know and what we need to know allows us to make a decision conscious of the risks associated with this decision. Perhaps there will be fewer surprises.

In both of these evaluations, we have excluded other material from political science to demonstrate what can be done with the set of questions and limited information and knowledge of the academic literature. Theoretical and empirical expectations and findings gathered from the substantive literature of political science can be compared with a particular scholarly article, a political speech, or a series of political statements. Those studying international communities characterized by varying frequencies of violence, for example, may have found that certain factors were related to low levels of conflict that were omitted by President Nixon. The discrepancies between the expectations and findings in the literature and that offered by a single scholar or politician can help to both identify inadequacies and guide attempts at eliminating these inadequacies. We turn, therefore, in the next three chapters, to a description and analysis of the major substantive areas of political science.

appendix
C

Satisfaction and revolution*

BY JAMES C. DAVIES

The J-curve is this: revolution is most likely to take place when a pro-longed period of rising expectations and rising gratifications is followed by a short period of sharp reversal, during which the gap between expectations and gratifications quickly widens and becomes intolerable. The frustration that develops, when it is intense and widespread in the society, seeks outlets in violent action. When the frustration becomes focused on the government, the violence becomes coherent and directional. If the frustration is sufficiently widespread, intense, and focused on government, the violence will become a revolution that displaces irrevocably the ruling government and changes markedly the power structure of the society. Or the violence will be contained within the system, which it modifies but does not displace. This latter case is rebellion. The following chart (Figure C–1) shows what happens as a society heads toward revolution.[1]

This is an assertion about the state of mind of individual people in

---

* [This article appeared under the title "The J-Curve of Rising and Declining Satisfactions as a Cause of Some Great Revolutions and a Contained Rebellion" in Hugh Davis Graham and Ted Robert Gurr (eds.), *Violence in America: Historical and Comparative Perspectives*, Vol. I, A Staff Report to the National Commission on the Causes and Prevention of Violence, June 1969, pp. 547–75.]

The author is professor of political science at the University of Oregon. He is author of *Human Nature in Politics* (New York: Wiley, 1963), editor of *When Men Revolt—and Why* (New York: The Free Press, forthcoming), and has written several influential articles on collective and revolutionary behavior.

[1] I wish to note that Janice Rademaker and Hendrik van Dalen gathered most of the statistical and many of the factual data presented here. Their work was indispensable to the completion of this paper. Ted Gurr made some generous and acute comments on an earlier draft that helped the reader to get more easily to the heart of the matter.

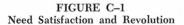

FIGURE C–1
Need Satisfaction and Revolution

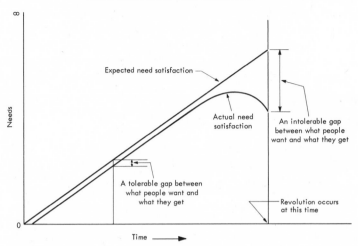

a society who are likely to revolt. It says their state of mind, their mood, is one of high tension and rather generalized hostility, derived from the widening of the gap between what they want and what they get. They fear not just that things will no longer continue to get better but—even more crucially—that ground will be lost that they have already gained. The mood of rather generalized hostility, directed generally outward, begins to turn toward government. People so frustrated not only fight with other members of their families and their neighbors. They also jostle one another in crowds and increase their aggressiveness as pedestrians and bus passengers and drivers of cars. When events and news media and writers and speakers encourage the direction of hostilities toward the government, the dispersed and mutual hostility becomes focused on a common target. The hostility among individuals diminishes. The dissonant energy becomes a resonant, very powerful force that heads like a great tidal wave or forest fire toward the established government, which it may then engulf.

This phenomenon of synergic unification of a public when frustration becomes widespread and deep is awesome in its tendency to erase hostility between people. It is akin to the feeling that develops in a quarrelsome household at times. A fighting family may just barely manage to hold together. The father may be unemployed and frequently drunk, the mother worn to a frazzle, the children quarrelsome as they displace the tensions generated by poverty and the frustrations of their fighting parents. The father, no longer able to provide for his family, may lose his authority within the family and strike out at those nearest to him. But when the landlord knocks on the door and announces that the rent must be paid by 10 o'clock tomorrow morning on pain of eviction, the family suddenly stops its own fighting, beats up the landlord, and throws him out on the street.

Such tension within the family is a microcosm of the tension within the national community; that is, among the individual members of the political society and among its conflicting regional, religious, racial, and socioeconomic groups. When the various segments of a deeply divided society suddenly sense that they all have the same enemy, the government, they can spontaneously unite for long enough to overthrow it.

CAUSES OF REVOLUTION AND REBELLION, PSYCHOLOGICALLY CONSIDERED

Revolutions and rebellions differ in result but have like origins. And the differences in origin are less ones of kind than of degree. Revolutions involve more segments of the population than do rebellions. The intensity of feeling in revolutions is probably greater and has taken a longer time to develop than in rebellions. The violent phase of a revolution is longer and more savage. The bitterness that lingers after the violence is likely to endure for decades or centuries after a revolution.

The difference is not in causes and the violent action or even in the long-range consequences so much as it is in the immediate result. Rebellions do not remove the established government but instead are contained, partly as the consequence of the use of violent force in large enough amounts to override the rebels' anger at the government. The rebels may choose to live with their frustrations rather than endure the blows of the police and the army and the dull, sick anguish of imprisonment. But rebellions also are contained within the established system to the extent that the government pays heed to the grievances that led to the rebellion. If the only response to extralegal violence is legal violence, then hatred of oppression becomes deeply imprinted in the minds of the momentarily silenced rebels. The hatred lingers and deepens like embers in dry tinder after firefighters have tried to beat to death a small fire.

As the American Declaration of Independence said in 1776, people do not for "light and transient causes" make a rebellion or revolution. What then are the grave and enduring conditions that produce frustrations in a broad and varied citizenry, that in turn produce the revolutionary state of mind?

The common condition appears to be the denial of satisfaction of those needs that are basic to all human beings. Not all needs (as for a new automobile) are basic, and not all basic needs are of equal revolutionary potential. Abraham Maslow has argued that man's basic needs are arranged in sequence, from the most to the least powerful. The most potent are the physical needs, which must continuously be satisfied for all people during their entire life. But when a person gains their satisfaction—as an infant, a child, and an adult—he does not then, animal-like, remain content with satisfying just these bodily needs. Soon after birth he demands affection and, if he gets it, he reciprocates affection toward others. But his physical needs persist, and if he is forced to choose, he will first satisfy his need for food and then his need for affection.

In early childhood the individual who has been regularly gratified in his physical and affectional needs does not then rest content with this mental state of affairs. He begins, usually no later than when he is 8 or 10 years old, to demand recognition as an individual who is worthy of his own regard for himself and of others' regard for him. In early childhood people begin to demand that others accord them respect. The respect of others is necessary if people are to acquire self-respect.

It is this kind of demand that lies so close to the surface of the Declaration of Independence, in the statement that all men are created equal and in the specific indictments of British rule—for example, in the great indignation expressed at the quartering of troops in private homes without the consent of the homeowners, and at the removal of trials at law from the Colonies to England. This demand is evident in the Declaration's "decent respect to the opinions of mankind," whose approval the American rebels sought.

And once these successive needs—the physical, the social-affectional, and the equal esteem or dignity needs—are sufficiently gratified, humans are not even then content: they then begin to look for that kind of activity that is particularly suited to them as unique individuals. Whether their competence is to be a ditchdigger, a powershovel operator, a construction foreman, a civil engineer or a building contractor, an architect, a mother, a writer, or a politician—they must do these things when they have become rather sure in the gratification of their even more basic physical, social, and esteem needs.

The crucial point is this: no human being so long as he lives is ever completely gratified in the satisfaction of his needs. Up to the moment of his death, he must eat and sleep; he must be with people; he has to be acknowledged as a distinct person; and he must realize his individual potential. When he ceases to do these things, he ceases to live. All of these needs of his have got to be gratified; they ultimately can be denied only by natural or by violent death. Armies and police forces can quash these natural and irrepressible human needs only by reducing human beings to animals and then killing them. The logic of this was stated in fictional form by George Orwell, in describing what was necessary for the perpetuation of dictatorship: "a boot, stamping in a human face, forever."

The Maslow need hierarchy is a necessary part of a psychological explanation of the causes of revolution. Marx to the contrary, revolutions are made not only by economically depressed classes and their leaders but by the joint effort of large numbers of those people in all social groups who are experiencing frustration of different basic needs. People deprived of career opportunities may join in revolt with people who have suffered indignities at the hands of employers, landlords, police, or military troops. They also may join with people who have suffered no indignities but are for the moment simply hungry.

The common characteristic of potential revolutionaries is that each of them individually senses the frustration of one or more basic needs and each is able to focus his frustration on the government. After this need frustration is generated, people begin to share their discontents and to work together. But preceding this joint action, there is no more conspiracy than there is among trees when they burst into flame during a forest fire.

THE J-CURVE AND PARTICULAR REVOLUTIONS

On the level of general theory, one can say precisely the same thing—in abstract terms—about each revolution and rebellion. But in some ways each revolution is unlike every other revolution. And from the practical research standpoint, directly comparable data are not available for all revolutions, particularly when they took place decades or centuries ago. In many nations now, the seeds of revolution are sprouting. But established governments in these nations are not likely to welcome social scientists in search of data by conducting public opinion surveys inquiring about attitudes toward the government.

In the interest of arriving at some conclusions and of arriving at the understanding that they are tentative, we can profitably consider particular revolutions.

The French Revolution of 1789

The French Revolution is the first of the great modern postindustrial revolutions. It is the first grand revolution after the grandest of all modern revolutions, the 16th-century Protestant Reformation.

The position of the various major social classes in France gives a major clue as to how the revolution came about. The relationships between these classes help explain also why liberty, equality, and fraternity did not arrive on the day they were declared to be human rights. The major segments of French society in the late 18th century were the well-known three estates: the clergy, the nobility, and then everybody else, who collectively were called the third estate for lack of a more precise term.

What is less well known are the proportions that each of these estates comprised of the total French population of about 23 million. There were, according to Georges Lefebvre, perhaps the greatest historian in 20-century France of the French Revolution, about 100,000 Frenchmen in the clergy (less than half of 1 percent); about 400,000 in the nobility (about 2 percent); and over 23 million in the third estate. The third estate included the high bourgeoisie, an economically, socially, and politically active group of merchants, bankers, and manufacturers. Also in the third estate were the petty bourgeoise—small merchants, bakers, artisans in wood and metal, and the growing body of skilled government bureaucrats. Finally, the third estate included workingmen, many of them the sons of peasants, and also the vast body of peasants. France, beginning its industrialization somewhat later than England, was still overwhelmingly an agricultural nation.

Even less well known than the proportions of each of the three estates in the total population is the proportion of land which each estate owned. Again, according to Lefebvre, the clergy owned about 10 percent of the land, the nobility somewhat less than 20 percent, the bourgeoisie about 20 percent, and the peasants all the rest. The heavy imbalance of landownership reflects only the most evident part of the land-tenure picture. Anywhere from 20 to 75 percent of the rural households in France before the revolution did not own any land. These peasants were either working as tenants to save money to buy land, or they had given up and were working as paid farm laborers. And in massive numbers they were drifting into cities to find work.

These peasants who aspired to landownership or who had achieved it saw themselves as facing an unending struggle to survive and to get a little ahead. As the industrial economy began to develop rapidly, the demand for farm products increased because so many people who once tilled and lived off the soil now worked for money in cities, which—as everywhere in developing nations undergoing industrialization—made ever-increasing, insatiable demands on the countryside to feed their people. Peasants, seeing the chance thus to move up the ladder from farm labor or land rental, were beset by a variety of inhibitors. There were the feudal dues (payment to landlords for the use of his flour mill, the exclusive right of landlords to hunt and fish, the reversion of land to a landlord if the peasant died without proper heirs, etc.); the duty to perform physical labor for public purposes (building public roads and other structures); the tithe (a 10 percent tax due to the church); and a variety of taxes payable directly to the national government through its local representatives and more specifically to the local collector, who took his lawful share of what he was able to extract from the peasant.

Peasants did not, in short, believe that they were beloved objects of solicitude of other segments of French society. Neither did their sons who went into the cities to work in factories and small shops or into mines to dig coal. Wages went up slowly in the 18th century, as we shall see later, and prices went up rather rapidly. Better off then when they left the countryside, they were nevertheless gradually getting worse off than they had been in years past in the city.

That portion of the bourgeoisie containing skilled artisans suffered some of the same taxing pains as did the landowning peasants. Their guilds were heavily taxed and so were their incomes. The high bourgeoisie, growing in wealth and power, suffered the disadvantage that the more systematically they ran their enterprises and kept record of profits and losses, the more they had to pay in taxes. And they believed the government was becoming increasingly subservient to the nobility.

The nobility saw the government as increasingly subservient to the bourgeoisie. With no respect for the dignity of inherited title, the government for a price was adding pseudonoble titles to wealthy men of no family, arrogantly designating these arrivistes as "nobles de robe" to distinguish them from the natural-born "nobles d'épée." The old nobles observed the new nobles buying country estates from increasingly vestigial but still very sworded noblemen. The nobles of the robe were enfolding, smothering, the nobles of the sword.

Old nobles, looking through dusty old documents, discovered a way to be with but not be of the modern mercantile-industrial world. They found that services and payments in kind were due them from peasants, many of whom had for centuries been free peasants. (Serfdom was first abolished, according to Tocqueville, in Normandy in the 13th century and was virtually nonexistent on the eve of the great 18th century revolution.) In short, landlords, seeing their economic advancement, their political power, and their prestige all threatened and actually diminished by the energetic and of course unhonorable bourgeoisie, began in the mid-18th century to reassert long-dead "rights" against peasants, who thereby saw not only their freedom, power, and prestige but also their economic welfare threatened and diminished.

The sworded nobles furthermore had little to do—few, if any functions in society to give their lives meaning. The government gradually was taking away—efficiently, effectively, and thoroughly—such governmental powers as nobles had possessed before kings could successfully establish national power. They were no longer needed to keep the peace, to adjudicate disputes among vassals and serfs, and most particularly to protect from violence their people, their peasants, their onetime serfs. Now the government acted, or tried or professed to act, directly in the behalf of the population at large. So the old nobles, sensing their loss of position in society as the new nobles of the robe began to emulate the sword-bearing style of life, began to emulate the new nobles in their wealth. And this meant evading such taxes as the capitation, by law payable by all people with incomes. It also meant using documents to enforce feudal dues, in many cases centuries after the reason for the dues had been reduced to legal paper, which now was hard to read and harder to justify.

The clergy, that one half of 1 percent of the population, had a few functions to perform. They kept records of births and deaths. They baptized. They warned souls of the need for grace and invoked God's grace. And they prayed, managed estates, and bottled wine, extracted the tithe from the peasants. And, for their recordkeeping and their divine intervention, they were freed of any tax payments.

These then were the major segments of society, each of which eyed every other segment and its members with suspicion and envy. Was that a tax collector coming? Was that a secret hoard of grain which that peasant or that landlord so hurriedly covered up? Where was that set of books of the merchant that were a true report of how rich he was getting? How much did that fat father pay the government to get his bright but unprincipled son the job as secretary to the resident government commissioner?

If individuals in each estate tended to suspect and envy individuals in all other estates, they all mistrusted and condemned the government. The monarchy asserted in the mid-15th century (during the reign of Charles VII) the power to tax anyone without the consent of any estate. In the 18th century, the crown was intermittently, and more frequently, beginning to use the power. It had to. France engaged in a nearly unbroken series of expensive wars in the 18th century. Good for members of all estates, as businessmen, landowning lords and peasants and the small class of workers, the wars were bad for businessmen and peasants as taxpayers. Starting in 1781, the government increased—but with an infirm hand—its efforts to collect taxes, demanding even that the nobility actually pay the taxes nominally due from it.

The government was thus disappointing the popular expectation of continued prosperity without cost. And until the French intervention in the American War of Independence, the wars were lost. The intervention in America gave France pride in somewhat vicariously defeating England, which in 1763 had virtually knocked France out of North America except for Louisiana. The financial crisis—which threatened and actually deprived high bourgeoisie, nobles, and now even clergy of wealth they had come to expect as their due—got worse. Inflation intensified. Lefebvre has calculated the rise in cost of living thus: in about 50 years before the revolution, prices went up some 65 percent and wages went up some 22 percent. Whether rich or poor, most people had enough excuse to displace at least some of their inter-state hostility onto the government. And in addition they had reason enough also to dislike and condemn the government, which either lost its wars or was unable to pay for the one war that it assisted in winning.

These growing tensions, increasingly directed toward government, were aggravated by events that amounted to bad luck at best and gullibility at worst. In 1786 France made a trade treaty with the England it had helped to defeat 3 years earlier in America. France agreed to reduce the tariff on textiles, which helped the then more efficient and mass-market-oriented English mills. In return, England agreed to reduce tariffs on wines and brandies, which England did not produce anyhow but imported from Portugal and France. The trade treaty went into effect in 1788.

In 1778, the French harvest of grain suffered from bad weather. That is, the weather was bad for grain and good for the vineyards. There was thus a nearly catastrophic shortage of grains for bread and a large surplus of wine to flood the English market after the lowering of the trade barriers. And the opening of war of Turkey against Russia and Austria diminished these countries as markets for French textiles, which now faced competition in French stores from cheap English cloth.

Unemployment rose along with the reduced demand for textiles. The abundant grape harvest dropped wine prices somewhat. Peasants who produced wine had to buy their food at higher prices. These economic dislocations chain-reacted to reduce the demand for everything but jobs and bread—the two goods that were in scarcest supply. Bread had never been so expensive since the end of the reign of Louis XIV in 1715, and so bread riots broke out in the major cities, and people in the cities began restlessly roaming out into the countryside to get food. Long-term rising expectations of a prosperous and peaceful economy and effective government were quickly disappointed. In the spring of 1789 and into the summer, the growing interclass hostility and growing hostility to government quickly burst into revolution, when the fear of physical deprivation quickly became real and immediate. The 18th-century developments are shown in Figure C–2.

The J-curve helps explain the French Revolution. The growing frustration of the land expectations of peasants, of the dignity expectations of landlords who wanted the status-wealth of the high bourgeoisie, and of the dignity and power expectations of the high bourgeoisie are all closely comparable to developments in other nations that have had revolutions. And so is the effect of sudden economic dislocation following long-term economic growth.

But the J-curve is not a total explanation of the French Revolution. At least in its intensity, the interclass hostility in France, not as such related to the J-curve, was unique. More or less independently of frustrated rising expectations in the 18th century, French society was already deeply fragmented. The internal war of all against all had already begun. The absorption of these forces, in conflict between classes and individuals, did temporarily deflect them from the government. But in the end the sheer hostility, as it became more intense, turned toward the government.

FIGURE C–2
The French Revolution

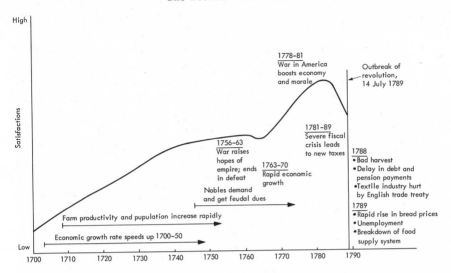

And in addition to the disappointed expectations and deflected inter-class hostility, there was in France in 1789 the visible and exciting example of the successful American Revolution. In 1968 French students followed the example of students in Japan, America, and elsewhere by rebelling against French universities and government. But this was only the second time the American revolutionary example had been followed: it had already been followed almost 180 years before.

The American Civil War of 1861

The difference between the terms "revolution," "rebellion," and "civil war" may be nothing more than this: revolution succeeds, rebellion fails, and civil war leaves the question open. All involve violence. In the Gettysburg Address of 1863, Lincoln referred to the ongoing conflict as "a great civil war"; at other times he called it rebellion and he never acknowledged the sovereign independence of the 11 Southern States that asserted it. It is not quite clear even a hundred years later that it was a rebellion or that it failed, but it is clear that the American Civil War did not end in Southern independence. It remains hard to characterize this most savage conflict. In proportion to the population of the time, this civil war produced the most catastrophic loss of life and property that America has ever suffered. The awesome depth of the conflict makes it important to explain.

The American Civil War is in some ways like the French Revolution of 1789, and in others like the Nazi revolution of 1933 examined in the next section. As in the French Revolution, the middle-class, entre-preneurial, and industrializing part of the nation was arrayed in battle against the landed aristocracy. Southern plantations fought a change in social institutions that would make them more suitable to the profound changes which capitalism and industrialization brought with them. But the American Civil War is unlike the French Revolution in the absence of joint action by both American bourgeoisie and landlords against the national government. If Southern landlords and Northern industrialists had combined against the government, it is quite possible the civil war would have resembled the Nazi revolution. It could have established an oligarchical dictatorship of the urban upper-middle-class and rural landlords, as in many 20th-century developing nations.

The American conflict does resemble the Nazi revolution in that it was initiated by conservative segments of society that were restive with the pace and direction of change. In both America before the Civil War and Germany before Nazism, an agrarian economy was being rapidly replaced by industry, and the hegemony of landed aristocrats was threat-ened by the growing political power of merchants and industrialists. Industrialization was about as recent in both countries—about two genera-tions, though its growth rate in Germany was greater. But the principal difference between America in 1861 and Germany in 1933 was in the orientation of the two revolutions: the latter was more progressive in its orientation in that there was a strong and real appeal in Nazism to those people who felt they had been denied equal opportunity to acquire education and technical skills. In America the South denied the desirabil-ity of education and anything other than agricultural technology.

The gradual rise and rapid decline in gratifications in pre-Civil War America occur in two cycles, one contained within the other. There had been a very long cyclical rise in expectations of Americans generally, from the beginnings of colonization, through independence, and down to the great growth of wealth in the early 19th century. There also was a shorter term cycle in Southern expectations, which rose from about 1789, when the national government was established, and began to decline in the mid-1850's. That is, there was a roughly 200-year cycle and within it a 70-year cycle of rising and falling gratifications. The latter cycle is set forth in Figure C–3.

The colonization of America in the 17th and 18th centuries provided a steady rise in expectations and gratifications until the 1750's and 1760's. But a common pattern of growth in the various colonies and a common determination on independence concealed some growing differences. In the northern colonies, from New England down to Pennsylvania, the dominant settlers were religious dissenters, radically modern in their indi-vidualism and anticorporatism. The democratic New England town meet-ings emerged from the institution of theoretical democracy in the New

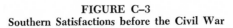

FIGURE C–3
Southern Satisfactions before the Civil War

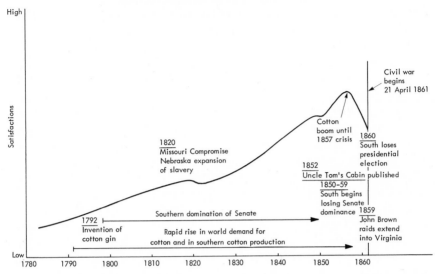

England church congregations. This democracy was an antithesis of the hierarchy in church and government that were so typical of England. This style of rule appeared also in Pennsylvania, dominated as it was by Quakers and their radically democratic ideology.

In Maryland, Virginia, the Carolinas, and Georgia, fewer of the settlers were democratically and individualistically oriented dissenters. Indeed there was a substantial influx of both Roman Catholics and their institutional cousins, Episcopalians. They were more accustomed to hierarchy and order established from above and they carried with them the nondissenting, establishment orientation of their English ancestors. There were, in addition, influxes of poor people with more individualistic and less establishment-oriented religious views, but they rarely were a major influence in the South, politically or socially, at any time before the Civil War, and they shared with the establishment-oriented plantationer class a dedication to the rectitude of slavery and to the virtues of the rural life.

Differences in institutions and values if anything became greater with the passage of time. Big cities of commerce and industry grew in the North and, with the exception of the great port city of New Orleans, never developed in the South. Agrarian development in the North was typified by family-sized farms. With their highly individualistic outlook, farmers had appreciable political power in the Northern state governments from the beginning of national independence. Agrarian development in the South was on the surface of things like growth in the North.

There were far more family-sized farms in the South than there were plantations, but the plantationers dominated Southern politics, using the issue of black inferiority to all white men very effectively in maintaining acquiescence by poor whites in the rule of the large landholders and slaveowners.

Inevitably, as industrialization and commerce developed in the North it began to urbanize rapidly. This process included not just a division of labor between farmers and city dwellers, but also a rapid growth in population. Correlatively and inevitably, an agrarian society like that in the South experienced a slower growth in population. The growth toward political equilitarianism in the North became more and more fundamentally opposed to the oligarchical domination of politics by the plantationers. And so began—more exactly, continued—the widening of the gulf between economic and social values and ways of life between North and South.

In national politics, the question of who should rule echoed continuously across the ever-eroding canyon between South and North. The Virginia dynasty was not a legend but a reality for a generation after independence. Excepting the brief and not very portentous administrations of John Adams (1797–1801) and his son John Quincy Adams (1825–29), there was an unbroken line of Southern Presidents of the United States, from Washington through Jefferson, Madison, Monroe, and Jackson. John Calhoun of South Carolina served as Vice President during J. Q. Adams' administration and the first term of Jackson's. From 1789 to 1837 the Presidency was almost continuously Southern.

This Southern domination became increasingly more romantic. The Southerners who became Presidents acted nationally, not sectionally. In Congress, the Missouri Compromise settled and unsettled (in 1820) the conflict over sectional representation. By this Compromise the South won the votes in Congress of the border state of Missouri, which was to be admitted as a slave state, and lost the free opportunity to expand its political power westward. The South did continue to dominate the Senate for another generation, judging at least by the 1854 Kansas-Nebraska Act, which, repudiating the Missouri Compromise, allowed slaves to come into these territories. Indeed the Senate was not just the last retreat of the South but also the only part of the government that did not reflect the ever growing social and economic dominance of the North.

The regional growth comparisons are awesome. In one decade, from 1850–60, the population of the South grew greatly—about 23 percent; in the same decade the non-Southern population increased a fantastic 43 percent. Although adequate economic trend data over time are hard to come by, in 1860 the North was producing over 90 percent by value of all manufactured goods. The proportion produced by the North had apparently been increasing rapidly as the war approached. The North was even exporting food (grains and livestock) to the agricultural South. And free farmers were saying politically that they did not want to compete, economically or socially, with plantationers whose fieldhands worked without pay.

These developments suggest, at least in hindsight, that the South was made to suppose that it could win a war against the growing industrial and commercial Yankee giant. But the South itself was enjoying, early in the 1850's, unprecedented prosperity. There was an almost insatiable world demand for cotton, of which the South had close to a world monopoly in production. The average annual production during the 1840–50 decade was 2.2 million bales; it increased to 3.4 million in the next decade. At the same time the average annual price during 1840–50 was about 8 cents per pound, rising more than 30 percent, to 10.6 cents, in the final prewar decade. Along with this—and an improvement in profit from tobacco and sugarcane production—came an increase in the price of prime field hands, the most commonly valuable category of slaves. Their price doubled during the 1850–60 decade, reaching as high as $1,500 per head, and the demand was enormous. It was not easy for Southerners to concede the rightness or the efficiency of an economy based on free labor.

But the little-diversified agrarian Southern economy was fragile. A particular weakness was the plantationers' custom of buying on credit advanced before the sale of their crops. Even before the 1775 War of Independence, it was common for Southern planters to be thus in long-range debt to English merchants. After 1783 there was one change: the creditors were now Northern merchants, mainly in New York. The South quite simply remained money-poor up to 1861 (and beyond). On a sellers' market, which the South enjoyed with some ups and downs until 1857, the system of credit worked well enough for Southern planters. And it worked even better for Northern creditors. To protect themselves from market uncertainties—and from individuals who were poor credit risks—Northern dealers would charge Southern buyers higher than normal prices. Southern buyers, when they were paid by credit paper at harvesttime, would sell the paper at a discount to pay their bills. So they paid twice at least: in the form of higher prices for the goods they bought, and lower prices for the credit paper they sold to pay off their annual debt.

This chronic low-intensity economic crisis, in the face of seemingly endless prosperity, is akin to the situation that produced the looting and burning of white-owned stores by Negroes in the 1960's—more than a century later: the Southern plantationers developed no affection for the big Yankee houses that had the goods and sold them at a price higher than a Yankee would have to pay. They were unable to set fire to the

New York stores and say "Burn, Baby, Burn." But they did try to destroy the Union.

Near the end of this cycle of rising and then declining political gratifications was the more immediate and very threatening economic crisis of 1857. It was an epitome of the Southern dependence on the North, of the dependence of any raw-material-producing colony on the financial and other economic circumstances of the diversified "mother country." In 1857 the South was hit by a panic in the New York commodity exchange market. For a time money exchange with England virtually ceased, and so did the effective demand for cotton in England. Although the Liverpool price was 18 or 19 cents a pound for cotton, in contrast to 10 cents a pound in New York, Southerners for the most part had to sell in New York. Many of them had already committed their crop to New York buyers and so were stuck; many who had not committed their crop needed money badly and were in virtually the same bind as those who had already sold their crops for future delivery. A Southern Senator in Washington saw the situation with a clear intelligence and passed his judgment: a cotton crop that could have sold for $100 million went for $65 million. To save irresponsible and selfish Northern speculators—who perhaps blamed the system for producing the money crisis—the South lost $35 million.

This was the final critical downturn in the gratifications of Southerners. They had lost political power that they had exercised so successfully in nearly a half century of Southern but Nation-minded Presidents of the United States. They had neared the final loss of their dominant power in the Senate, where so often they held a veto over laws demanded by Northerners. And now, in a process that so starkly showed their economic thralldom to the North, they had to save their economic masters to the tune of a loss of a third of the value of their major crop—and the nation's major export.

The growing and now enormous tensions found release in secession. The eventual outcome of the 1854 Kansas-Nebraska Act, which in 1854 still offered some hope of restoring the balance of sectional power in the Senate, soon became clear. An honest referendum on the slavery issue indicated an 8-to-1 majority in Kansas in favor of entering the Union as a free state. After liberating a few slaves in Kansas, that madman and self-styled liberator, John Brown, in 1859 made a raid in search of arms on the U.S. arsenal at Harpers Ferry. But Harpers Ferry was not in Kansas; it was in Virginia. And it was clear where John Brown now proposed to commence the liberation of slaves.

So the South began to secede. South Carolina was the first to take the step, on December 20, 1860. And South Carolina fired the first shot, on the federal Fort Sumter in Charleston Harbor, on April 21, 1861. The Civil War had begun as the ever-romantic South came to the end of its neofeudal dream. Its expectations of freedom to continue to expand its wealth and way of life were shattered by the events of the late 1850's, in Congress and in the mercantile houses of New York.

The Nazi revolution of 1933

The Nazi revolution was a German and a world catastrophe. It led to the partial destruction and the partition of a population that had been growing in unity, civilization, and recognition since the Protestant Reformation that Luther led, since the tremendous spurt in industrialization in the late 19th century, and since the surge of nationalism that took the form of empire building and them, in 1914, of war.

Germany was the first to experience a successful reformation, that major advance toward establishing the equalization and individuation of men. For whatever reasons, it was the last major European nation to undergo that profoundest of modernizers: industrialization. In one sense the first modern popular revolution took place in Germany in the 16th century, before industrialization had developed anything like its modern factory system anywhere. In another sense Germany never had a post-industrial revolution comparable to the French Revolution. The German Reformation was universalist in its equalitarian principles and so was the French Revolution. There was a messianic quality to the equalitarian beliefs of the German Reformation of the 16th century, the French Revolution of the 18th, and the Russian of the 20th. These revolutions spawned and nurtured many popular movements in the world. But the Nazi revolution—the nearest counterpart to the postindustrial French Revolution—was not universalist. It was particularistic, intensely nationalistic, and imperialistic, proposing to subject and exploit both Slavic and Gallic peoples to the control and enrichment of the Germanic. It was a kind of revenge for the world recognition that came to France and Russia after their universalist revolutions, renown that had stifled Germany between two peoples that felt their own superiority to Germans.

The growth in vitality of German society and culture was relatively steady and continuous, perhaps for centuries up to 1918. Surely it was continuous since the tariff union (developing from 1819–1844) that intensified the trend, under Prussian domination, toward economic unity. With the growth of an enormous iron and steel industry, the basis was laid for building warships, artillery, and rifles. Construction of these commodities made war and expansion a euphoric dream that called for realization. In 1870, in battle, Germany defeated the France that had been the terror of Europe just two generations before. Within months, in January 1871, came the seige and surrender of Paris. Within days after the surrender of Paris came the formal inauguration of the unified German empire, when the Prussian king was crowned Emperor William I. The curves of rising expectations and gratifications were steadily rising, for Germans as individuals and as a nation.

In such a short analysis it is not possible to specify steps in the progress of Germany upward to its dismaying and unacknowledged defeat in world war in November 1918. It is clear enough that the long-range trend, accelerating rapidly after the tariff union and the 1871 unification, was upward. It is clear that the 1918 defeat came as a profound shock. It was sufficiently stunning and ambiguous to be regarded as only a temporary setback by those elitist individuals who believed in an imperial destiny and by those ordinary Germans who had a deep pride in their country. All these had entrusted basic decisions to the government. Under two emperors and such gifted paternalistic rulers as Bismarck and the Krupp family, the government had given them economic prosperity, social security, and world prestige.

Again, as in the analysis of the American Civil War, there was a centuries-long J-curve and a decades-short one. For present purposes, we can commence the analysis of the final rise and decline with the ambiguous 1918 defeat, recalling only that the advances up to 1918 had been real and enormous and remained in the memories of perhaps most Germans.

Both the French and the German Nazi revolutions were preceded by military defeat. But the former nation could not so easily turn the blame outward as could the latter. In the French case, the Seven Years' War, ending in 1763, was a virtually total defeat by England in North America. The vicarious French victory over England at Yorktown in 1781 produced independence for the United States and near-bankruptcy for France. The military action was far from France. England did not make demands intimately affecting Frenchmen in France in 1763 and the government's financial crisis in 1781 could hardly be blamed by Frenchmen on the defeated British.

With Germany after the 1918 Armistice it was different. The Allies blockaded German ports and then occupied just enough German territory to hurt pride and business badly. German Communists, exalted by the Russian example, threatened their countrymen with total destruction of the established system, already shaken by the loss of the emperor. Germans therefore could readily displace blame and thereby dissociate the glories of an ever-greater German nation from the trickeries of external and internal enemies who sought only their own aggrandizement and German degradation. This hope for restoration of recently and meanly lost greatness was a very central part of the mental outlook of perhaps most Germans in the 1920's.

The continuation of hope and of pride in being German formed a cement that kept the nation from the disintegration that France experienced in the late 18th century. There was not quite the war of all against all that characterized prerevolutionary French society. Internal hostility was less personal and the enemies were more symbolic. The Allies, the French, the Communists, the Jews, and capitalists were the enemies rather than one's neighboring peasants, one's landlord, one's boss in the shoe factory, or the arriviste wealthy bourgeois who bought one's estate.

The impersonal contacts with enemies in Germany were such as to reinforce displacement of the internal tensions of an economy that had suffered the consequences of vast military expenditure, in an all-out war from 1914 to 1918. It was easier to forget the sanctions (governmental and industrial) against industrial strife than the more comfortable fact of punitive and unrealistic reparations. It was the government that initiated currency inflation. But the effect of the inflation on the internal economy could be overshadowed in people's minds by its effect on the French enemy, especially since the inflation was an effort to defeat the French and Belgian military occupation of the Ruhr Basin, starting in January 1923, by watering down the high price of reparations. German workers, who did strike in large numbers in this period, often regarded the French and Belgian occupying forces (and their attendant business experts who took over management control of the big enterprises) as the enemy. And then they could also blame those German capitalists, many of them Jews, who skillfully made fortunes out of the inflation. Because their customs made them stand out—particularly in the abstract—the Jewish capitalists were easier to blame than the German ones. And middle-class Germans could blame the Communists as agitators of the proletariat. In many such plausible ways, blame for Germany's ills could be projected outward. These plausible and sufficiently genuine external and internal enemies limited the tendency, which was never notably strong, of Germans to blame themselves for their problems, which in the 1920's indeed became severe.

The underlying optimism (a continuing heritage from the imperial and Reformation eras) and the surface displacement of responsibility for contemporary problems probably combined to encourage an irrepressible optimism in the mid-1920's. The inflation was a trauma. It began in August 1922 and ran wild for more than a year, until November 1923 when efforts at drastic monetary reform were undertaken. But the 1920's nevertheless were times of hope and progress in Germany. If the inflation wiped out private savings and insurance policies, it also wiped out internal public debt, and in April 1924 the Dawes plan promised a large influx of external capital for reconstruction. Though there were peaks of unemployment (1.5 million in January 1923, 2 million in February 1926, and 1.4 million in January 1928), the trend in jobs was generally upward. Taking the prewar year 1907 as a base of 100, by 1925 the number of gainfully employed had increased to about 127, and by 1933 had increased to 128. Again taking 1907 national population as a base of 100, by 1925 it had increased only to 102 and by 1933 to 106. In short, the proportion of the population that had jobs, roughly a decade after World War ended, was a fourth larger than a decade before the war ended.

Up to 1929, economic conditions in Germany generally improved. And then, starting in July 1929, there was a steady, unremitting increase in unemployment until some time in the first quarter of 1933—that is, until after Hitler came to power on January 30, 1933. At the peak of unemployment, sometime in 1932, between 5.6 million and 7.3 million were unemployed. This was about three times the previous peak of about 2 million in February 1926 and 10 times as high as the 560,000 people who were out of work in July 1928.

The depression hit hard in other ways. Germans, who as we noted had lost all their savings in the inflation, had begun to save again. Savings had increased by about half between 1928 and 1930. In the next year, 1931, the amount of money in savings accounts declined about 6 percent. This hurt many kinds of people, perhaps most seriously the lower middle class. And the shortage of work, statistically a cold figure, became a chilling reality, particularly for the working class. Germans on the average in 1928 worked 7.7 hours per day. By 1932, the hours worked per day had declined to 6.9—roughly by 10 percent.

What this adds up to, in summary, is that fewer people were working; those who worked were working fewer hours. And more money had to be drawn out of savings than could be put in. The sense that work and thrift would pay off, as Germany and Germans rose out of the defeat in war and the disgrace in postwar inflation and occupation, was rapidly replaced with despair. The gap between expectations and gratifications yawned wide, for perhaps a large majority of Germans. The gap was filled first with Nazi words and then with deeds as the economy was revived and geared toward war.

We have become so sensitive to the impact of ideology—perhaps as a consequence of the enormous amount of it generated and broadcast throughout the world since the 1917 Russian Revolution—that we tend to explain the success of the Nazis in terms of the racist, irrational rhetoric that stems from *Mein Kampf*. However nicely it fit the German mood in the late 1920's, the words would have found few ears if there had not been recurrent and at last catastrophic economic crisis. Figure C–4 shows the series of crises.

The physical needs of millions of people were deeply denied. The standard diet of the unemployed consisted largely of potatoes and margarine. Working-class people might have been a force to oppose the racist or at least antiproletarian appeals of the Nazis. But unemployed people, particularly when they have suffered for several years, are more inclined toward apathy than activity. Those whose physical survival was

FIGURE C–4
Economic Satisfactions and Nazi Revolution

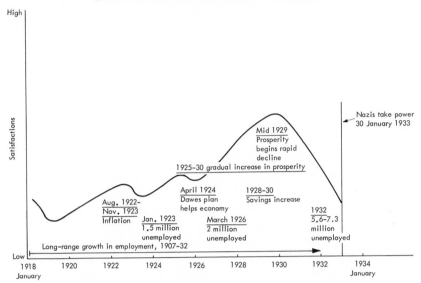

not so directly endangered—those who had enough to eat—were threatened in virtually all walks of life with a regression to the economic level of 1919–23.

Interclass conflict took different form in pre-1933 Germany from that in pre-1789 France. In the German instance, intergroup conflict seems to have been less pronounced, at least on anything approaching the personal level of hostility that prevailed in France in the late-18th century. Nevertheless various segments of the society did show hostility toward others, however vague its form and ill-defined its object. There was a high degree of symbolic hostility between labor and capital in Germany, but the number and intensity of strikes declined greatly from 1925 on. At first this decline was probably due to the rather general prosperity of the mid-1920's. Later (1920–32) it was probably due to the acuteness of unemployment, which led men to fear a strike because they would then be faced with a diet of potatoes and margarine. The conflict between labor and capital was thus more abstract and ideological than real, and took place more in politics than outside factory gates. As such it was inevitably attenuated. Its savagery diminished to a rather generalized hostility, perhaps on both sides.

The petty bourgeoisie, the *Kleinbürgertum*, is now almost fabled as the hard core of anti-Semitism. Indeed it may be that from this social group came those who formed the mobs that quite concretely smashed Jewish shops. In any case, the frustrated expectations of the petty bourgeoisie must have been compounded of the loss of their savings along with the fear that they would retrogress into the mass of pitiably poor people, whence they thought they had emerged by a combination of thrift and hard work.

One major segment of German society that saw its expectations frustrated were those who hoped for a resurgence of the nation that had fought so valiantly in the World War. This segment consisted principally of two groups—the military elite, those who were indeed Junkers or who styled themselves as such; and the returned veterans who after the war were met not with victory parades but often with contempt and derision. Even more crucially, veterans were often faced with unemployment or unemployability—the latter including many of those from whom military life had been their first successful occupation. They had no GI bill to train or retrain them for useful work. Thinking themselves heroes returned, they often found themselves drifters and bums. From this subgroup came many of the early Nazi rank and file. From the other subgroup, the officer caste, came those who first supported more traditionally nationalist political parties than the Nazis, who then stood by and observed the arrant Nazis with mingled contempt and envy, and who at last became the willing instruments of the Nazis when the glorious war clouds gathered again.

The pervasive German attitude in the late 1920's seems to have been one of bafflement rather than of active support for the Nazi movement or widespread intergroup hostility. Labor was inhibited by fear of loss of jobs. Many of the middle class were disconcerted by their recurrent failure to better themselves. Members of the upper middle class could not believe that things were getting as bad for so many people as clearly was the case. And the old aristocracy remembered only the glories of feudalism and war or of the sheltered academic life.

It is this stunned state of mind that produced a high measure of political apathy or of active contempt for the inadequate efforts of the republican, parliamentary government to govern. The Nazi revolution was not just a coup d'etat: it had broad popular support. But it did depend for its rise to power on the growing political irresoluteness of people who had hitherto been politically more self-confident (labor and the upper middle class). And it depended on a high degree of involvement and participation on the part of those whose frustrations—whether military or economic—coincided with the medley of themes played by the Nazis. The Nazi revolution depended on the support of people whose desperation and consequent dissociation from reality led them to ignore, tolerate, and even take part in violence they would otherwise have abhorred.

The black rebellion of the 1960's

The black uprisings in America in the 1960's clearly amount to a rebellion, but they are not in any precise sense a revolution like those of France in 1789 or Russia in 1905 and 1917. However, the differences between these revolutions and the black rebellion are largely quantitative. The latter involves a widespread joint commitment to rather fundamental change among all segments of Negro society in the country: change in the political power structure of the country in all political units—cities, counties, states, and nation. And these changes, involving all blacks and all parts of the political community, have been accompanied by the violence that is a universal element of revolution.

The differences between revolution and the black rebellion derive from several facts: Negroes constitute only about 11 percent of the national population and therefore are numerically incapable of enforcing changes to the same degree as in a nation where a substantial majority is frustrated by the established government. The constitutions and laws of the national and most state governments have not contained many restrictions that discriminate against people on racial grounds—quite the contrary.

So there has been no basic change in principles. The Constitution and law of the land have been used or developed in ways that make them instruments to achieve changes in the nonlegal social practices and customs of discrimination. And there has been a sufficiently developed sense of commitment to equality as a major social value to make the equalizing of opportunities for black people a process against which most whites could not readily fight. They could not readily deny the applicability of their principles to those who newly have demanded equality. And that portion of the nation which frankly accepted the principle of racial inequality lost the savage Civil War. The very slow struggle for racial equality and human dignity for blacks commenced with Lincoln's 1863 Emancipation Proclamation and the military defeat of the South two years later.

What is striking, in a comparison of this (and other) contained rebellions with the great revolutions, is that the Negro rebellion appears to have been preceded by the same J-curve of expectations that are at first gratified and then frustrated. The same reaction patterns of this level of analysis appear to have developed in the minds of American blacks as have developed in the minds of those who have become revolutionaries in previous eras and other countries.

The difficulty in seeing this likeness relates to the vast gap between what whites and blacks have gotten in America. This gap has made it hard to see just what advances blacks have made and when. Those who as blacks and whites believe in equality have emphasized the vast and continuing inequalities. Black or white, they do not see what advances have been made. In the 1960's, when conditions were better than in the 1860's, or than in the 1930's, the expressions of discontent have been at their maximum. The new words and deeds of discontent can be understood only if one appreciates that profoundly deprived people are often incapable of expressing their discontent. In short, to understand why the black rebellion has occurred, it is necessary to see how black people had already developed.

At the end of the Civil War, Negroes were perhaps as near to minimal survival in the psychological sense, as human beings, as they had been since their initial transportation from Africa. They had lost the security of provision for food, clothing, shelter, and physical safety that had been fairly well assured them as long as they docilely accepted their position as slaves. They could no longer be sure that the master would provide for them. They had, often, to forage for themselves, like war refugees everywhere when crops have been destroyed and normal patterns of collaboration in productive work have been shattered. Overjoyed at their emancipation, they could use their freedom no more effectively than could concentration camp inmates in Germany when the doors at last swung open in early 1945. They could concern themselves really with only the satisfaction of their physical needs, which freedom is not and equality and dignity are not.

Those who must concentrate only on survival usually do not revolt: they are too hungry. This preoccupation simply with staying alive if anything strengthened in the late decades of the 19th century as the practice of lynching—the killing by mobs rather than by lawfully or other systematically employed force—continued. Between 1882, when records of lynchings were first kept, down to 1941, lynchings averaged 78 per year. The constant fear that one might be arbitrarily killed, maimed, or injured was one of the day-to-day facts of life for most blacks, particularly until the early 1920's. Lynching and physical injury could be said to have declined to a relatively minor worry—comparable perhaps to the level of worry about automobile accidents in the 1960's—in the late 1930's and the 1940's: the average for 1937–42 was five per year and for 1943–48 less than three per year. But the level of general health remained low and so did life expectancy.

The process of moving up off the even, flat plane of survival itself was of course continuous. But it was so slow that it seems best to date the first major upturn, from concern for mere survival for most blacks, as the beginning of the Second World War. Responding to the threat of a large demonstration, a repetition of something akin to the 1932 veterans' march on Washington, Franklin Roosevelt in 1941 issued an executive order prohibiting discriminatory hiring practices in all defense industries, and establishing the Fair Employment Practices Commission (FEPC) to administer the order. Though it worked unevenly and in many cases not at all, it nevertheless was a major basis for advance above subsistence for Negroes. By war's end, some 2 million blacks were employed in war industry, and the FEPC reported that 1,300,000 of these had gotten jobs in consequence of its efforts.

What could have been a cataclysmic frustration of rising expectations for blacks at war's end turned out not to be. The successful efforts to avoid a post-war recession, which would have witnessed the old (and still common) practice of discharging Negroes first, benefited blacks as well as whites. There was no widespread and sudden drop in Negro employment. Instead, the pace of rising economic opportunity continued. In 1946 the CIO and AFL trade-union organizations undertook a drive to organize Negro workers in the South and to integrate them into existing unions. By 1948, FEPC legislation had been passed in six states, taking up some of the slack when the ending of war contracts removed the protection of the wartime FEPC. Symbolically, and a bit more, the first Negro was admitted in 1947 to major league baseball, Jackie Robinson; there were 14 major league Negro players in 1951; by 1954 all but 3 of the 16 major league teams were integrated. Racially integrated low-cost public housing after the war began the breakdown of discrimination in this basic concern of life. In 1956 all public housing in Washington, D.C., was desegregated. In 1962 President Kennedy issued an order prohibiting discrimination in any housing that was either financed or had mortgage insurance under a Government program. It was estimated that this affected a fourth of all future housing construction in the nation.

These advances relate to jobs and housing and therefore to the physical needs, but they also—notably in the case of sport participations—have overtones of equal dignity. Advances that more directly related to this profound, nonphysical need for equality included the following:

The admission of Negroes into the category of commissioned officer: 500 Negro officers in the Army in 1943, 7,500 by war's end; and 28 officers in the Navy in 1944, 50 by war's end.

The integration of 90 percent of all Negro army personnel into unsegregated units by 1953 and complete integration a year later.

The first desegregation of interstate buses in 1946, of railway dining cars in 1950, and of railway passenger cars in 1952.

The long series of steps designed to desegregate education, commencing with the court order to the University of Oklahoma in 1948 to admit on a segregated basis a graduate student who was black, to the University of Texas in 1950 to admit on a nonsegregated basis a Negro to the law school, down to and beyond the landmark 1954 case which ordered the integration of public secondary and primary schools "with all deliberate speed."

The similarly long series of steps to end discrimination in the voting process, starting with the court invalidation in 1944 of the white primary closed to blacks and continuing with the 1954, 1964, and later civil-rights acts, which increasingly protected and enforced the right of blacks to register and vote in all elections.

The range and number of national and state legislative and judicial and administrative efforts to see that black people were accorded equal dignity is very large indeed. Repeatedly in the 1940's, 1950's, and early 1960's it gave evidence to Negroes that progress was being made. Their expectations inevitably rose from the near-ground level before the second World War to what proved increasingly to be excessively optimistic. Acts of legislatures, court, and administrative agencies—and of private groups and citizens—to equalize life opportunities for black people had never quite fulfilled their initial purpose. This brings us to the matter of promise and performance, to assessment of the gap between the expectations aroused by legislation, executive order, and court decision, on the one hand, and realization of equality, on the other.

The killing by lynch mobs dwindled to one case in 1947 and two in 1948. A new kind of killing of blacks began and at times something like the old lynch mob operated again. In 1952 a top state NAACP official in Florida who organized a campaign to secure the indictment of a sheriff charged with killing a Negro prisoner was killed by a bomb. After the 1954 commencement of public school integration, there were some 530 cases of violence (burning, bombing, and intimidation of children and their parents) in the first four years of integration. Schools, churches, and the homes of black leaders were bombed and many people were killed in these bombings. Federal troops were brought into Little Rock in September 1957 to integrate the high school; during the following school year (1958–59), public schools were closed in Little Rock.

In short—starting in the mid-1950's and increasing more or less steadily into the early 1960's—white violence grew against the now lawful and protected efforts of Negroes to gain integration. And so did direct action and later violence undertaken by blacks, in a reciprocal process that moved into the substantial violence of 1965–67. That three-year period may be considered a peak, possibly the peak of the violence that constituted the black rebellion. It was violence mostly against white property and black people. It merits reemphasis that during this era of increased hostility, progress continued to be made. Indeed, the occurrence of some progress intensified both the white reaction to it and the black counteraction to the reaction, because every time a reaction impeded the progress, the apparent gap widened between expectations and gratifications.

Direct (but not violent) action by Negroes began in late 1956 with the bus boycott in Mongtomery, Alabama, which endured for over a year and succeeded. It was precipitated when a Negro woman got on a city bus, sat down in a front seat, was ordered to give up her seat to a white man, and refused. The bus boycott soon came under the leadership of Dr. Martin Luther King, Jr., whose belief in nonviolent resistance—and the mild temper of blacks in Montgomery at the time—succeeded in keeping the action relatively peaceful.

Direct violent action began in April 1963 in Birmingham, Alabama, in what may be called the first full-scale concerted violent encounter of blacks and whites in recent years. Seeking integration of such facilities as lunch counters, parks, and swimming pools, the blacks in Birmingham, most of them young, were met with water hoses, police dogs, and violent acts of police and white people. The number of demonstrators increased to some 3,000 and there were 1,000 arrests. The repressiveness of the police united a hitherto-divided black community in Birmingham. And it produced perhaps the first major case since the second World War in which Southern blacks threw rocks and bottles at police. From this time on, violence deepened and spread among blacks. The Birmingham riots immediately touched off a response in other cities—according to one estimate, 758 demonstrations in the 10 weeks following the Birmingham violence. And in six weeks of that 1963 summer, blacks (in Birmingham and elsewhere) succeeded in getting some 200 lunch counters and other public facilities desegregated.

The combined effect of substantial, though slow, progress in employment, housing, education, and voting did not have the effect of quieting blacks or stopping the Negro rebellion of the 1960s. The full-fledged riots of Los Angeles in 1965 and Newark and Detroit in 1967 have been amply studied, at least from the descriptive viewpoint. But there is a tendency to see these events in isolation. It is recognized that riots in one place will touch off riots in another or—more likely—in several others, but the social-contagion theory (including the contagion of seeing African nations liberated after the Second World War) by no means gets to the roots of the rebellion. And neither does the notion that blacks are frustrated and are striking out rather blindly at the centuries of repression. If 300 years of repression have been too much, why were 200 or 280 not enough to produce rebellion?

What is striking is the time sequence of events. As in major historic revolutions, the events relating to the 1960's rebellion consist of a rather long period of rising expectations followed by a relatively brief period of frustration that struck deep into the psyches of black people. And I suggest that from the 17th to the early-20th century there has been very little development beyond mere physical survival for virtually all black people in America (and in Africa). It is significant to note that in the prosperous 1960's, there was no sharp or sudden rise in unemployment of blacks. There was no marked deprivation of material goods to which blacks had become accustomed. But there was, starting notably in 1963, not the first instance of violence against blacks but a sudden increase in it. This resurgence of violence came after, and interrupted, the slow but steady progress since 1940. It quickly frustrated rising expectations.

This increase in violence, commencing so to speak with the firehoses and police dogs in May 1963 in Birmingham, affronted not only the physical safety of the demonstrators, thereby reactivating anxiety and fear of bodily harm itself—the most basic of human concerns. This increase in violence also affronted the dignity of black people as human beings. Black people sensed that their various and continuously rising expectations, now confronted with violence, were to rise no more.

In addition to this violence between whites against blacks and of blacks against whites, there has been an explosive growth of private acts of violence of blacks against blacks. This has newly activated the fear for physical safety itself. And the ever-growing congestion in the slums has worsened housing conditions.

White people who fail to understand their own past and their own ever-rising expectations (if we have one car, we must have two; if we finished four years of college, our son must become a doctor or a lawyer) are puzzled at the dissatisfaction of blacks who have made such considerable progress since the Second World War. But what would be odd about blacks, and indicate that they indeed had some special nature, would be for them to be satisfied in present circumstances. The very rapidity of their advance makes them expect to continue its pace. The very low point from which they started makes them expect to reach equality within a few years or at the very most a few decades. Their mental processes are operating in an altogether normal manner. They would be less than human if they acted otherwise.

Figure C–5 and Table C–1, the latter devised by Harmon Zeigler with

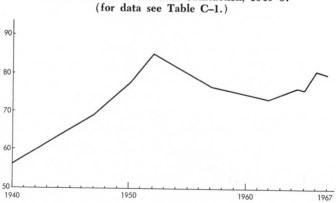

FIGURE C–5
Index of Nonwhite Economic Satisfaction, 1940–67
(for data see Table C–1.)

the assistance of Jerry B. Jenkins, represent one striking index of the origin and time sequence of black frustrations. He chooses, as the items to form his index, average family income and average years of schooling. He divides the former by the latter, for the total U.S. population and

TABLE C-1
Origin and Time Sequence of Black Frustrations
Explanation

Col. 1: $\dfrac{\text{Social want satisfaction}}{\text{Social want formation}}$ = systemic frustration

Col. 2: $\dfrac{\text{Social want satisfaction (nonwhite)}}{\text{Social want formation (nonwhite)}}$ = frustration (nonwhite)

Col. 3: Index of satisfaction (nonwhite)

Col. 4: Index of frustration (nonwhite)

	1	2	3	4
	Average Family Income Divided by Average Years of Schooling for—		*Nonwhite Satisfaction*	*Nonwhite Frustration*
Year	*Total Population*	*Nonwhite Population*	*Nonwhite % of Total Population Frustration Level (100% = Equality of Want Satisfaction and Want Formation between Nonwhites and Total)*	*% Difference between Nonwhite and Total Population (100% − Col. 3)*
1940*	$\dfrac{\$1,231}{8.4} = 146.3$	$\dfrac{\$489}{5.8} = 84.3$	$\dfrac{84.3}{146.3} = 57.5$	42.5
1947	$\dfrac{\$3,031}{9.0} = 336.8$	$\dfrac{\$1,614}{6.9} = 233.9$	$\dfrac{233.9}{336.8} = 69.4$	30.6
1950	$\dfrac{\$3,319}{9.3} = 356.9$	$\dfrac{\$1,869}{6.8} = 274.9$	$\dfrac{274.9}{356.9} = 77.0$	23.0
1952	$\dfrac{\$3,890}{10.1} = 385.1$	$\dfrac{\$2,338}{7.1} = 329.3$	$\dfrac{329.3}{385.1} = 85.5$	14.5
1957	$\dfrac{\$4,971}{10.6} = 469.0$	$\dfrac{\$2,764}{7.7} = 359.0$	$\dfrac{359.0}{469.0} = 76.5$	23.5
1960	$\dfrac{\$5,620}{10.6} = 530.2$	$\dfrac{\$3,233}{8.2} = 394.3$	$\dfrac{394.3}{530.2} = 74.4$	25.6
1962	$\dfrac{\$5,956}{11.4} = 522.5$	$\dfrac{\$3,330}{8.6} = 387.2$	$\dfrac{387.2}{522.5} = 74.1$	25.9
1964	$\dfrac{\$6,559}{11.7} = 560.6$	$\dfrac{\$3,839}{8.9} = 431.3$	$\dfrac{431.3}{560.6} = 77.0$	23.0
1965	$\dfrac{\$6,957}{11.8} = 589.6$	$\dfrac{\$3,994}{9.0} = 443.8$	$\dfrac{0.5740}{0.7627} = 75.3$	24.7
1966	$\dfrac{\$7,436}{12.0} = 619.7$	$\dfrac{\$4,628}{9.2} = 503.0$	$\dfrac{0.6223}{0.7666} = 81.2$	18.8
1967			79.8	20.2

* 1940 income figures are actually for 1939, and are for families and unrelated individuals.
SA: 1952. (73d ed.), p. 111: median school years (1947, 1957, and 1964–67).
SA: 1965. (86th ed.), p. 112: median school years 1960.
SA: 1966. (87th ed.), p. 340: median family income: (1947, 1950, 1952, 1957, 1959, 1960, 1962, and 1964).
NOTE—The frustration index and tables were devised by Harmon Zeigler with the help of Jerry B. Jenkins.

for the nonwhite population (which is about 95 percent black), from 1940 to 1967, using U.S. Census Bureau data. The increase and decrease in the gap between what an average family and a nonwhite family of given educational level gets in income becomes Zeigler's measure of frustration.

If black and white workers with the same amount of education were earning the same income, there would be no difference in the indexes between the two categories of people. As the chart indicates, nonwhites were closest to earning the same amount as the total population in 1952. They rose from 58 percent in 1940 to 86 percent in 1952, but declined after 1952 to a low of 74 percent in 1962. They did not return to their relative status of 1940, but they lost substantial ground compared with where they were in 1952.

If the education-income relationship were the only one involved in producing frustration in people as their expectations and gratifications diverge, we could have expected a peak of unrest sometime in the mid-1950's. It came later—by my reckoning in 1963. This suggests that the gap formed from the increased incidence of violence on the part of police and white citizens provided the quantum of energy necessary

FIGURE C–6
The Black Rebellion of the 1960's

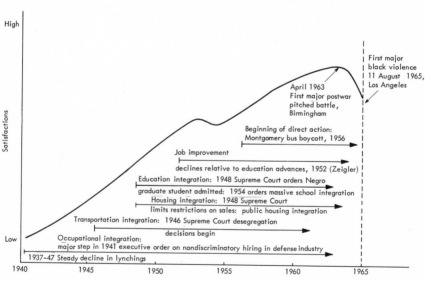

to raise black frustrations to the point of rebellion. Figure C–6 shows the developments.

Two ways are possible of resolving the problem that arises when the expectations-gratifications gap develops—and perhaps there are others.

One way to close the growing gap is to attempt to deprive blacks in America of all the gains that they have made since at least the beginning of the Second World War. These gains have been mostly in the satisfaction of their physical needs (in jobs and housing); their social and their dignity needs are beginning to gain prominence. In George Orwell's phrase, we may call this the technique of the boot stamping in a human face forever. If white people were to attempt and even succeed in so reducing black people to a life that consisted of trying to stay alive— the life they lived under slavery and, most of them, for two to four generations after emancipation—black rebelliousness could be contained. In the process white people would be reduced to the same animal-like behavior that they themselves were imposing on blacks, just as concentration camp guards and concentration camp inmates came to resemble each other in appearance and behavior.

A second way to resolve the problem is to recognize and help them to satisfy their expectations, which fundamentally are the expectations which degraded white people in decades and centuries long past have themselves achieved—notably the recognition of their equal dignity and worth. It is not to be supposed or hoped that black people then will at last become satisfied, any more than white people who achieve dignity become satisfied. But at least those blacks who have achieved dignity will then be that much closer to becoming fulfilled human beings, able at last to realize themselves in the climate of self-respect that is necessary for people to grow.

Student rebellions of the 1950's and 1960's

These rebellions seemingly commenced first among university students in Japan and then began in the United States and in Western and Central Europe. Partly because of space limitations, it is impossible to assess the J-curve as a device for explaining these particular rebellions. Part of the reason for deferring an attempt to do so lies in the continuing complexity of related events.

It is true, for example, that living quarters and classrooms for French students were getting progressively worse as the postwar French wave of newborn children reached university age. Expectations rose and were frustrated, contributing to the May 1968 riots. It is true that the 1964 Berkeley riots followed soon after enforcement of a previously unenforced rule against on-campus fund solicitation for off-campus organizations. Expectations had risen and were frustrated. And it is true that American university students who were raised with expectations of a bright future have seen their hopes disappointed when faced with military service in Vietnam. These explanations may be the central ingredients of the rebellious mood.

But these phenomena are not quite new. Students have previously been crowded and otherwise disappointed. What is new is the occasional use of violence. The reasons for resort to this technique are not clear. The amount of violence—as distinguished from nonviolent direct action, which people tend incorrectly to read as violence—is not great but it is real. When black people, who have been the victims of violence for centuries, use violence, it is comprehensible. When white students use it, the reasons remain obscure enough to cause at least this writer to postpone an attempt to explain.

SOME TENTATIVE CONCLUSIONS

We have seen that the J-curve is a necessary though not sufficient part of the explanation of at least several revolutions and some contained rebellions. This J-curve is a psychological, not a sociological explanation. The units of analysis are individual human beings. They may fall into visible categories (like blacks or students or working men or peasants), but their mental processes that relate to frustration and aggression are fundamentally the same. That is, we are positing that anyone deprived of food—whether his normal circumstances include the simple diet of poor people or the elaborate one of rich people—will suddenly become inclined to break any social convention to get food. We are also supposing that anyone who is physically secure in the provision of food, clothing, health, and physical safety will seek to establish and strengthen social ties and then to seek equal dignity. The demand for these things is so profound that constitutions and laws have to be made to adapt to the demands—not the demands to constitutions and laws.

If the ever-emerging expectations of people are gratified without too much resistance by those whose similar expectations have already been gratified, then revolution and rebellion are unlikely. If they are not, orderly political processes are displaced by violence. It was that way with our ancestors; it is that way now. And it is that universal a phenomenon. Lawmakers as well as clerks, businessmen as well as laborers, professors as well as students would react the same if suddenly deprived of the goods and dignity they had come to expect in the normal course of life. They would be less than human if they too did not become angry.

part III

Approaches to the
systematic study of politics

chapter

8

Selected approaches to the study of macro political problems

In the second chapter of this book, on eternal issues of politics, we noted that many of the problems with which political scientists currently deal are ones which have appeared over and over again in the history of political thought. In the third chapter, dealing with concepts and generalizations, we discussed the distinction between macro and micro political concepts. Briefly, a macro concept is one which refers to the characteristics of some kind of aggregate or collection of individual units, for example, a national political system. Macro political problems, then, are those which occur at the macro level of analysis. Many of the eternal questions of politics are, in fact, macro problems. For example, the great questions of stability and change in political systems are macro political problems. In this chapter, we are going to focus critical attention on several approaches which political scientists have used to examine macro political problems.

Before we turn to an examination of these approaches, an important question must be raised. Why do we need an "approach" to study macro (or any other) political problems? In fact, what do we mean when we use the term "approach"? We are using the term to mean a loosely interconnected and sometimes less developed set of theories or hypotheses. An approach implies an orientation to looking at the world in a particular way, guided by a particular set of assumptions that certain factors are going to be significant, employing a particular set of concepts and ultimately hoping to provide a basis for explanation and prediction. We need approaches of some kind, however ill-developed, to help us to make sense out of the confusion of data that exists "out there" in the world.

Without some guiding orientation, we would not know how to select the relevant phenomena for investigation. Approaches are necessary, but a word of warning must be added here. There is no guarantee that a given approach is useful. We suspect that many approaches employed by political scientists involve little more than the proliferation of new words for old things. Approaches must be evaluated in terms of the functions which they perform. Therefore, we will ask the following questions of each approach:

1. Does the approach stimulate our thinking about a problem? Does it communicate some useful ideas to the student of the subject? In short, does it help to define and identify the factors relevant to a problem?
2. Does the approach provide a useful way of organizing data in a particular area? Does it help to make some order out of the raw data?
3. Has the approach led to useful research?
4. Does the approach include generalizations necessary to the explanation or prediction of the phenomena that we are interested in?

Of course, the ultimate payoff for an approach is in providing answers for important political questions.

We are going to examine a number of approaches to macro political problems in the context of the way in which the approach illuminates (or fails to illuminate) a particular macro problem of some general interest. The problem we have chosen (that which we ultimately want to explain or predict) is *political change*. By political change we mean more than the change of leaders which takes place periodically in systems characterized by regular elections. In focusing on political change as a macro problem, and defining it rather loosely, we mean that a nation has moved from one kind of political system to another through some process, revolutionary or evolutionary. In other words, we are confining the use of change here to refer to fundamental and far-reaching changes. The organization of our discussion will be as follows:

1. We will introduce the basic assumptions and vocabulary of each approach.
2. We will illustrate the approach through an example or examples in political science.
3. We will examine the possible application of the approach to the problem of political change.
4. We will discuss the utility and limitations of the approach.

The approaches examined will be: systems analysis and functional analysis, communications, political culture, and conflict.

SYSTEM AND FUNCTION

Systems analysis and functional analysis are closely related, and we shall therefore discuss them in the same section. The idea of viewing political phenomena as a *system* is an old one in political science. What is suggested by the notion of system? The first assumption is that the system is made up of parts which are interdependent:

By "interdependence" we mean that when the properties of one component in a system change, all the other components and the system as a whole are affected. Thus, if the rings of an automobile erode, the car "burns oil"; the functioning of other aspects of the system deteriorates, and the power of the car declines.[1]

A second assumption is that a system can be distinguished from its environment, from the things that are not in the system; that, in fact, there is a boundary between the system and its environment. If we cannot distinguish a system from its environment, if we cannot say where a system begins or ends, then we cannot know whether a system has changed or not.

Also, fundamental to the idea of a system is the conception of exchanges between the system and its environment. The system is not closed to outside influences, and it in turn may influence its environment. The exchanges into the system are usually called inputs and the exchanges from the system to its environment are called outputs. These notions may be clearer if we look at Figure 8–1 and think in terms of a particular

FIGURE 8–1
A Sketch of the Systems Approach to Politics

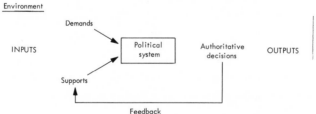

SOURCE: David Easton, *A Framework for Political Analysis* (Englewood Cliffs, N.J.: Prentice-Hall, 1965), p. 112. Used with permission.

political system. The figure gives a general sketch of a systems approach to the political system. Suppose that the system in question was the Supreme Court of the United States. The inputs into the system are divided into two types: demands and supports. Demands involve requests for action (or inaction) on the part of the system. In the case of the Supreme

---

[1] Gabriel A. Almond and G. Bingham Powell, *Comparative Politics: A Developmental Approach* (Boston: Little, Brown & Co., 1966), p. 19.

Court, the act of appealing a lower court decision may be seen as a demand. Supports refer to the sense of attachment which citizens have for the system. Generally, these may be of two types. Support may be long-term and bear little relationship to the issue under immediate consideration; on the other hand, support may vary with the particular decision. In the United States, there is probably a widespread sense of attachment to the institution of the Supreme Court. The Court's decision is its output. The idea of "feedback" is that the decision, once made, becomes part of the operating environment of the system—the public reaction to the decision, its effect on the level of support (if any), its quieting or stimulating of demands, the fact that the decision is now a precedent for the Supreme Court and other courts, and so on.

At the general level of a political system, demands originate because the things that are valued in society are scarce and are matters of conflict. The noted political scientist David Easton, a proponent of the systems approach, views politics as involving the authoritative allocation of scarce values—it is the political system which determines who gets what, where, when, and how.[2] In fact, politics would be unnecessary if values were not scarce. It follows that one macro problem of very great concern is how a political system converts demands into authoritative outputs, and who wins and who loses in the process. Another major focus of attention of systems theorists in political science and sociology has been on the question of how systems manage to cope with stresses from their environment—the questions of system maintenance, system persistence, or system stability.[3] We will touch on both of these questions when we examine the treatment of a specific political problem using a systems and functional approach.

Another major assumption of the systems approach seems to be the idea of a normal operation of the system (a "healthy" system state) and some mechanisms which serve to maintain that normal operation. It is convenient to link that assumption with the introduction of the closely related ideas which go by the name of "functionalism." The basic question posed by functional analysis is this: What effect or consequence does a particular element of a system have on the operation of the system as a whole? Functional analysis in the social sciences stems from an organic analogy. For example, we might ask what function a particular organ such as the heart plays in the normal operation of the body. Of course, the heart has the functional consequence of pumping blood throughout the body. Without some such mechanism, the body

---

[2] David Easton, "An Approach to the Analysis of Political Systems," *World Politics*, vol. 9 (April, 1957).

[3] William C. Mitchell, *Public Choice in America* (Chicago: Markham, 1971); and Talcott Parsons, *The Structure of Social Action* (New York: McGraw-Hill, 1937).

would die. Functional analysis considers the consequences of different elements in a system for the maintenance of that system.

All of this implies the assumption that we know what the normal operation of the system is and that we know what must be done in order to keep it operating in that fashion. This latter assumption can be called that of the "functional requirements" or "functional requisites" of the system. In the case of the human body, we know that blood must be pumped throughout the body to maintain its normal operations. It is not always that easy in social or political science. The sociologist Robert Merton has commented, "embedded in every functional analysis is some conception, tacit or expressed, of the functional requirements of the system under observation. . . . this remains one of the cloudiest and empirically debatable concepts in functional theory."[4] This problem cannot be simply handled *by definition*. We cannot define a system in terms of a set of characteristics and then turn right around and say that these same characteristics are the conditions which must be met for the system to persist. Thus, we cannot, for example, define a society as a collection of individuals with a minimum degree of interaction and then say that a minimum degree of interaction is necessary for a society. If we do that, we convert an empirical statement, which presumably could be refuted by evidence, into a statement which is circularly true and which cannot be refuted.

Several concepts related to functional analysis must now be clarified. First, there is the distinction between functional consequences and dysfunctional consequences: "*Functions* are those observed consequences which make for the adaptation or adjustment of a given system; and *dysfunctions*, those observed consequences which lessen the adaptation or adjustment of the system."[5] Not all elements in a system necessarily have positive (functional) consequences for the system in which they are found. They may have nonfunctional consequences or they may function negatively. For example, there is some disagreement among political scientists as to whether high rates of political participation are functional or dysfunctional in political democracies.[6] In addition, the distinction between functions and dysfunctions highlights the fact that parts of systems may have multiple consequences, both positive and negative. Perhaps high rates of political participation weaken some aspects of democracy and strengthen others. Therefore, one must consider the "net aggregate effects" of aspects of systems.[7]

---

[4] Robert Merton, *On Theoretical Sociology* (New York: Free Press, 1967), p. 106.

[5] *Ibid.*, p. 105.

[6] Jack L. Walker, "A Critique of The Elitist Theory of Democracy," *American Political Science Review*, Vol. 60 (June 1966), pp. 285–95.

[7] Merton, *op. cit.*, p. 105.

A second major distinction is between manifest and latent functions. Manifest functions are consequences which are consciously and overtly intended by the actors in a system. For example, the manifest function of organizing an interest group may be to attempt to influence the course of public policy through lobbying and other activities. Latent functions are those which are unconscious and unintended. An interest group which is formed with the manifest purpose of lobbying may perform the latent function of fulfilling social needs for its members. It is extremely important to recognize that social actions or institutions may have latent functions, for, as Merton notes, ". . . any attempt to eliminate an existing social structure without providing adequate alternative structures for fulfilling the functions previously fulfilled by the abolished organizations is doomed to failure."[8] This point cuts two ways in thinking about the consequences of political change or political reform. First, as Merton notes, one must be aware that structures which are changed may be performing unseen but desired functions, which will have to be fulfilled in other ways.[9] Second, in bringing about change, the very policies we enact may simultaneously bring about other changes which are neither anticipated nor desired.[10]

We have now introduced some of the basic assumptions and vocabulary of systems and functional analysis. Our treatment has necessarily been abstract and brief. In order to flesh out our discussion, we now turn to an example of systems analysis and functional analysis in political science: Richard Fenno's treatment of the "problem of integration" in the United States House of Representatives' Appropriations Committee.[11] The Appropriations Committee deals with questions relating to the allocation of money for the various substantive programs enacted by the Congress. For the purposes of the study, the Committee was treated as a political system. Fenno defines his problem in terms which indicate that he believes that a minimum degree of "integration," a "working together or a meshing together or mutual support among . . . roles and sub-groups," is a functional requirement for the Committee. "No political system (or sub-system) is perfectly integrated; yet no political system can survive without some minimum degree of integration among its differ-

---

[8] *Ibid.*, p. 135.

[9] Merton's classic treatment of the "functions of the political machine" is a very good example. In short, Merton suggests that in urban areas in the United States, political machines performed many latent functions (such as social welfare functions) which political reformers tended to overlook (*ibid.*, pp. 125–36).

[10] Some would argue that many social welfare policies (such as urban renewal and welfare itself) have actually impeded some of the goals which were intended by the programs.

[11] Richard Fenno, "The Appropriations Committee as a Political System," *American Political Science Review*, Vol. 56 (June 1962), pp. 310–24.

entiated parts."[12] It is clear that Fenno regards the "normal performance" of this Committee as an exercise in avoiding, minimizing, and resolving conflicts.[13] This is the other side of the coin of Committee integration.

Fenno explains the integration of the Committee in terms of five mechanisms or structures which have that functional consequence: "(1) the existence of a well-articulated and deeply rooted consensus on Committee goals or tasks; (2) the nature of the Committee's subject matter; (3) the legislative orientation of its members; (4) the attractiveness of the Committee for its members; and (5) the stability of Committee membership." He argues that the content of the consensus on goals and tasks is primarily to *"guard the Federal Treasury."*[14] Fenno notes, for example, that Committee members have developed a distinctive vocabulary to describe their task, using such phrases as "wielding the meat axe" and going over budget requests with a "fine-toothed comb."[15] The subject matter of the Committee increases integration, because appropriations can be seen more easily as a "business" or "efficiency" operation rather than as a matter for policy conflict. The legislative orientation of the members of the Committee is also important, for members are recruited on the basis of their conformity to certain norms of conduct: "Responsibility," "balance," "ability to get along."[16] The attractiveness of the Committee is its ability to satisfy the needs of the members: "Such satisfaction in turn increases the likelihood that members will behave in such a way as to hold the group together."[17] Finally, a high degree of stability in membership increases the chances of developing stable leadership, norms of behavior, and informal mechanisms of accommodation.[18] This, in brief summary, is Fenno's account of the high degree of integration of the Committee.

He also argues that the high degree of integration of a subsystem of a total system, such as the Appropriations Committee in the House of Representatives, may have functional consequences for larger systems. For example, "party groups have a relatively small influence upon appropriations decisions."[19]

For our purposes, we are not so much interested in the actual content

---

[12] *Ibid.,* p. 310.

[13] He says: "Conversely, integration is also defined as the degree to which a committee is able to minimize conflict among its roles and its sub-groups, by heading off or resolving the conflicts that arise" (*ibid.*).

[14] *Ibid.*

[15] *Ibid.,* p. 312.

[16] *Ibid.,* p. 313.

[17] *Ibid.,* p. 314.

[18] *Ibid.,* p. 315.

[19] *Ibid.,* p. 323.

of Fenno's study as the way in which it illustrates the concepts of system and function. In particular, with reference to this study, we want to point out the following characteristics: the selection of a subsystem embedded in a larger system for analysis, the fact that the boundaries of the systems are determined by formal criteria (membership in a committee), the specification of a functional requisite (committee integration), the concern with the survival of the system and "conflict avoidance," and the suggestion of certain functional relationships which constitute hypotheses (e.g., that consensus on goals leads to integration).[20] We note these characteristics here because they will be significant in our overall evaluation of systems and functional approaches.[21]

Although both systems analysis and functionalism have frequently been associated with the study of political stability, we may inquire as to whether the approaches have anything to contribute to an understanding of our general illustrative problem for this chapter, political change. Easton's systems theory does take as its central question the maintenance of the system, but Easton defines the system so broadly that there is room for a wide variety of structural changes within systems that survive. Thinking in terms of the interdependencies of elements within a system, in terms of inputs of demands and supports, and in terms of feedback relationships may lead to some interesting hypotheses about the possible sources of political change. Thus, Easton develops the concept of "stress" on the system which results from (1) an overflow of demands into the system, or (2) a decline below the minimal level of support, or (3) more likely, some combination of (1) and (2).[22] Easton argues that political systems (of whatever kind) operate within "normal ranges" and that if stress on the system drives it out of its normal operating range, adaptive or adjustive changes in the system will result or, ultimately, the system will not survive. Suppose that we are concerned with a democratic system, and the normal range of political participation in elections is somewhere between 55 and 80 percent. If participation should suddenly shoot up to 99 percent or drop sharply to 10 percent, this could well be an indicator of extreme stress on the system, and we might predict a change in the basic operating characteristics of the system. Two points should be made about the consequences of stress. First, in coping with stress,

---

[20] The reader might ask himself if consensus on goals and integration are not close to being the same thing—something we warned about earlier.

[21] For a contrasting case study, stressing the consequences of a lack of integration in a committee, see Richard Fenno, "The House of Representatives and Federal Aid to Education" in Robert L. Peabody and Nelson W. Polsby (eds.), *New Perspectives in the House of Representatives* (Chicago: Rand McNally, 1963), pp. 195–235.

[22] David Easton, *A Systems Analysis of Political Life* (New York: John Wiley & Sons, 1965), chaps. 4 and 14, and *A Framework for Political Analysis* (Englewood Cliffs, N.J.: Prentice-Hall, Inc., 1965), pp. 90–101.

a system may alter its internal characteristics, e.g., a democracy may change to a nondemocracy. Second, there is no guarantee that a system will be able to cope with all forms of stress—although it is unlikely, the system may in fact not survive in any form.

Functionalism, as well as systems theory, has often been directed toward problems of political stability. Nevertheless, some of the key ideas of functionalism may have a role in helping us understand the sources and consequences of political change. Just as the notion of interdependence may lead us to expect changes in one aspect of society to be reflected in changes in other aspects, so too may the concepts and assumptions of functionalism lead us to look at the data of politics in a new light. Take, for example, the notion that there are functional requisites which must be met if systems are to survive. If we can identify these for particular systems, then we will have at the same time uncovered some of the conditions which might cause the system to fail to survive, to change.[23] If integration is necessary for a political system, and if integration falls below a given level (Easton's "normal range"), then we are led to expect (by the functional approach) the *disintegration* of the system. The concept of dysfunctions, also, alerts us to sources of change, for these are elements which work against the maintenance of a given system. If dysfunctional elements predominate over functional ones, again, we would expect a change in the system. Finally, the concept of latent functions cues us to the possibility that unintended political change may result from intended political change.

As we will discuss below in our evaluation, we do not mean to suggest that either systems analysis or functionalism begin to provide an adequate explanation of political change. What they do provide is an orientation, a way of looking at things, which may lead the observer to ultimately arrive at such an explanation.

We turn now to an evaluation of systems and functional approaches in political science. First, we will make some cautionary remarks about possible problems of these approaches. In defining a system, we must be able to distinguish what is in the system from what is outside the system. We must establish the boundaries of the system. The establishment of system boundaries, however, involves the investigator in the dilemma of how much interdependence is necessary before we consider

---

[23] This is a point noted long ago by Aristotle and recently restated by Michael Weinstein: "Implicit in a description of the factors that favor the persistence of political systems is an analysis of the tendencies that make for political change." *Systematic Political Theory* (Columbus, Ohio: Charles E. Merrill, 1971), p. 9. However, expecting the identification of functional requisites to lead directly to the identification of the conditions associated with disintegration assumes that a political system is approximately closed. That is, it may not be the absence of the functional requisites associated with survival that leads to the breakdown of the political system, but, rather, the presence of other conditions *plus* the functional requisites.

a set of elements a system. Although we have noted that systems analysis and functionalism are often asserted to be useful because they free us from the study of formal institutions, it is also frequently the case that the boundary question is resolved by assuming that systems are coincident with "natural" boundaries—geographic (society of the United States) or institutional (the United States Congress). It is true that, it being a matter of definition, we may arbitrarily select any set of elements as a system; but, as with other matters of definition, there are empirical questions which bear on that selection. Ultimately, we must ask: Is there a sufficient degree of interrelationship in order to make the definition of a system tenable?

A second problem to be aware of is that the central question posed by the systems approach (as developed by David Easton), the question of system persistence, may not be a very interesting question, because most systems do persist.[24] The persistence question is so broad that it excludes many interesting political phenomena. For example, although revolutions occur in political systems, the systems themselves persist—in that sense, revolutions are just another form of system adaption.

A third problem is the temptation to confuse description with value judgments in these approaches. Almost without realizing it, we may shift from a statement that "this is the way the system does function" to "this is the way it ought to function." Part of the problem may stem from the effort to establish the "normal operations" of the system and from the concern with the stability of systems. But what is "functional" for system stability may be "dysfunctional" from another perspective— one which values something other than system stability. The concepts functional and dysfunctional are relative to the system states one prefers.

Finally, functionalism is prone to a series of unnecessary assumptions to which Merton has called attention:

1. The assumption that every structure has a function, the "postulate of universal functionalism."
2. The assumption that systems are functionally unified, the "postulate of functional unity."
3. The assumption that a given function can only be fulfilled by a given structure, the "postulate of functional indispensability."[25]

The first point suggests that we need not assume that every social or political institution or practice has a positive function to perform. Some may function negatively and some may have no functional consequences at all. The second calls attention to the fact that the degree of integration or unity of a system is a *variable*—it may not be fixed at a relatively

---

[24] See the review of Easton by Philip E. Converse, *American Political Science Review*, Vol. 59 (December 1965), pp. 1001–1002.

[25] Merton, *op. cit.*, pp. 79–91.

high level. As the Fenno article indicates, one of the things we may want to explain is the variability of the level of integration in systems. Finally, we cannot assume that only one structure can fulfill a requisite function. If, for example, integration is necessary for system survival, we need not assume that there is only one way for a system to be integrated.

Earlier, we suggest that an evaluation of approaches may be made in terms of four criteria: (1) the stimulation and communication of thinking about the problems of politics, (2) the organization of data about politics, (3) the stimulation of useful research about politics, and (4) the explanation and prediction of political events. We have indicated our belief that systems analysis and functionalism may contribute a useful, if limited, orientation to political problems—in particular, we mentioned some of the general insights which might be gleaned with respect to political change. The concepts of systems analysis may also provide a useful way of organizing data—particularly the notion of inputs, outputs, and feedback. It is less clear that these approaches have stimulated useful research in political science. At times, it appears there is more talking about the approaches than applying them. Nevertheless, we may mention several areas of research which may be influenced by the approaches: (1) the study of political socialization,[26] (2) the study of comparative political development,[27] (3) the study of the legislative system,[28] and (4) the study of the international political system.[29]

There is a general consensus, we believe, that neither systems theory nor functional analysis provide for explanation and prediction in the sense in which we described the terms earlier.[30] Fundamentally, this is because neither approach is a theory as we have used the term. Neither provides specific expectations of relationships or hypotheses. Both are orientations to political phenomena, providing a set of categories within which to work. Easton has observed that "what we call theory in political research often takes the form of conceptual analysis rather than the formulation

---

[26] The concept of support has led to a concern with the origins of support, and some evidence points to the importance of the early childhood learning experiences.

[27] See Almond and Powell, *op. cit.*

[28] John Wahlke *et al.*, *The Legislative System* (New York: John Wiley & Sons, 1962).

[29] Morton Kaplan, *System and Process in International Politics*, (New York: John Wiley & Sons, 1957).

[30] A claim might be made that functional analysis is explanatory. The argument might be stated as follows: system X is functioning adequately; for system X to function adequately, function Y must be performed; structure Z performs function Y; therefore, Z is explained by its contribution to Y. The argument is invalid because of the fact that structures other than Z may be able to perform Y. This is the idea of functional equivalents. See Alan Isaak, *Scope and Methods of Political Science* (Homewood, Ill.: Dorsey Press, 1969), pp. 229–231.

of generalizations. . . ."[31] The observation is certainly true, and particularly true of systems and functional analysis. But the admission that they involve "conceptual analysis rather than the formulation of generalizations" is the admission that they do not involve explanation, for concepts cannot explain anything. This does not mean that conceptual analysis is unimportant; it simply means that conceptual analysis ultimately must lead to the formulation of testable generalizations.

As a concluding comment about systems and functional analysis, we may fairly say that both share a set of methodological problems which must be kept in mind, that neither provides for explanation and prediction, but that they may be useful in the communication of political ideas and in illuminating and organizing particular political problems.

COMMUNICATIONS

The communications approach is an area which is closely related to that of systems and functions. The relationships are suggested by the following observations:

1. Input-output models have as a basic element exchanges which are symbolic—that is, communications. For example, demands and supports are often registered via communications, as when a citizen writes his congressman about a pending piece of legislation.

2. Within systems, one of the major links between elements of the system (or between subsystems) is the communications system. For example, within the Congress, formal and informal means of communication link the various committees (the subsystems) together.

3. Any analysis of a systems capacity to respond to environmental stress must include an analysis of its ability to receive, analyze, store, and react to communications. For example, a study of legislative activity in Congress would have to be concerned with the capacity of congressmen to receive and analyze information on the topic under consideration.

4. System outputs must, in the final analysis, be communicated if they are to be effective. If, for example, Congress passes a piece of legislation but the information is not distributed to the affected parties, the legislation will in all likelihood fail.

These points strongly suggest that the extent to which a systems approach is successful will be largely dependent upon the handling of communications variables.

The communications approach, however, implies more than concern with communications variables. It implies a set of concepts and assumptions which represent a distinctive orientation to the political world. The

---

[31] Easton, *A Systems Analysis of Political Life, op. cit.*, p. 11.

approach derives from an analogy between human social and political systems and the study of information flows in self-regulating machines and computers.[32] The basic assumptions of the communications approach derive from this fundamental analogy and are as follows: (1) that every human organization, political or nonpolitical, is held together by communications; (2) that important aspects of human communication can be understood by the study of and analogy from the simpler communication processes of machines.

What is communication? According to Karl Deutsch,[33] the prime proponent of communications theory in political science, it is the transmission of information. Thus, the communications approach calls attention to a particular aspect of the political universe, the exchange between systems or subsystems of political (and politically relevant) information.

A number of important concepts are associated with communications analysis. The first is the idea of a communications network or "learning net." In the language we have been using, the learning net is a system (a set of interrelated parts) which has the following capabilities:

1. Sensory capabilities—the capacity to pick up relevant objects out there in the environment of the learning net.
2. Interpretative capabilities—the ability to distinguish some kinds of objects from others.
3. Memory and recall capabilities—the ability to draw upon past experience and stored instructions to know how to deal with current situations.
4. Decision-making capabilities—given the input or information and the memory and recall capabilities, the network can make decisions and respond.
5. Finally, and critically, learning capabilities—after an initial decision has been made and carried out, there is new input of information, the results. This new information is fed back into the system, and corrections can be made for errors.[34]

The machine analogy which Deutsch uses to describe the learning net is a radar-operated antiaircraft system. Any decision-making system can be thought of in these terms. If we think in terms of political decision making, we can treat Easton's original conception of a political system as a learning net. For a political system to function, demands must be picked up (or communicated to) the system. For a system to cope with demands, they must be distinguished, since it is patently impossible for

---

[32] This approach is sometimes called cybernetics. The father of this approach was Norbert Wiener. See *Cybernetics* (New York: John Wiley & Sons, 1961).

[33] Karl Deutsch, *The Nerves of Government* (New York: Free Press, 1966). Our discussion will follow Deutsch closely.

[34] *Ibid.*, pp. 80–91.

a system to respond to all demands. A political system does not respond (and could not respond) to each demand as if it were a totally new thing which had never been dealt with in the past. There must be some established ways of processing demands and some ideas of what appropriate responses are. A political system must be able to reach some decision on the basis of information, goals, and stored capabilities (memory). Finally, it must read the feedback to the decision and act on that information. Of course, it is not inevitable that political systems will correct errors in decision making.

A second major concept is that of "information." Deutsch defines information as the "patterned relationship between events."[35] Information is not the event itself, but the communicated patterns or symbols which describe the events. For example, information to a political decision maker might be the communication that a civil disturbance has occurred or that there is a high rate of unemployment. Information is transmitted along "channels." These may, of course, be the channels of the communication media (television, newspapers, radio), the private channels of government (the State Department cable, the interdepartmental memo), or the informal processes of interpersonal communication. To the extent that there is loss or distortion of information along a channel, to that extent the channel is inefficient. The classic notion of the spread and magnification of a rumor gives some idea of the potential for distortion in a communications channel. Clearly, it is critical that political decision makers have relatively efficient channels of information.[36] Information has the desirable scientific properties that it can be recorded, measured, and analyzed. A final, key concept in communications is feedback. As we indicated earlier, the communications network takes into account the results or consequences of its action, and if the mechanism is working correctly there should be a diminishing series of errors.

The description of the communications approach as developed by Karl Deutsch suggests the image of a political system as a conscious, goal-seeking mechanism which can take information inputs, refer to memory, make decisions, read feedback, and correct errors. It follows from this image that the study of the amount and flow of communications within systems (or between systems) may tell us a lot about the type of political system which can be sustained. For example, the requirements of responsiveness to public opinion and competition of political viewpoints within a democratic political system suggest that there ought to be: (1) communication flowing both from political leaders to the public and from

---

[35] *Ibid.*, p. 82.

[36] Of course, one of the important things to keep in mind about political decision making is that it does take place in a world of *imperfect* information. Decision makers cannot be aware of all the relevant information and cannot be sure of all of the consequences of their decisions.

the public to political leaders, and (2) relatively open channels of communication in the society and access to alternate sources of information.[37] The first reflects the notion that in democratic systems, leaders must be aware of and responsive to public opinion; the second is based on the idea that political competition depends upon the free flow of ideas and access to political information. In the language of communications analysis, in a democratic system information must be exchanged with some minimum degree of accuracy between leaders and nonleaders. The notion of leaders reacting to the feedback of public response to policies is also important in democracies.

Empirical research supports the hypothesis that communications development is an important factor related to the degree of political competition in political systems.[38] In a study of 76 nations, Cutright found that a measure of communications development had the highest correlation with political development (as measured by indicators of political competition) of any socioeconomic indicator.[39] Cutright argues that his evidence suggests the interdependence of social and political factors in development. From this perspective, nations which do not fit the general pattern (high communications development, high political development; low communications development, low political development) may be expected to adjust (or change) to achieve a balance between the two factors. Thus, viewing these two factors as interdependent may lead to predictions about political change in "deviant cases."[40]

Additional analysis of the Cutright data by Donald J. McCrone and Charles F. Cnudde lends further substance to the argument for the significance of communications for democratic systems. One of their conclusions is of prime importance here: "Democratic political development occurs when mass communications permeate society."[41] According to their analysis, communications development is a final, critical stage in the development of democracy.

We have argued that one might use a communications perspective to develop expectations about the extent of communications development in *democratic* systems. We have briefly noted some research which supports that inference. What about the possible use of a communications

---

[37] Lester Milbrath, *Political Participation* (Chicago: Rand McNally, 1965), p. 151. We are not prepared to argue here what the exact ratio of opinion giving to opinion receiving should be in a democratic system. For one conception, see C. Wright Mills, *The Power Elite* (New York: Oxford University Press, 1959), chap. 13.

[38] Phillips Cutright, "National Political Development" in Nelson W. Polsby *et al.* (eds.), *Politics and Social Life* (Boston: Houghton Mifflin Co., 1963), pp. 569–82.

[39] *Ibid.*, pp. 574–75.

[40] *Ibid.*, p. 581.

[41] "Toward A Communications Theory of Democratic Political Development," *American Political Science Review*, Vol. 61 (March 1967), p. 78.

orientation for the study of political change generally? The first point to note is that the control of communication flows, both from an input and an output side, will have a lot to do with the direction and rate of change within systems. For example, one of the things which highly traditional, conservative, and stable societies would try to avoid (if they want to maintain those characteristics) is communication with the outside world. It follows that a condition of political change may well be a change in the nature or content of communications in society.

The communications perspective also allows us to envision the conditions in which political systems might be subject to stress and to change. Systems which are relatively inefficient in gathering information about their operating environments will undoubtedly make errors in decision making. If the reading of feedback follows the same pattern and the course is not corrected, the political system may eventually find itself in a state of collapse.[42] Surely, one condition preceding revolutions in political systems is that the information gathered by the rulers is inaccurate about such situations as the extent of citizen support of the regime. Thus, the leadership may be prone to see dissidents as only a "small group of agitators" when the number of dissatisfied citizens is actually much larger.

Finally, given this perspective, it is possible to conceive of a political system as "programmed" to be more or less oriented to the promotion of change. As Deutsch observes, the political system is "a major instrument for either retarding or accelerating social learning or innovation. . . ."[43] This view suggests that the political system has a certain degree of independence in restricting or promoting change in society.

In evaluating the communications approach, we should be aware of the fact that the approach is based on an analogy with the communications processes of machines and, as with all analogies, there are points of dissimilarity as well as similarity. "The test by which we discriminate between a false analogy and a good analogy consists in the extent of actual structural correspondence between the two systems from which the analogy is drawn."[44] This test is ultimately made in terms of whether the analogy suggests "new observations, experiments, or predictions that can be confirmed by the facts."[45] The communications approach, based on the analogy with machines, would seem to be most applicable to rather closed systems, with limited inputs and specified goals.[46] Political systems may not reach that degree of closure and may have multiple, and even conflicting, goals.

---

[42] Deutsch, *op. cit.*, p. 193.

[43] *Ibid.*, p. 254.

[44] *Ibid.*, p. 78.

[45] *Ibid.*, p. 80.

[46] In other words, it is more applicable to nondemocratic systems.

The communications approach may indeed stimulate useful thinking about the political world and may aid in communicating political ideas of some importance, because some of the major concepts of political science can be conceptualized in communications terms. As an illustration, Deutsch has conceived of a number of important political concepts such as cohesion and integration in communication terms:

> If we can measure information . . . then we can also measure the cohesion of organizations or societies in terms of their ability to transmit information with smaller or larger losses or distortions in transmission. . . . If we think of an ethnic or cultural community as a network of communication channels . . . we can measure the "integration" of individuals in a people by their ability to receive and transmit information on wide ranges of different topics with relatively little delay or loss of relevant detail.[47]

In addition, to the degree that the approach simply calls attention to the theoretical significance and empirical import of the communications variables, it would appear to be useful to political scientists. We have illustrated, in our discussion of the close relationship between communications development and democratic development, the significance of communications variables.

In much the same way as systems analysis and functionalism, communications does provide a scheme for organizing data, again in terms of an input-output-feedback model. As far as stimulating useful research, there has been a modest stream of research using a communications perspective, including work on nationalism and international integration.[48] With respect to explanation and prediction, the evaluation must be the same as that made of systems and functions. Communications is not so much a theory as it is an analogy and an orientation; as such, it cannot yield the expectations of relationships (hypotheses) which can ultimately lead to explanation and prediction.

POLITICAL CULTURE

The notion that culture is important for explaining human behavior is derived from the disciplines of anthropology and sociology. In a general sense, culture may be thought of as the distinctive pattern of symbols, beliefs, values, and feelings in a given society. A culture is conceived as having a degree of permanence or stability—it is something which is passed on from generation to generation. Its importance in explaining social behavior is simply this: the culture defines the way we look at

---

[47] *Ibid.*, p. 150.

[48] Karl Deutsch, *Nationalism and Social Communication* (Cambridge, Mass.: The MIT Press, 1953).

the world and delimits the range of culturally appropriate responses to situations.

What is "political culture"? Gabriel Almond and Sidney Verba define it in this way: "The political culture of a nation is the particular distribution of patterns of orientation toward political objects among the members of the nation."[49] Three key elements of this definition need to be examined. First, there is the idea of a "distribution of patterns." This suggests that political culture is viewed as being something which individuals in a system hold *in common* with some degree of permanence. Second, there is the concept of "orientation." In a general sense, this term is used to refer to a psychological property of individuals:[50] At this point, then, culture refers to psychological orientations of individuals which occur in some pattern, with some frequency and relative permanence in a given system. Finally, what makes something a "political" culture is that the orientations are toward political objects. Putting these three things together, an example of political culture in the context of American politics would be the widespread belief (psychological orientation plus pattern or frequency) that citizens ought to be active in politics (the individual, in this instance, is viewed as a political object).[51]

The definition of political culture carries within it the most obvious assumptions of the approach. One is that systems are characterized by distinctive patterns of political orientations. The accompanying assumption is that these patterns are important for the explanation of important political phenomena. Political culture is a complex and many-faceted notion, and we shall now elaborate on some distinctions relative to the concept.

Psychological orientations to politics include three types: cognitive, affective, and evaluative.[52] Cognitive orientations are factual beliefs about the political system, e.g., that a citizen can (or cannot) make himself heard in the decision-making process of the political system. Affective orientations are the feelings one has about the political system, e.g., an emotional reaction (positive or negative) to the symbols of the regime such as the flag. Evaluative orientations are the value judgments about the political system, e.g., the belief that a particular set of institutions is the right one for your society (the evaluation that the system is legitimate).

For Almond and Verba, the objects of the psychological orientations

---

[49] Gabriel Almond and Sidney Verba, *The Civic Culture* (Boston: Little, Brown & Co., 1963), p. 13.

[50] The reader may wonder why political culture is a macro concept if it is based on individual orientations. The reason is that the culture is defined in terms of the *aggregate* of individually held orientations—it is a collective property of systems.

[51] This is, in fact, a widely shared norm of American politics. See *ibid.*, chap. 5.

[52] *Ibid.*, p. 14.

are: (1) the system itself,[53] (2) the inputs to the system, (3) the outputs of the system, and (4) the role of the self in the system.[54] This way of organizing the orientations derives from a systems perspective. The modes of orientation and the objects can be combined into classification systems of types of political cultures, as in Figure 8–2. For example,

FIGURE 8–2
Types of Political Cultures: Frequencies of Orientation toward Various Objects

Types of Political Culture	Political Objects*			
	System	System Outputs	System Inputs	Self
Parochial...........	zero or near zero	zero or near zero	zero or near zero	zero or near zero
Subject.............	high	high	zero or near zero	zero or near zero
Participant.........	high	high	high	high

SOURCE: Adapted from Gabriel A. Almond and Sydney Verba, *The Civic Culture: Political Attitudes and Democracy in Five Nations* (copyright © 1963 by Princeton University Press), Table 2, p. 17. Little Brown and Company, Inc. © 1965. Reprinted by permission.
* Zero or near zero means that almost no one in the system has orientations toward this object; high means that almost everyone in the system has orientations toward this object.

we can consider the frequencies with which certain orientations are present or absent in a given system. In the parochial political culture, the frequencies of orientations to all political objects are near zero. In fact, one might call this situation the absence of a political culture, since no distinction is made between political objects and other kinds of objects. An example of a "pure" parochial political culture would be a very simple and traditional tribal society. In a subject political culture, most citizens are oriented to the system and its outputs but are not oriented to the input side (demands and supports) or to the role of the self in the system. An example of a "pure" subject political culture would be an absolute monarchy. In the participant political culture, most individuals are oriented to all objects of the political system. A "pure" type of participant political culture would be a direct democratic system.

A second typology can also be developed from the orientations and objects. The focus in this typology (see Figure 8–3) is on whether the

---

[53] Easton divides the political system into three component parts: (1) the government (the group which actually makes the authoritative decisions at a given moment in time), (2) the regime (the basic constitutional arrangements of the society), and (3) the political community (the set of persons who are bound together in the political system). See Easton, "An Approach to the Analysis of Political Systems," *op. cit.*

[54] Almond and Verba, *op. cit.*, p. 14.

FIGURE 8–3
Types of Political Cultures: Positive and Negative Orientations

Types of Political Culture	Modes of Orientations		
	Cognitive	Affective	Evaluative
Allegiant............	Positive	Positive	Positive
Apathetic...........	Positive	Neutral	Neutral
Alienated...........	Positive	Negative	Negative

Source: Adapted from Gabriel A. Almond and Sydney Verba, *The Civic Culture: Political Attitudes and Democracy in Five Nations* (copyright © 1963 by Princeton University Press), Table 3, p. 22. Little Brown and Company, Inc. © 1965. Reprinted by permission.

orientations to political objects are positive, negative, or neutral. In the case of the "allegiant" political culture, cognitions, feelings, and evaluations are all positive. Individuals in this system have a positive attachment to the system, and the expectation would be that with this high level of support, the system would be stable. In the "apathetic" political culture, cognitions are positive (present) but feelings and evaluations are neutral. This, too, might be a very stable system. In the "alienated" political culture, cognitions are present but the feelings and evaluations are negative. Presumably, the alienation from the political system presents the potential for instability in the system due to a lack of support.

These two typologies of political cultures are both idealizations, and no real-world political systems are expected to conform exactly to the specifications, i.e., there are no purely parochial political cultures. These ideal types may be used as bench marks to measure deviations from the extreme cases. For example, we may wish to know if a political culture is more subject or more participant. In addition, real-world political systems are conceived as being mixed political cultures containing components of parochial elements, subject elements, and participation elements or mixtures of allegiance, apathy, and alienation. Political cultures are mixtures at two levels. At the individual level, a person may be a parochial on some aspects of the political system (as when a citizen does not know what the government is doing in a policy area), a subject on some other aspects (as when a citizen is aware of what the government is doing but does not think that he can do anything about it), and a participant on others (as when a citizen knows what the government is doing and thinks he can do something about it). At the system level, the population may be seen as containing different proportions of allegiants, apathetics, and the alienated.[55]

Two other important concepts are the idea of a "subculture" and

[55] *Ibid.*, pp. 21–26.

the idea of the "civic culture." Within political systems, there may be distinctive patterns of political orientations among certain groups which deserve to be treated separately from the rest of the population. These are referred to as subcultures. One example of a subculture might be a group which was markedly deviant from the rest of the population along one of the orientations we have mentioned, e.g., a group characterized by extreme parochialism in a highly participant political culture. Almond and Verba also introduce the notion of the "civic culture," a mixed political culture in which participant and allegiant orientations predominate but "participant political orientations combine with and do not replace subject and parochial orientations."[56] The civic culture is considered to be a modern political system, but with strong elements of traditionalism, and with subject and parochial orientations limiting the amount of participation.[57] We will discuss the significance of this concept when we take up the utility of the political culture approach for the study of political change.

As an example of the use of the concept of political culture in political science, we will review briefly Patterson's descriptive study of "The Political Culture of the American States."[58] After noting that the American political culture as a whole has been characterized (by Almond and Verba) as "allegiant, participant, and civic," Patterson examines some regional and state variations in the American political culture.[59] He notes that there are variations in five areas: (1) basic attitudes, (2) political identification, (3) participant-subject orientations, (4) political styles, and (5) political socialization. We will mention one example from each area.

In the area of basic attitudes, Patterson argues that there are regional differences in "tolerance of nonconformity," with the South less tolerant as a region.[60] Political identification refers to "pride in governmental institutions."[61] Patterson contends that "pride in governmental and political institutions is highest in New England, the South Atlantic states, and the Mountain states, and lowest in the East South Central part of the country."[62] As for participant-subject orientations, he found that the South as a region is characterized by more people with a low amount

[56] *Ibid.*, p. 30.

[57] *Ibid.*, pp. 29–30.

[58] Samuel C. Patterson, "The Political Culture of the American States" in N. Luttbeg (ed.), *Public Opinion and Public Policy* (Homewood, Ill.: Dorsey Press, 1968), pp. 275–92.

[59] *Ibid.*, p. 279.

[60] *Ibid.*, p. 281.

[61] *Ibid.*, p. 283.

[62] *Ibid.*, p. 284. The data referred to is that gathered by Almond and Verba, *op. cit.* The regional differences could not be totally explained by regional differences in education.

of a measure he calls "citizen duty."[63] With respect to styles of politics, he notes that "though the demagogic-hortatory political style is by no means limited to them, Louisiana and Mississippi political cultures seem to be dominated by this style."[64] With regard to political socialization, the learning of political attitudes and behavior,[65] Patterson notes that "southern children learn different attitudes toward racial equality than children in other regions of the country."[66] We are not concerned with the causes or consequences of these variations in political culture here; however, the ultimate significance of this study would be in provoking attempts to explain the variations or to observe the consequences of them for political behavior. An interesting aspect of Patterson's findings is that they lend credence to the argument that the South may be considered as a political subculture in the United States.

Can the concept of political culture aid in the understanding of political change? Before turning directly to that question, it is necessary to make two other observations. First, it should be obvious by now that there is (potentially) a close connection between political culture and a system-functional approach to politics. A political culture can be conceived as interdependent with the political system, functioning either to maintain that system or to weaken it. Thus, and this is the second point, there flows from the political culture orientation the *hypothesis* of a congruence between political culture and political system characteristics. Almond and Verba make the argument in this way:

. . . . by examining the relationship between political cultural tendencies and political structural patterns, we can avoid the assumption of congruence between political culture and political structure. The relationship between political culture and political structure becomes one of the most significant researchable aspects of the problem of political stability and *change*. Rather than assume congruence, we must ascertain the extent and character of the congruence or incongruence.[67]

A related functional proposition stems from the congruence hypothesis. It suggests that the political culture contributes to the ongoing maintenance of the system. For example, Almond and Verba raise the question: "Is there a democratic political culture—a pattern of political attitudes that fosters democratic stability, that in some way 'fits' the democratic political system?"[68] Their answer is yes, and the pattern of political attitudes which fits the democratic system is what they call the civic culture.

---

[63] Patterson, *op. cit.*, p. 287.

[64] *Ibid.*, p. 288.

[65] We will discuss political socialization in more detail in the chapter on micro approaches.

[66] Patterson, *op. cit.*, p. 288.

[67] *Op. cit.*, pp. 32–33.

[68] *Ibid.*, pp. 337–338.

Their argument is based on the assumption that democracies need to achieve balance between a number of potentially stressful factors:[69] participation and passivity; power and responsiveness; norms, perceptions, and activity; involvement and apathy; the management of affect, consensus, and cleavage.[70] One illustration should give the flavor of their position. We know that politics is not salient for most citizens in the United States most of the time. But a sense of civic obligation suggests that citizens ought to be interested and to participate in politics. Almond and Verba argue that this inconsistency allows for a balance in the system between a need for political elites to operate freely and with a good deal of flexibility (the need for effective leadership) and the need for a check on elites (need for responsiveness of elites): "If issues arise that individuals consider important . . . the inconsistency between attitudes and behavior acts as a latent or potential source of political influence and activity."[71]

After this digression, we are in a better position to examine the utility of political culture for the study of political change. From what we have said, there is a possibility not only of a congruence between political culture and political structure but also of a lack of congruence. The supposition would be that a lack of congruence would be stressful on either the political system or the political culture or both. Suppose, for example, that there was a predominantly subject orientation in a democratic political system. There might well be pressure for a return to equilibrium—a balance between orientations toward a more passive role for citizens and a political system in which citizens are regarded as passive—a nondemocratic system. The general point is that a lack of congruence between political culture and political system may contribute to system instability and political change. In addition, the concept of political subcultures alerts us to the possibility that there are collections of individuals who deviate from the basic cultural norms in a political system. Subcultures, therefore, may provide a source of "lack of integration" in the system and a stimulus for political change.

We turn now to a brief evaluation of the political culture perspective. First, we will consider some problems associated with this approach. In studying the relationships between political culture and other political system characteristics, we must be certain to have a definition of political culture which is independent of our definition of the political system. We cannot infer the political culture from the character of the political system. If we commit this fallacy, then we will have "demonstrated" a relationship between political culture and political structure solely by

---

[69] Note here the assumption, similar to Easton's, that political systems need to cope with stress produced by their environments.

[70] *Ibid.*, pp. 337–360.

[71] *Ibid.*, pp. 348–349.

definition, circularly. A related problem is the tendency to treat political culture as a deus ex machina which is called upon to explain everything. If someone inquires why the United States has a two-party system, it is due to the American political culture. If someone asks why the Italian political system is fragmented, it is traced to the Italian political culture. If someone else wants to explain the nature of interest group conflict in Great Britain, he may be referred to the ubiquitous political culture. When we fail to specify precisely what we mean by political culture, there is a strong temptation to use it to "explain" that which we cannot otherwise explain.

In terms of our criteria for evaluation, political culture stacks up as follows. First, the notion does communicate an important idea—namely, that political behavior is constrained to some degree by dominant modes of orientations to politics within given systems. Second, there is some organization capacity to the concept, in particular, in the development of typologies of political cultures.[72] Third, several interesting hypotheses and research applications do flow rather directly from the approach, for example, the hypothesis of a congruence between political culture and political structure. Finally, as with the other approaches, political culture does not provide explanations or predictions, since a concept cannot explain or predict anything. In addition, we must be careful not to attempt to use political culture to explain everything.

In conclusion, political culture has become an important concept in political science, not only at the political systems level but in many other realms.[73] It must be tied down empirically, as we have discussed with reference to all concepts. And, as we will discuss in Chapter 10 on integration, the concept provides a potential link between macro and micro levels of analysis.

CONFLICT

Generally, the conflict approach, unlike communications and political culture approaches, is not explicitly linked to the systems approach. Like the communications approach, however, conflict is considered to be a process linking a sequence of behaviors. In the case of conflict, these behaviors are defined to be directed toward the goal of obtaining resources, positions, or personal satisfaction. Consequently, many political scientists consider conflict to be the essence of politics. More specifically, a conflict process can be defined as an ongoing contest between two or more people representing themselves or others for rewards or values which are in scarce supply (not everyone wanting rewards can obtain

---

[72] Particularly when political culture is closely allied with system.

[73] For example, the "rules of the game" in the study of legislative systems. See Wahlke *et al., op. cit.,* chap. 7.

them). The rewards are usually defined in terms of what the people involved in the conflict believe them to be; for some it may be territory, for others it may be the enactment of a law giving them access to an election booth.

Many people think of conflict as "bad" and cooperation as "good." Others, however, suggest another way of looking at conflict and, consequently, a different kind of value judgment about conflict.[74] Consider two conflict patterns—a cleavage conflict and an overlapping conflict. These patterns are shown in Figure 8–4. A cleavage conflict refers to

FIGURE 8–4
Patterns of Conflict

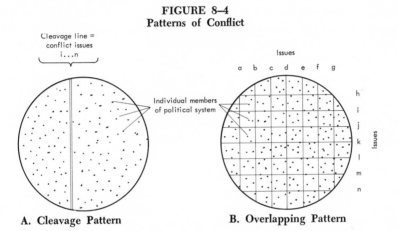

A. Cleavage Pattern   B. Overlapping Pattern

a pattern in which conflict issue after conflict issue divides people, groups, or nations the same way. The same people are always allied together and always have the same enemies. If some of these people develop into a permanent and hopeless minority (or majority) that always loses, they will presumably be more likely to choose violent means to redistribute the wins and losses in the political system, neighborhood, city, nation, or international system.

The overlapping pattern of conflict in a political system is one in which conflict issues divide people different ways. People both win and lose, are members of minorities and majorities, and change allies and supporters depending upon the nature of the particular conflict issue. This is the pattern that has been associated with the pluralist conception of democracy.[75] This pattern implies that people will perceive that today's

---

[74] Lewis Coser, *The Functions of Social Conflict* (New York: Free Press, 1964); and James S. Coleman, *Community Conflict* (New York: Free Press, 1957).

[75] This conception is very much like Dahl's description of the American political system, which we described in Chapter 2: It depends on the following assumptions: (1) most people belong to more than one group, (2) groups tend to be overlapping in membership, and (3) all groups "get heard" in the decision-making process.

"enemy" will be the "friend" that they need tomorrow to win on another issue. If a political system can be characterized as approximating an overlapping pattern of conflict, people are not expected to resort to illegal or violent means to win; for it would not be in their self-interest to eliminate a potential supporter on a future conflict issue. In other words, this pattern is a no-war conflict pattern. Before we could make these predictions, however, we would have to assume that all of the conflict issues are roughly equivalent in importance to all people.[76] Otherwise, a person could not be expected to lose gracefully on an issue about which he felt very intensely nor be satisfied about being a member of the winning group only on what he perceived to be unimportant issues. Thus, our decision about whether a conflict is "good" or "bad" may well depend on the type of conflict that we perceive it to be.

These patterns raise several macro level questions: (1) How and why does one pattern develop in a particular political system? (2) What could cause change from one pattern to another? (3) Do we in fact find that groups of people behave in a manner consistent with the predictions of the two patterns? (4) Will the cleavage pattern eventually lead to the disintegration or breakdown of the political system? (5) Are the two patterns associated with different cooperative patterns?[77]

Although these patterns characterize political systems rather than individuals, they also raise questions linking conflicts and the individual to the political system. How will a typical conflict develop in a system that has a cleavage pattern? Differently from one developing in an overlapping conflict system? Will a conflict develop further and last longer in one type than in the other type? Will individuals behave differently in a situation that can be characterized as being more like one pattern than the other?

These linkage questions lead us to a consideration of two quite different assumptions about conflict behavior: the rational conflict assumption and the nonrational conflict assumption. The choice of assumptions makes a difference, because the assumption will partially determine what are considered to be relevant concepts and behaviors. When the rational assumption is employed, the study of conflict concentrates on strategies, preferences, payoffs, risks (the probability of incurring costs), coalition formation rules, rules determining the selection of strategies, and decision rules terminating the conflict.[78] The nonrational or irrational assump-

---

[76] Elmer Schattschneider, *The Semi-Sovereign People* (New York: Holt, Rinehart & Winston, 1960), p. 67.

[77] Notice that conflict is not conceptualized here as being the opposite of cooperation; rather, both conflict patterns suggest different bases and patterns of cooperation to carry on the conflict.

[78] Among the studies approaching research on conflict this way are: William H. Riker, *A Theory of Political Coalitions* (New Haven: Yale University Press, 1962); Thomas C. Schelling, *The Strategy of Conflict* (New York: Oxford Uni-

tions[79] are found in studies focusing on images of enemies, persecutions, hostilities, trust, displacement, expansion and contraction of the scope of conflict, violence, rebellion, demonstrating, war, crises situations, conflict takeoff, and the socialization and polarization effects of conflict on the development of the conflict and on the perceptions of the participants to the conflict.[80]

The conflict studies which assume that the participants are rational define this rationality in terms of the rules that the participants use to determine a choice of strategies. If a participant bases his choice of strategy on a maximization rule, he is trying to guarantee himself (absolutely or probabilistically) that he will win more than the other participants or the most that can logically be obtained given the structure of the conflict and the known payoffs (the wins and losses associated with the joint choices of the participants). A rule that guarantees that the worst thing that can happen to a participant is to incur the smallest of the possible costs is called a minimax decision rule. The selection of a strategy will be determined by his conscious consideration of all his preferences, payoffs, and risks as well as his opponent's choices.

Approaching the study of a conflict this way implies that we would not look for behavior that was inconsistent with the strategy selected or the structure of the conflict; if we found such behavior, we might ignore it as being outside of the boundaries of the statement of our problem. For example, the participant's response to his opponent's action is *not* expected to be dictated by the participant's observation that the opponent looks very much like his father. If we feel, however, that the assumption that the selection of a conflict strategy based on rational criteria determines all subsequent conflict behavior is inconsistent with the characteristics of the types of conflict we want to study, we will then look for other (nonrational or irrational) factors that may predict that behavior. What part does previous learning play in conflict? If we

---

versity Press, 1963); Anatol Rapoport, *Fights, Games, and Debates* (Ann Arbor: University of Michigan Press, 1960).

[79] The nonrational assumptions make no commitment to either the total rationality or irrationality of conflict participants. Instead, conflict behavior is assumed to consist of more or less rational behavior, and attention is focused on linking different conflict behaviors to the characteristics of the participants or the situation. In contrast, an irrationality assumption would imply that every conflict behavior is a response to a stimulus that has nothing to do with the nature of the conflict issue or the situation. Such behavior would be entirely unconsciously determined.

[80] Several studies have included this assumption: Dina A. Zinnes, "Hostility in International Decision-Making," *Journal of Conflict Resolution*, Vol. 11 (September 1962), pp. 237–43; Ole R. Holsti, "The 1914 Case," *American Political Science Review*, Vol. 58 (June 1965), pp. 365–78; Ole R. Holsti, "The Belief System and National Images: A Case Study," *Journal of Conflict Resolution*, Vol. 6 (September 1962), pp. 244–52; Bernard N. Bass and George Dunteman, "Biases in the Evaluation of One's Own Group, Its Allies and Opponents," *Journal of Conflict Resolution*. Vol. 7 (March 1963), pp. 16–20.

learned from our parents and friends to consider people with certain characteristics to be enemies or less than human, how will we behave if we find ourselves competing with such people in politics? Will our behavior be different in the same conflict situation if our opponent does not belong to an "enemy" group? Most people would expect to find different behavior.

Since these two differing assumptions about conflict behavior refer to the individual or micro level, the question arises: What is their relevance for the macro questions we raised in the first part of this section? The answer is that the questions we posed require making assumptions about how people will behave in a cleavage system or an overlapping conflict system before we can talk about change in these patterns. This point will perhaps be clarified if we first diagram a general model of conflict development, in Figure 8–5, and then use an example[81] to illustrate how different conflict systems are likely to affect conflict development and behavior.[82]

Taking the cleavage pattern first, we can say that the probability of any given event becoming a conflict issue is much higher in the situation where the event affects the winners favorably and is perceived to have disadvantageous effects on the losers, although the probability of any event becoming a conflict issue is very low (how many of the millions of events that occur every day become conflict issues?). An event occurring in a situation approximating an overlapping conflict pattern, such as a British military plane flying over Maine, is not expected to have a very high probability of being transformed into a conflict issue. If we contrast two very similar events occurring in different situations—the British plane flying over American territory in an overlapping conflict situation and a Chinese military plane flying over Alaska in a cleavage conflict situation—we can see why there appears to be nothing intrinsic in events that automatically make them candidates for conflict issues. Rather, it depends upon how they are perceived, how they affect people, and whether people believe that they can do anything about the situation. In both hypothetical instances, if the British and the Chinese knew that our radar detection systems left something to be desired, we might feel less secure about our defenses, and we could either lodge diplomatic protests or attempt to intercept their planes with missiles or planes.

If, however, both events are transformed into conflict issues, the speed

---

[81] Contrary to the previous sections of this chapter, we will use a hypothetical example here, because there is no study which has tested all the hypotheses implied by the stages of conflict development. The example we use will be consistent with a collection of research findings about particular hypotheses tested on different conflicts.

[82] Figure 8–5 is adapted from Coser, *op. cit.*, Coleman, *op. cit.*, and Schattschneider, *op. cit.*, whose works are the basis for our discussion of conflict development.

FIGURE 8–5
Conflict Development in a Political System

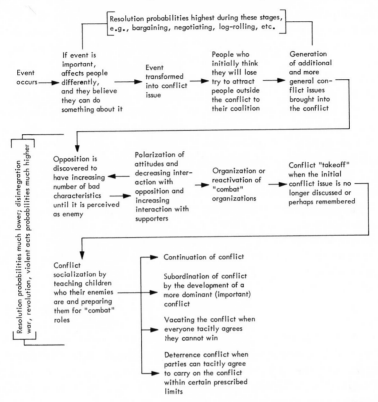

of the transformation is likely to be much faster with the cleavage pattern. For one thing, there has been little past communication between the Chinese and the Americans and, more importantly, they do not share the same allies. In the British–United States case, the Canadians, French, or others would probably try to prevent a split between the British and the Americans, because they would not want to choose sides if such a conflict did develop. This latter factor would affect the time that it would take to expand the scope of the conflict. The United States and China would already have different sets of allies who might not feel so strongly about preventing the development of a new conflict. It should be noted, though, that if the initial reticence of the allies of both the United States and Britain to choose sides were overcome by further development of the conflict, the conflict might develop a much wider scope. The potential allies of the United States and Britain are also allies of large numbers of other nations which could be pulled into the conflict via these links.

The addition of new issues and the generalization of these issues would also be expected to occur more quickly in the cleavage conflict system; for issues from past and continuing conflicts are known to all the participants. Chinese aid to North Vietnam and North Korea and the American protection of the Nationalist Chinese Government on Taiwan would quickly be on everybody's lips. Even with the meeting of Chinese and American leaders, an incident could quickly throw us back to the general conflict issue of "Communism versus Yankee imperalist dogs." On the other hand, it has been some time since we have been involved with the British at that level. If the initial conflict issue was not resolved as we would expect it to be, it would take some time to elevate past disagreements to the general level. In fact, we can't even think of an American-British equivalent for "Communism versus Yankee imperalist dogs." Multiple and general issues serve, of course, as a basis for building larger coalitions; people who may not be motivated to take supportive positions on the initial issue may be attracted by another issue about which they care more intensely.

Once the conflict is generalized and the enemies clearly identified as warmongers, however, there is no reason to expect that the speed of polarization will vary greatly with the type of conflict system. In the conflict cleavage system, polarization will reinforce and perpetuate the cleavage pattern. Polarization, if it occurs, in the overlapping conflict system may presage a change in that pattern. Once most people cannot tolerate the thought of losing, the assumption of equivalently important issues of the overlapping conflict pattern is violated, and we do not expect the more moderate conflict behavior. Leadership, planning, and organization for combat begin to appear now. Since such organization takes time, time again distinguishes the two conflict patterns. If such organizations are available in a cleavage system, they only have to be put into a state of readiness.

Many conflicts appear to remain at this stage for some time while others very quickly arrive at the takeoff point. Once a conflict has taken off, its continuation is independent of the issues. Consequently, formal negotiations, if they are occurring, will be largely ceremonial in nature. They could hardly be otherwise; for how can we negotiate Communism versus Yankee imperialism or British Tories versus Yankee upstarts?[83] It has been noted that increased interaction between opponents occurs shortly before the outbreak of hostilities, but these exchanges frequently bypass formal diplomatic channels.

At this point, there are many hypotheses but little evidence for predicting what will happen to the conflict. If it continues, conflict socialization

---

[83] Calling American leaders "running dogs of imperialism" (or American policeman "pigs") effectively removes the people so labeled from the human race and allows us to ignore the rules of conduct governing our relations with human beings. You don't have to treat a pig courteously.

(or learning who your enemies are) will probably affect the very youngest members of the group. The villains in comics will take on the racial and cultural characteristics of the opponents, and children will begin to learn addition working problems about the number of enemy dead and wounded. Without redirection from a more important and threatening conflict issue, people socialized into conflict roles are slow to change their enemy images, particularly in cleavage conflict systems.

In terms of our larger concern with political change, it is not surprising that many see major feedback relationships between conflict and change, i.e., conflict produces change and change produces further conflict. Since many conflict issues arise over events that change the status quo for some people, this seems a reasonable expectation. Recalling our two patterns of conflict, however, suggests that conflict is not necessarily associated with significant change as we have defined it. The stable overlapping conflict system would accommodate demands and over time produce slower change in the authoritative redistribution of resources. A conflict that took off in such a system, however, would be likely to produce a major political realignment,[84] no small change in any political system. Institutionalizing the conflict by organizing combat organizations symbolizes the increasing cohesion and cooperation consistent with a major political alignment. The cleavage system, with its greater potential for disintegration, could as one possibility divide into two separate nations or groups. This would mean major changes in leadership, governmental organization, resources, and population.

As far as the model of conflict development itself is concerned, we would probably not expect significant changes in the distribution of resources, positions, or leadership in the early stages of conflict development. The potential for this would appear to be highest at the polarization and organization stages.

With some variations, this process model of conflict development appears to grossly describe international conflicts as well as fluoride controversies in American communities.[85] Despite the high level of interest in conflict behavior and its correlates and the enormous amount of research devoted to the topic, few attempts have been made to construct a conflict model with its domain of applicability clearly defined by its assumptions. So we are left wondering if a conflict over a school bond issue is equivalent to the Middle East conflict.

Like most process models, the model of conflict development we have

---

[84] For example, some have been predicting that racial conflict in the United States will lead voters in the Southern states to switch their party allegiance to the Republican Party. It seems clear that the Arab-Israeli conflict has led to the development of the Palestinian guerilla movement, which has affected the support by many for the more conservative Arab and Persian leaders.

[85] Coleman, *op. cit.*

presented here describes from the vantage point of hindsight rather than successfully predicting or explaining future conflict development. This means that the conditions associated with conflict development are fairly clearly identified and defined. As with the previous approaches we have discussed, this also means that we are missing the crucial elements for adequate prediction and explanation. This is apparent when we recall the rational and nonrational assumptions. Although it seems reasonable to expect that the concepts associated with the rational assumption—strategies, risks, preferences and decision rules—would be appropriate to the early stages of conflict development before the participants have moved beyond a give-and-take mentality, this has not been investigated. Even in the more advanced stages of a long-standing conflict, we might expect that those charged with the conduct of the conflict would become sufficiently expert in their role so that they too could think largely in loss-gain terms. The appropriateness of these assumptions for different stages of conflict development is in part ambiguous, because the behavioral assumptions themselves have not always been linked to behavior in the real world. Until they are, we will not have a clear understanding of the effects of conflict on people or on the political system.

CONCLUSIONS

In this chapter we have examined some of the ways that political scientists have chosen to look at macro political problems. In each instance we have noted the basic assumptions and concepts of the approach, an application in political science, the possible insights of the approach to the macro problem of political change, and an evaluation of the approach. This discussion is summarized in Table 8–1. In concluding, we wish to emphasize two areas. The first is the close connection between the various approaches that we have examined. The second is the uses and limitations of approaches or orientations to political phenomena.

As ways of looking at the macro political world, the approaches we have outlined in this chapter share many common properties. For example, they share the view that political, social, and cultural systems are interdependent, linked, so that changes in one part will result in changes in the other. This assumption is explicit in all the approaches with the exception of conflict, where it remains for the most part at the implicit level. This is an important perspective, because it means that we cannot afford to neglect the complex interrelationships—the web of relationships, if you will—between the society and the political system. In a very real sense, political change (or stability)[86] is rooted in social change (or stability) and vice versa. In addition, three of the approaches share a concern

---

[86] Stability may mean a steady rate of change, while change may mean a change in the rate of change.

TABLE 8–1
Review of Selected Approaches to the Study of Macro Political Problems

Approach	Major Assumptions	Key Concepts	Major Problems
Systems— functions	1. Interdependence 2. System boundaries 3. Requisite functions 4. Persistence 5. Normal ranges	1. System 2. Boundary 3. Input 4. Output 5. Demand 6. Support 7. Feedback 8. Function 9. Functional requisite 10. Dysfunctional 11. Manifest function 12. Latent function	1. Defining system boundaries 2. Determining functional requisites 3. Assumptions of "universal functionalism," functional unity," and "functional indispensability"
Communications	1. Analogy with machines 2. Organizations tied together by communications	1. Learning net 2. Information 3. Channel 4. Feedback	1. Limitations of analogy with machines
Political culture	1. Patterns of political orientations 2. Political culture shapes political system	1. Political culture 2. Political orientations 3. Parochial 4. Subject 5. Participant 6. Allegiant 7. Apathetic 8. Alienated 9. Mixed culture 10. Culture 11. Civic culture 12. Subculture	1. Need for independent definitions 2. Cannot be used to explain everything
Conflict	1. Conflict-normal activity 2. Nonrational-rational decision-making behavior	1. Strategies 2. Risks 3. Payoffs 4. Preferences 5. Polarization 6. Crisis 7. Cleavage 8. Overlapping	1. Hindsight description 2. Rational domain of application not clearly distinguished from nonrational domain 3. Stages of conflict development more analytically than empirically clear

with system maintenance, persistence, balance, or equilibrium. This idea is suggestive of a striving for adaptation on the part of political and social systems.[87] We must, of course, be careful not to take these notions too literally or assume that all societies will have achieved stability or will have achieved it in the same way. These ideas draw attention to the ways in which political and social systems react to stress.

Another set of ideas common to the first three approaches are the concepts of input, output, and feedback. The images suggested here are of systems responding to their environment and their responses becoming part of their environment. This circular flow, from environment to system to environment, is a simplification which helps us to comprehend the nature of the political process. As an illustration, in the United States in the late 19th and early 20th centuries, there was a demand from the public for the regulation of trusts. In response to that demand, the Sherman Anti-Trust and Clayton Acts were passed. There is a general consensus among observers that those acts have not accomplished their original objectives in terms of limiting trusts. Nevertheless, the public policy decisions have provided what Murray Edelman calls "symbolic gratification"[88] for various groups in the population, and they have become part of the new operating environment of the political system. Proposals to abolish the acts would probably not be politically feasible.[89]

Finally, the communications, political culture, and conflict approaches in particular call explicit attention to the symbolic aspects of politics. Communications and political beliefs are significant for the study of politics. If politics involves conflict about the authoritative decisions made for a society, the process by which these decisions and beliefs about these decisions are communicated takes on great significance and suggests that we need to develop linkages between these approaches.

At the beginning of this chapter, we argued that approaches are necessary to make some sense or order out of the political world. The interpretation of any political event, actor, or act will be guided by some theoretical or conceptual framework, no matter how deeply buried. It is important to know the presuppositions, the assumptions, which underlie such perspectives. Approaches are necessary in order to simplify and highlight particular, and limited, aspects of reality. The world is too complex to be dealt with as a whole. At the same time, we must then remember that we are dealing with a selected (and limited) aspect of the whole when we adopt a particular orientation.

---

[87] Systems don't strive for anything, of course; this is a shorthand way of saying that people in these systems do these things.

[88] Murray Edelman, "Symbols and Political Quiescence," in Charles F. Cnudde and Deane E. Neubauer (eds.), *Empirical Democratic Theory* (Chicago: Markham, 1969), p. 99.

[89] *Ibid.*, p. 107.

chapter

9

Selected approaches to the study of micro political problems

In discussing political problems, we have divided them into two levels of analysis: macro and micro. In the previous chapter, we discussed a number of approaches to macro political problems. Although the distinction between the two levels in any given situation is relative (see our comments in Chapter 3), it is clear that many of the interesting micro political questions relate to the behavior of individuals. We would like to be able to describe, explain, predict, and evaluate the political behavior of individuals or groups of individuals. Why? There are many reasons, some more theoretical and academic, some more practical. For example, a political scientist may want to explain why people vote the way they do in order to illuminate the problem of "voter rationality" in a democratic society.[1] A practicing politician may seek the same answer in order to help formulate campaign strategy.[2] The point is that both are interested in micro political behavior.

Among others, two important micro political questions have been extensively studied. These are: (1) Who participates in politics and why? and (2) Why do people adopt the political positions that they do; e.g., why are some people liberal and some conservative?[3] In this chapter

[1] V. O. Key, *The Responsible Electorate* (Cambridge, Mass.: Harvard University Press, 1966).

[2] Dan Nimmo, *The Political Persuaders* (Englewood Cliffs, N.J.: Prentice-Hall, 1970).

[3] For an introduction to these two general questions, read Lester Milbrath, *Political Participation* (Chicago: Rand McNally, 1965), and Angus Campbell *et al.*, *The American Voter* (New York: John Wiley & Sons, 1964). We shall make repeated references to these two works in this chapter.

we will examine four interrelated approaches—psychological, group, role, and socialization—which have been applied to these two micro political problems and others.

A GENERAL APPROACH TO MICRO POLITICAL BEHAVIOR

To tie the four micro approaches together, we will present a general orientation to the study of micro political behavior. This is a general sketch which performs somewhat the same function of organization which the basic input-output model of the systems approach performs at the macro level. In addition, the general micro approach highlights several basic assumptions we make about the study of human behavior.

We call the general approach the "environment–individual characteristics–response"[4] approach. In Figure 9–1, the approach is outlined with

FIGURE 9–1
A General Approach to the Study of Micro Political Behavior

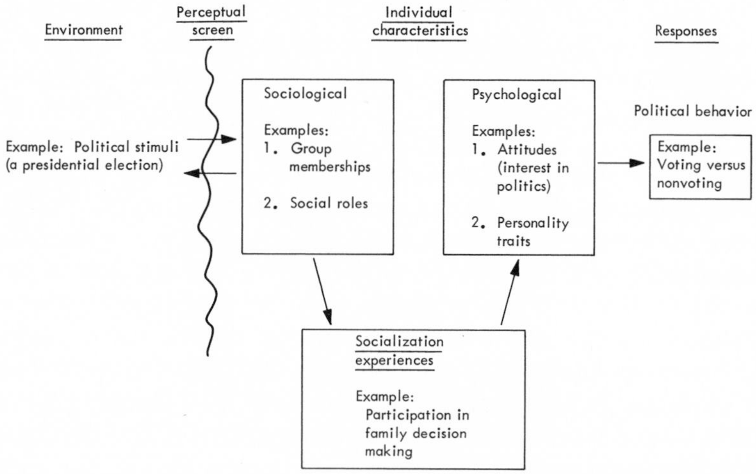

illustrations of where the various factors we will discuss fit into the general approach. Environment refers to everything outside the individual which potentially impinges upon him. The electorate is part of the environment of an elected official. This book you are reading is part of your environment. It is clear that no one can be attuned to everything which is potentially in his environment. A perceptual screen regulates (to some degree) which stimuli get in and which stimuli are kept out,

---

[4] We have borrowed and modified the terminology of Fred Greenstein in *Personality and Politics* (Chicago: Markham, 1969), p. 36. Sometimes the same ideas are labeled the S-O-R (stimulus-organism-response) approach.

distorted, or modified. Ordinarily, what gets through the screen is influenced by the characteristics of the individual. For example, people who are already interested in politics are more likely to be receptive to political stimuli in their environment than those who are not interested in politics.[5]

For purposes of simplicity, we have divided the characteristics of the individual into two broad categories, sociological and psychological. The sociological characteristics are those which identify the individual as belonging with other individuals in groupings on the basis of shared characteristics such as age, sex, race, social class, occupation, education, group membership, and so on. Broadly speaking, psychological characteristics refer to the aspects of individuals related to the contents of their minds: attitudes, beliefs, values, or personality.

Finally, responses are the behaviors of individuals. Normally, this is what we want to explain. Since there is no such thing as nonbehavior on the part of individuals, what we are interested in explaining is why an individual did one thing rather than another (why he voted for one candidate instead of another) or why one person behaved differently than another (why one participated in politics and the other did not).[6]

The major assumption illustrated by the environment–individual characteristics–response sketch is that *all* human behavior is the product of an interaction between the environment of an individual and his characteristics. The sketch, therefore, gives us some idea of where to look for explanations of individual behavior. A second assumption is that the individual characteristics labeled "psychological" are largely the product of the earlier impact of the environment on the individual. That is, attitudes, as well as other psychological characteristics of individuals, are influenced by our previous experiences. There is a particular term which is used to describe the learning of important psychological characteristics—socialization. An individual's socialization will depend largely on his history and his previous environment and experiences, and will provide an important part of the explanation of his behavior. A third, and related, assumption is that the sociological characteristics of the individual will place him in the circumstances which increase the likelihood of particular kinds of socialization experiences. In part, this is why we expect (and find) that individuals with similar sociological characteristics tend to have similar attitudes and behaviors.[7] The fourth assumption, which we men-

---

[5] Milbrath, *op. cit.*, p. 44.

[6] Of course, we speak of explaining individual cases as a convenience. The reader should keep in mind, in line with our expectation that generalizations in the social sciences will be statistical, that we mean explaining the behavior of sets of individuals.

[7] These relationships are, of course, imperfect, and one of the interesting puzzles (at times) is to try to explain why they are as weak as they are. For example, see the material on the relationship between social class and voting behavior in Campbell *et al.*, *op. cit.*, chap. 12.

tioned previously, is that the characteristics of the individual will influence (through the mechanism of a perceptual screen) which stimuli get in, are kept out, or are modified. The kind of person a man is influences the kind of world that he thinks he lives in. Finally, this sketch does not explain or predict any particular behavior; it is merely a commonsense guide to where to look for such explanations.

Within this general approach, we will examine the four more specific orientations to micro political behavior, each of which makes a distinctive contribution to the understanding of that behavior. We will introduce the basic vocabulary and assumptions of each approach, summarize a research application or applications in political science, suggest the possible contribution of the approach to a general micro political problem (political participation), and evaluate the strengths and weaknesses of each approach.

PSYCHOLOGICAL APPROACHES

We begin our examination of approaches to the study of micro political problems with individual psychological characteristics. We are going to divide this discussion into two broad categories: attitudes and personality traits. Both may be defined generally as *predispositions* to respond to environmental stimuli in a characteristic manner. That is, both attitudes and personality traits are characteristics which are not directly observable (they are mental things) and which are activated by conditions in the environment of the individual. For example, identification with the Republican Party is a characteristic of an individual (an attitude) which may be latent until activated by some event in the environment of the individual, such as a political convention. The only way that we can observe psychological characteristics of individuals is to present them with some stimulus which will activate the predisposition.[8]

A major assumption of our perspective on psychological approaches is that these predispositions intervene between environmental stimuli and behavior, and that the explanation of behavior most frequently requires knowledge of both.[9] For example, if we distinguish two types of environmental situations, a low stimulus situation and a high stimulus situation, we can predict different behaviors for collections of individuals. Angus Campbell has distinguished high stimulus elections from low stimulus elections.[10] A high stimulus election has as a prime characteristic a larger

---

[8] Thus, one way of finding out the partisan identification of an individual is to ask him: Which party do you feel yourself closer to? This is a stimulus.

[9] Greenstein, *op. cit.*, chap 2.

[10] Angus Campbell, "Surge and Decline: A Study of Electoral Change" in Campbell *et al.*, *Elections and the Political Order* (New York: John Wiley & Sons, 1966), p. 41.

flow of political stimuli from the media, e.g., an American presidential election; a low stimulus election has a correspondingly smaller flow of such stimuli. Therefore, we expect and do find higher voter turnout in a high stimulus election, which allows us to trace part of the explanation of differences in turnout to environmental differences. However, we will achieve a more complete understanding of these differences if we also examine the attitudes of the electorate—their interest in and concern about the outcome of the election. Thus, both environmental conditions and individual predispositions interact to provide an explanation for varying levels of voter turnout.[11]

When we use the term "attitude," we shall be referring to a predisposition to respond in a characteristic manner to a narrow and specific set of social or political objects, as in the observation that Senator X has a conservative attitude toward social welfare policies. A little later, we will contrast our use of the term attitude with our definition of personality trait. Why are we concerned with the concept of attitude in studying political behavior? The most obvious answer is that we believe that there is a connection between attitudes and behavior. Therefore, we should make that assumption explicit here and also qualify it. We do believe that attitudes are related to behavior. At the same time, we do not expect that in a given circumstance there will necessarily be a one-to-one relationship between a specific attitude and a given behavior.[12] Why? One answer is that environmental circumstances may so tightly constrain behavior that a given attitude is irrelevant. For example, although a person may dearly love his cat, if a fire threatens both his cat and his wife and only one can be saved, we know which one will have to perish. This illustration also points up the possibility of "attitudinal conflict"—a situation which we will discuss later as having important consequences for behavior.

In considering the relationship between attitudes and political behavior, a number of important aspects of attitudes need to be taken into account. Lane and Sears, in their informative work on *Public Opinion*,[13] list the following dimensions of opinion:

1. *Direction.* This means approval or disapproval. An individual is either pro or con with respect to busing to achieve school desegregation.

2. *Intensity.* This is the depth of emotional commitment to a position. An individual may be strongly or weakly pro (or con) with respect to busing to achieve school desegregation.

---

[11] *Ibid.*, pp. 41–45.

[12] In fact, there are some classic studies which have found discrepancies between attitudes and behavior. For example, R. T. Lapiere, "Attitudes Versus Actions," *Social Forces* (1934), pp. 230–37.

[13] (Englewood Cliffs, N.J.: Prentice-Hall, 1964), pp. 6–16.

3. *The public opinion context.* This is the question of how the attitude or opinion fits with opinions held by others in a system. Is it deviant or modal? It is important to know whether an individual's opinion is supported by or opposed by others.

4. *Stability.* Is the attitude durable over time or is it relatively unstable? Are attitudes toward busing stable or unstable?[14] This may be important from the perspective of officials who seek to implement policies based on the busing concept.

5. *The informational context.* How much information does an individual have in support of (or opposition to) his position? With respect to busing, for example, is he aware of the court decisions on which the concept is based?

6. *The organization of attitudes.* This refers to the degree to which an attitude fits with other attitudes one holds—are they interrelated or isolated from one another? To what extent does knowledge of one attitude of an individual allow prediction of other attitudes? Does the person who opposes busing also hold other attitudes which place him against integration?

7. *The consistency of opinion.* Closely related to organization, this refers to the degree to which opinions are logically consistent with each other. Thus, if someone is opposed to busing because it is "harmful to children" when busing involves integration, it would be logically inconsistent to support busing in another circumstance (school consolidation for instance) in which integration was not an issue.

8. *The policy component of an attitude.* This refers to the policy implications of the attitude. In the case of our example, the policy implications are clear—individuals are for or against busing. However, other policy positions may flow from this basic attitude; one may favor state aid to private schools as a result of being against busing.

9. *Salience.* This refers to the importance of a question at a given moment in time. Given different historical circumstances, the salience of opinions will vary from time to time. Attitudes against busing only became salient after certain events (court decisions) make the issue a real one for many people.

Why is it important to consider these dimensions of attitudes? If our concern is with the relationship between attitudes and behavior, then we will often have to take these aspects of opinion into account in making the connection. Suppose that we are interested in the potential for violence arising out of a school busing controversy. What aspects of opinion might we have to be aware of in assessing the likelihood of violence?

---

[14] On the low stability of American political attitudes, see Philip E. Converse and Georges Dupeux, "Politicization of the Electorate in France and the United States" in Angus Campbell *et al.*, *Elections and the Political Order, op. cit.*, pp. 285–88.

It may help to make this discussion of attitudes and political behavior a little less abstract by considering a specific piece of research using the concept of attitude. In their monumental study of American voting behavior, the authors of *The American Voter* develop a predictive model of electoral choice based on six "partisan attitudes."[15] The six attitudes which they use to try to predict the vote are:

1. Attitude toward the Republican candidate.
2. Attitude toward the Democratic candidate.
3. Attitude toward the parties as managers of government (involving questions of efficiency, corruption, and so on).
4. Attitude toward the parties in terms of domestic policy concerns (involving questions concerning the state of the economy and so on).
5. Attitude toward the parties in terms of foreign policy concerns.
6. Attitude toward the parties in terms of which is more favorable to the groups one is a member of.

In essence, these six attitudes cover a voter's orientation to the candidates, to the issues (in a broad sense), and to his perception of self and group interest. It is the authors' argument that if they can capture the direction and intensity of these six attitudes immediately prior to the vote, then they can do a very efficient job of predicting the way a collection of individuals will vote. For an idea of how partisan attitudes relate to the vote, let us take one specific illustration: attitude toward the Republican candidate, Dwight D. Eisenhower. Each individual respondent in the study was categorized according to the direction and intensity of his response toward Eisenhower. The data in Table 9–1[16] show the percentage

TABLE 9–1
Influence of Candidate Orientation

	Attitude Toward Eisenhower		
	Very Unfavorable	*Neutral*	*Very Favorable*
Voting for Eisenhower..............	6%	44%	98%

Source: Adapted from a table in Angus Campbell *et al.*, *The American Voter* (New York: John Wiley & Sons, 1964), p. 34, Used with permission.

voting Republican (for Eisenhower) in the extreme categories of attitudes and at the neutral point (neither positive nor negative). Not unexpectedly, there is a very regular relationship between attitude toward

---

[15] Campbell *et al.*, *The American Voter, op. cit.*, chap. 3.

[16] From *ibid.*

the candidate and voting for him. The relationship weakens, of course, as the attitude becomes more neutral (less intense). In fact, using all six partisan attitudes, the authors were able to predict accurately the direction of the vote for 86% of the electorate for the 1956 presidential election.[17] This is an impressive rate of prediction, although there remain "errors." It should be kept in mind that these findings are not presented as a complete explanation of why people vote the way they do. We do not consider, for example, the question of how people develop their partisan attitudes.[18]

Before we return to the contribution of the concept of attitude to the study of political participation, it would be well to call attention to two aspects of the study of attitudes which seem especially fruitful. One, which we mentioned earlier, is the phenomenon of attitude conflict. Often individuals do not behave the way we might expect them to on the basis of a single characteristic. A possible explanation for this "deviant" behavior is attitude conflict. Suppose that we found someone who liked Eisenhower in 1956 but did not vote. How are we to explain this? Suppose that we also found that this individual felt that the Republican Party was bad for the economy. This is a situation in which one attitude propels the individual in one direction (vote Republican) and the other propels him in the opposite direction (vote Democratic). Assuming that the two conflicting attitudes are held with relatively the same intensity, one possible resolution of the conflict is to refuse to choose—to fail to participate. There is some theory and data to support the contention that attitudinal cross-pressures lead to withdrawal and lower rates of political participation.[19]

A second perspective worth mentioning is the *functional* orientation to attitudes.[20] This is an application of functionalism to the study of individuals as systems. The question raised by this approach is: What are the functions of attitudes for individuals? The psychologists Smith, Bruner, and White have postulated three basic functions of opinions: (1) the object appraisal function, (2) the social adjustment function, and (3) the externalization function. The first function, object appraisal,

---

[17] *Ibid.*, p. 38.

[18] *Ibid.*, chap. 5. The authors feel that the weight of the evidence leads to the conclusion that partisan attitudes derive from partisan identification (not vice versa) and that partisan identity stems from the family. Thus, an oversimplified account of their argument would look like this: family partisan identification leads to offspring's identification leads to partisan attitudes leads to the vote. For a sophisticated treatment of the data relating to the causal orderings leading to the vote which generally supports the inferences made in *The American Voter*, see Arthur Goldberg, "Discerning a Causal Pattern among Data on Voting," *American Political Science Review*, Vol. 60 (December 1966), pp. 913–22.

[19] Campbell *et al.*, *The American Voter, op. cit.*, pp. 40–42.

[20] M. Brewster Smith *et al.*, *Opinions and Personality* (New York: John Wiley & Sons, 1956).

refers to "the process of testing reality in order to assess its relevance to one's ongoing enterprises."[21] This might be called the self-interest or rational function of opinion. The relevance for political behavior is obvious—one frequent assumption is that political behavior is largely rational, directed toward perceived self-interest.[22] The second function, social adjustment, "involves a process in which information about how other people regard the object engages with his motives to affiliate or identify himself with them or to distinguish himself from or oppose them."[23] Again, the relevance of the concept of the social adjustment function to political attitudes is clear. A frequent hypothesis is that political attitudes reflect the social groups to which we belong or with which we identify.[24] Finally, there is the externalization function, which involves "response to an external event in a way that is colored by a person's unresolved inner problems."[25] This function draws attention to the deeper psychological functions of opinion—the fact that the attitudes we have may not reflect so much the way the world is, but the way we are personally. It has frequently been asserted that there is a connection between individual personality traits and political attitudes and behavior.[26] We will examine this general area in the section following our discussion of attitudes and political behavior.

Why should we be concerned with the functions of attitudes? First, because the approach calls attention to the multiple consequences which attitudes may have for the individual. Second, and relatedly, there are some practical implications of being aware of the multiple consequences of attitudes. Suppose that you are interested in changing the attitudes of a group of people relative to the school busing controversy. Knowledge of *why* people hold the attitudes they do (in a functional sense) may help you to plan a strategy for changing attitudes. For example, if you know that the group of people hold antibusing views for an object appraisal reason (i.e., that busing would be physically or psychologically harmful to children), then evidence to the contrary should alter the opposition. On the other hand, if the attitudes are held in conformity to a group standard, then the group position must be changed before

[21] M. B. Smith, "Opinions, Personality and Political Behavior" in Nelson Polsby *et al., Politics and Social Life* (Boston: Houghton Mifflin, 1963), p. 213.

[22] Anthony Downs, *An Economic Theory of Democracy* (New York: Harper & Row, 1957).

[23] Smith, "Opinions, Personality and Political Behavior," *op. cit.*, p. 214.

[24] We will examine material relative to this hypothesis in the section on groups and micro political behavior. For a good general discussion, see Seymour M. Lipset, *Political Man: The Social Bases of Politics* (Garden City, N.Y.: Doubleday & Co., 1960), chaps. 6–8.

[25] Smith, "Opinions, Personality and Political Behavior," *op. cit.*, p. 214.

[26] We will examine some of this material below. For an excellent review of the status of this literature, see Greenstein, *op. cit.*

we would expect individual attitudes to change. Finally, if the attitudes are held for an externalization function, we would not expect rational appeals to have much impact in terms of altering attitudes. We would have to understand the personal needs of the individuals which are satisfied by their attitudes and perhaps find some other outlet for them.[27]

We turn now to the utility of the concept of attitude for the study of political participation (the question of who participates in politics and why). In terms of our general sketch of the factors related to behavior (Figure 9–1), it would make sense to consider attitudes an important influence on any behavior, including participation or nonparticipation. What sorts of attitudes might be expected to relate to political participation?[28] Political scientists have discovered a number of attitudes which relate to rates of political participation. One prominent example is an attitude which has been variously called "sense of political efficacy" or "sense of civic competence."[29] In brief, what this means is that people who believe that they are, or can be, effective in politics are more likely to participate than those who believe they are not, or cannot be, effective. Evidence gathered in a variety of studies supports this expectation. As an illustration, one study found that 46 percent of those who made the lowest scores on a measure of political efficacy were nonvoters, while only 6 percent of those who made the highest scores were. On the other hand, only 3 percent of the low scorers on political efficacy made high scores on a measure of political participation, while 28 percent of those who were high scorers on efficacy were also high on participation.[30] The findings are summarized as follows: ". . . persons who feel efficacious politically are much more likely to become actively involved in politics. . . ."[31] Some other attitudinal correlates of political participation are listed in Figure 9–2.[32] We use the term "correlates" to indicate that the causal orderings of the relationships are not simple to disentangle. Although we believe that these attitudes do lead to participation (as indicated by the arrow in the figure), it also makes sense to believe that the act of participation may reinforce or undermine the attitudes indicated by the feedback arrow in the figure. In any case, there is substantial evidence that these attitudes are related to participation.

The second psychological approach to micro political behavior which we are going to consider is that which focuses on personality traits.

---

[27] Smith *et al.*, *Opinions and Personality*, *op. cit.*, pp. 276–79.

[28] For a summary, see Milbrath, *op. cit.*, pp. 50–64.

[29] Angus Campbell *et al.*, *The Voter Decides* (Evanston, Ill.: Row, Peterson & Co., 1954); and Gabriel Almond and Sidney Verba, *The Civic Culture* (Boston: Little, Brown & Co., 1963).

[30] Milbrath, *op. cit.*, p. 56.

[31] *Ibid.* (emphasis removed).

[32] *Ibid.*, pp. 50–64.

FIGURE 9–2
Attitudinal Correlates of Political Participation

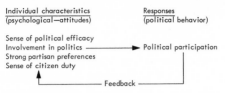

What is a personality trait? Earlier we defined an attitude as a predisposition to respond in a characteristic manner to a relatively narrow set of social or political objects. In contrast, a personality trait is a predisposition to respond in a characteristic manner to a broad range of social or political objects regardless of their substance or content. When we speak of personality traits in this sense, we mean that the individual tends to respond in a similar way to a wide variety of stimuli. For example, if we say that someone has an "aggressive personality," we mean that he is aggressive in many circumstances. In addition, although both attitudes and personality traits are thought to be largely learned behaviors resulting from socialization, it is expected that personality traits are primarily the result of childhood experiences and are correspondingly long-standing and difficult to modify or change.

What is the significance of the concept of personality traits for the study of micro political behavior? We can suggest a number of reasons for believing that the use of this concept might be fruitful. For one, there is the possibility that personality traits and attitudes are related. The suggestion would be that certain personality types would tend to hold characteristic political attitudes—that political attitudes are in fact rooted in more deep-seated personality structures. Perhaps the most famous hypothesis of this variety is that of the "authoritarian personality."[33] Briefly, this hypothesis is that individuals who have a deep-rooted need for unquestioning submission to authority (as well as some other personality characteristics which we need not go into here) will tend to hold distinctive political and social attitudes: anti-Semitism, ethnocentrism (generalized prejudice), and political and economic conservatism.[34] It is believed by some that authoritarian personalities have a high potential for susceptibility to fascist political ideas. Despite extensive methodological criticism and controversy, a wide range of evidence supports the contention that there is a relationship between the measure of authoritarianism (called the F-scale) and a number of right-wing political beliefs.[35] In

---

[33] T. W. Adorno *et al., The Authoritarian Personality* (New York: Harper, 1950).

[34] *Ibid.*

[35] See Greenstein, *op. cit.,* p. 106, n. 26.

our examination of a specific piece of research relating to personality traits and political behavior, we will have occasion to return to the question of the relationship between conservative political beliefs and personality.

A second, and related, reason for being concerned with personality traits is that personality may also relate to the way in which people hold their political attitudes. That is, some students of political psychology have argued that personality may not be so important for the content of political beliefs as for the style and manner in which political beliefs are held. A criticism of the concept of authoritarianism has been that it is tied to a particular set of political attitudes—right-wing ones. The psychologist Milton Rokeach has attempted to develop a general measure of authoritarianism which is independent of political content.[36] He has called this concept "dogmatism." Rokeach believes, and has uncovered some evidence to support his contention, that dogmatics will tend to have dogmatic political (as well as social, economic, and religious) belief systems regardless of whether the beliefs are right-wing, left-wing, or even of the center.[37]

We have noted that there are hypotheses which suggest connections between personality traits and both the content and structure of political attitudes. There are also general expectations of relationships between personality traits and political behavior. This is the third reason to consider personality traits potentially significant for the study of micro politics. Perhaps the most widely known hypothesis relating personality traits to political behavior is the contention that individuals seek political power in order to fulfill a craving for status and power over others. This idea was formulated by Harold Lasswell. He suggested that private motives, developed early in life, particularly the power motive, might become displaced onto public objects such as a political office. These motives would than be rationalized by the individual in terms of the public interests.[38] It is important to note here, as with the multiple functions of attitudes, that there will seldom be a single motivation for becoming active in politics. The evidence for the proposition that politicians generally have a greater need for power over others than nonpoliticians is not convincing.[39]

Examining a specific piece of research on personality traits and politics may help to illustrate the potential and the problems of this approach. The political scientist, Herbert McClosky, examined the relationships between a wide variety of personality characteristics and a set of political

---

[36] Milton Rokeach, *The Open and Closed Mind* (New York: Basic Books, 1960).

[37] *Ibid.*

[38] Harold Lasswell, *Psychopathology and Politics* (New York: Viking Press, 1960).

[39] Milbrath, *op. cit.*, pp. 81–82.

beliefs which he labeled conservatism.[40] In order to understand the study, it is important to know that McClosky attempted to develop an attitude scale to measure conservatism. This scale is based on the translation of some classical statements of conservative ideology into specific items. For example, one of the classical conservative statements is "man is a creature of appetite and will, 'governed more by emotion than by reason'. . . ."[41] Another is that "men are naturally unequal, and society requires 'orders and classes' for the good of all." A typical item which presumably is intended to capture the latter sentiment is: "It's not really undemocratic to recognize that the world is divided into superior and inferior people."[42] There has been some controversy about whether McClosky is "really" measuring conservatism. We have taken the position that such exchanges are rather sterile. What is interesting is that whatever he is measuring, there emerges from his study a set of intriguing findings relating political ideology and personality. In comparing extremely high scorers on his scale, "extreme conservatives," with the extremely low scorers, "liberals," the following relationships are found: "The figures demonstrate with overpowering effect that conservatives tend . . . to score on the more 'undesirable,' poorly adapted side of these personality variables."[43] As an illustration, while 62 percent of "extreme conservatives" score high on "paranoid tendencies," only 16 percent of "liberals" score high on that measure.[44] There is a regularity to the data McClosky presents which is impressive. In part, McClosky explains his findings by suggesting that conservative beliefs derive from more fundamental personality needs: ". . . conservative doctrines may tell us less about the nature of man and society than about the persons who believe these doctrines."[45]

It is not our intention here to go into the methodological problems of this type of research. We simply wish to note the following points about the study of the relationship of personality and ideology. First, one must develop reliable and valid measures of both personality traits and political ideology. This is no easy task in itself. The terms reliable and valid are similar to the requirements which we introduced in Chapter 3 for good scientific concepts: empirical import and theoretical signifi-

---

[40] Herbert McClosky, "Conservatism and Personality" in Polsby *et al., op. cit.,* pp. 218–31.

[41] *Ibid.,* p. 220.

[42] *Ibid.,* p. 221.

[43] *Ibid.,* p. 226.

[44] *Ibid.,* from a table on p. 226.

[45] *Ibid.,* pp. 227–28. For an article which uses a different methodology and develops different conclusions about the relationship between conservatism and personality, see Robert A. Schoenberger, "The New Conservatives: A View from the East," in Schoenberger (ed.), *The American Right Wing* (New York: Holt, Rinehart & Winston, 1969), pp. 280–98.

cance. For a measurement to be reliable, we must provide evidence that we can replicate the results. For a measurement to be valid, we must provide evidence that the concept functions in theoretically important generalizations. And, as with most problems in the social sciences, validity and reliability are matters of degree. Second, one must be concerned about whether there is in fact a relationship between the two concepts. Since both personality and ideology will probably be measured by some sort of attitude scale, care must be taken that the operational definitions of the two are in fact independent of each other. If they are not, then it is no surprise to find that personality and ideology are related. For example, if the McClosky personality items were simply restatements of the ideas which formed the basis of the measure of political ideology, then the relationships between the two measures would be due to this lack of independence. Third, one must investigate the causal ordering of the relationships. Is it the case that personality predispositions lead to the development of congruent political attitudes? Finally, one must be concerned with the question of whether personality or ideology ultimately have anything to do with political behavior.[46] All of these considerations, and more, stem from a concern with questions like those raised by McClosky's study.

Political scientists have also investigated the question of whether personality characteristics have anything to do with political participation. Earlier, we noted that individuals with a high sense of political efficacy tend to be more active in politics than those with a low sense of political efficacy. One of the findings at the more general, personality trait level is interesting given the previous finding. Measures of "ego strength" or "personal efficacy" also show a significant positive relationship with participation.[47] This means that individuals who have a sense of self-confidence are more likely to participate than those who lack such self-confidence. There is also a positive relationship between personal efficacy and political efficacy. One can speculate that confidence in oneself generally transfers to the political realm. Thus, a tentative causal model relating the three variables can be developed: sense of personal efficacy leads to sense of political efficacy, which leads to political participation. This model would fit our general expectation that personality traits are developed prior to attitudes specific to the political realm. Nevertheless, the remarks we made about the McClosky research apply equally here. In addition, we have not exhausted the examination of personality factors which might relate to participation.[48]

---

[46] For example, McClosky found little relationship between his measure of conservatism and party affiliation. McClosky, *op. cit.*, p. 231.

[47] Milbrath, *op. cit.*, pp. 60, 76–78.

[48] For a review, see *ibid.*, pp. 72–88.

We turn now to an evaluation of psychological approaches to the study of micro political problems. Our general comments will apply to both attitudes and personality traits. Where the comments apply only to one approach, we will so indicate. We begin with some cautionary remarks about these approaches. First, we must take note of the measurement problems. Psychological concepts, which are mental things, must be observed indirectly. Often attitudes and personality traits are measured with interviews and questionnaires. Numerous attempts have been made to develop scales which measure concepts such as "liberalism-conservatism," "political efficacy," "authoritarianism," "dogmatism," and many others. There are countless pitfalls in the path of those who attempt to measure psychological concepts. As an illustration, there is the phenomenon of "response set."[49] Investigators have discovered that some people tend to respond to questionnaire items in terms of their form rather than their content. For example, some people tend to agree to such items regardless of what they say. Such a tendency may be correlated with a lack of education. Now suppose that you had developed a scale in which positive agreement with the items indicated "high authoritarianism." Then you find out that people with low education tended to be authoritarians. It could be that what you were really observing was the tendency of people with low education to display an acquiescent (agreeing) response set.[50] This, of course, is only a single illustration of the multiple problems of psychological measurement.

A second caution, to repeat something which we said earlier, is that we should not expect that attitudes will necessarily predict behavior, that personality traits will necessarily predict attitudes, or that personality traits will necessarily predict behavior. Of course, in many instances we are hoping that these relationships will obtain. But, as in the case of the potential relationship between personality and political beliefs, the functional approach reminds us that "persons with similar underlying personality characteristics are capable of holding different political beliefs, and those with similar beliefs may differ in underlying personality characteristics. . . . political orientations are often acquired haphazardly, without engaging deeper personality sources."[51] As an example, one does not have to explain the political conservatism of a wealthy businessman by his personality; a more parsimonious explanation might be rational self-interest.[52]

A final, and related, caution is that in many instances, personality

---

[49] For a discussion, see Douglas N. Jackson and Samuel Messick, "Content and Style—Personality Assessment," *Psychological Bulletin*, Vol. 55 (July 1958), pp. 243–52; and Greenstein, *op. cit.*, pp. 101–102.

[50] *Ibid.*, pp. 114–65.

[51] *Ibid.*, p. 124.

[52] Schoenberger, *op. cit.*

explanations of behavior are superfluous, because individuals with different personalities behave substantially in the same way. For example, behavior which is tightly constrained by environmental circumstances is not likely to show much variation by personality. In a totalitarian political system, personality could not tell us much about electoral choice, since there is typically only one choice on the ballot.[53]

In terms of evaluation, we will continue to employ the criteria developed in the last chapter: (1) communication and stimulation of ideas, (2) organization of data, (3) development of research, and (4) explanation and prediction. However, since we are not dealing with a particular psychological school or approach in this chapter, our remarks will have to be quite general. It would appear that psychological approaches are fruitful in stimulating and communicating important ideas relative to the explanation of micro political behavior. This point can be substantiated by posing the following question: How satisfied are we likely to be with accounts of micro political behavior which simply report correlations between social characteristics and political behavior? It seems clear that we will want to employ psychological variables in order to understand such relationships. For example, we know that there are correlations between social class and the direction of voting behavior—individuals in the working class tend to vote for parties of the left and individuals in the middle and upper classes tend to vote for parties of the right.[54] To try to understand this relationship, we are likely to make reference to intervening attitudes of the individuals. We might make reference to ideology, self-interest, class consciousness, or some other psychological state—the point is that a psychological perspective helps to clarify such relationships.

A general psychological orientation, such as the environment–individual characteristics–response approach outlined at the beginning of this chapter does provide a useful organizational scheme for variables potentially related to micro political behavior. By adopting a broad definition of psychological approaches, including attitudes, we may safely say that psychological approaches have stimulated a wide variety of useful research in political science.[55]

Finally, psychological approaches may lead to explanations and predictions of micro political behavior. Following the example we used with respect to class and voting behavior, we find that knowledge of the psychological social class identification of individuals provides better pre-

---

[53] For discussions of the conditions in which personality might play a role in political behavior, see Lane, "Political Personality and Electoral Choice" in Polsby *et al., op. cit.,* pp. 232–33.

[54] Lipset, *op. cit.,* chap. 7.

[55] For one summary of politically relevant research, see Greenstein, *op. cit.,* pp. 163–84.

diction of political attitudes and behavior than knowledge of the social class defined by objective criteria, e.g., income, education, occupation.[56]

Although we have not begun to exhaust what could be said about psychological approaches to the study of politics, we have said enough to indicate the importance of such approaches for the study of micro political behavior and the many hazards which present themselves in using such approaches. We turn now to a consideration of the relevance of the concept of the group for the study of micro political behavior.

GROUPS AND MICRO POLITICAL BEHAVIOR

The concept of "group" would often be characterized as a sociological characteristic of individuals. It should be made clear, as we just indicated in our example of social class and voting behavior, that the group may be a sociological category and may also have, or not have, a "psychological reality" for the individual. This distinction should be kept in mind as we discuss the utility of the group concept for the explanation of individual political behavior.

Some scholars have gone so far as to argue that the group should be the central concept in political science.[57] Although not many political scientists would go this far, it is clear that the concept or related ones are frequently employed in the investigation of the antecedents of micro political behavior. Why has the concept been considered significant by political scientists? There are at least four general hypotheses which probably account for this fact.

1. Group conflict is often thought to be the major explanation for political outcomes in society. As Charles Hagan has put it, ". . . values are authoritatively allocated in society through the process of the conflict of groups."[58]

2. The number and kind of group memberships within society are often thought to have major implications for political system characteristics. In particular, it is argued that if the individuals in a society belong to many groups and those groups have conflicting political goals, this situation is conducive to democratic stability. This is referred to as the multiple group or overlapping group membership thesis.[59]

---

[56] V. O. Key, Jr., *Public Opinion and American Democracy* (New York: Alfred A. Knopf, 1961), p. 143.

[57] Arthur F. Bentley, *The Process of Government* (Cambridge, Mass.: Harvard University Press, 1967).

[58] "The Group in Political Science" in Roland Young (ed.), *Approaches to The Study of Politics* (Evanston, Ill.: Northwestern University Press, 1958), p. 40.

[59] Because this condition, it is argued, leads to political moderation on the part of group members. David Truman, *The Governmental Process* (New York: Alfred A. Knopf, 1951), pp. 508–16.

3. The groups one is a member of are thought to influence the socialization experiences of the individual. Thus, one would expect a degree of correspondence between group memberships and political attitudes and behavior.

4. The groups one is a member of may influence current attitudes and behavior by providing standards, cues, rewards, and punishments for conformity to group positions.

It is the latter two general hypotheses which have the greatest implications for micro political behavior, for they both suggest relationships between group memberships and political behavior.

As we indicated earlier, there are a number of ways of approaching the problem of defining the concept of group. We shall examine the approach taken by the political scientist David Truman.[60] He distinguishes categoric groups, interaction groups, institutionalized groups, and potential groups. Categoric groups are collections of individuals who share at least one common characteristic. Individuals who share sociological characteristics such as age, race, sex, education, and so on, are members of categoric groups. An infinite number of categoric groups may be constructed by the investigator. Members of categoric groups need not be aware of or interact with each other. Individuals who do share characteristics may, however, provide the basis for more interesting groups if they interact with one another on the basis of their shared characteristics. Thus, the people interested in the preservation of an animal species threatened with extinction share a common characteristic. They may become interesting politically when they begin to communicate and act together on the basis of that shared set of attitudes. They may even form an "institutionalized" group. These are groups characterized by a high degree of stability, uniformity, formality, and generality. An institutionalized group will have a formal organization.

A critical concept for Truman is that of the "potential" group. We have actually already illustrated the concept with the threatened species example. A potential group is a categoric group where the common characteristic is a set of shared attitudes. In effect, this is a collective predisposition to respond given the appropriate circumstances. Note that this definition of group has shifted attention from sociological categories to psychological characteristics (attitudes). The concept of potential group is significant to Truman for he uses it (1) to explain why groups are formed, through disturbances in the equilibrium (balance) of individuals who form potential groups, and (2) as part of the explanation of the stability of the American political system. In effect, Truman argues that there is a comprehensive potential group committed to the democratic

---
[60] *Ibid.*, chap. 2.

rules of the game.[61] Truman's group concepts are summarized in Figure 9–3. A group becomes a political interest group when it seeks to implement its goals by activity directed toward the political system.[62]

FIGURE 9–3
Truman's Group Concepts

Categoric	*Potential*	*Interaction*	*Institution*
Group	*Group*	*Group*	*Group*
(a)	$(a + b)$	$(a + b + c)$	$(a + b + c + d)$

a = at least one shared characteristic
b = shared attitude or attitudes
c = interaction
d = stability, uniformity, formality, generality, organization

We turn now to specific research applications of the group concept to give more concrete illustrations of how it is used in political science. Both illustrations have to do with group influence on voting behavior. The first is concerned with more contemporary influences; the second with influences during the socialization process concentrating on the family.

In *The American Voter*, the degree of group influence on the individual is presented as a function of a triangle of relationships between the group and the individual, the group and the political world, and the individual and the political world. In terms of the first relationship, the authors suggest that "the higher the identification of the individual with the group, the higher the probability that he will think and behave in ways which distinguish members of his group from non-members."[63] This is a statement of the proposition that psychological identification with the group will provide for more distinctive behavior than mere membership in a categoric group which lacks such identification. Data are presented which support this contention. For example, among members of union households, those who were "highly identified" with the union voted 28 percent more for the Democratic Party (64 versus 36 percent) than those who were "weakly identified" with the union.[64] Among all the groups studied, this finding was repeated to a greater or lesser degree. The second aspect of the conditions making for group influence on the individual is the relationship of the group to the world of politics: ". . . as perception of proximity between the group and the world of politics becomes clearer, the susceptibility of the individual member of a group to influences in political affairs increases."[65] The group

---

[61] *Ibid.*, pp. 512–15.
[62] *Ibid.*, p. 37.
[63] Campbell *et al.*, *The American Voter*, *op. cit.*, p. 168.
[64] *Ibid.*, p. 169.
[65] *Ibid.*, p. 171.

must somehow be perceived by the individual as salient for politics, and the group standard must be communicated to the group members. A classic example of "proximity" is when the candidate for office is a member of the group. Again, data are presented which illustrate the proposition. For example, the percentage of votes cast by Catholic voters for Catholic congressional candidates in races involving non-Catholics was 61 versus 49 percent by non-Catholic voters.[66]

The propositions relating the group and the individual and the group and the political world are pictured in Figure 9–4 as two sides of a

FIGURE 9–4
Influence of the Group on Individual Behavior

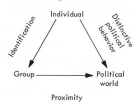

triangle which influence the relationship of the individual to the political world. Therefore, even though we are interested in this particular instance in the contemporary influence of the group on the individual, we would ultimately have to inquire into the origins of the individual's identification with the group and into the circumstances under which the group is or is not perceived as salient politically.[67]

As a second research illustration of the use of the concept group, we turn to a study by Herbert McClosky and Harold E. Dahlgren of "Primary Group Influence on Party Loyalty."[68] Although this study is concerned with both contemporary and past influences of a number of primary groups, we are going to concentrate on evidence relating past socialization experiences to political behavior and on the influence of the family as a socialization unit. In the group study reported in *The American Voter* which we just examined, the groups were collections of individuals who more than likely did not associate directly with each other. McClosky and Dahlgren's research looks at primary group influence: "those small, face-to-face, solidary, informal and enduring coteries that we commonly experience as family, friendship and occupa-

---

[66] *Ibid.*, p. 176.

[67] *Ibid.* In an interesting observation, the authors note that the political party identification uniquely fits the model of group influence: ". . . proximity is at an upper limit, for the party has a central position in the world of politics. In all major elections, its salience is absolutely high: one candidate is always a group member, the prime group goal is victory" (pp. 180–181).

[68] In Polsby *et al., op. cit.*, pp. 255–70.

tional peer groups."[69] The authors point out that there is substantial evidence which suggests the importance of primary groups for the development of political attitudes and behavior.[70] One illustration is the recurring finding that about three fourths of Americans share the partisan identity of their parents.

The major hypothesis which we are going to illustrate here is that the primary group influence on party loyalty in terms of the stability of those attachments to a particular party will vary with "the strength of the family's initial political indoctrination."[71] Although the indicators of the strength of family political indoctrination are indirect, some suggestion of the impact of the socialization process on later political behavior can be gleaned from data reported in this study. For example, voters who share partisan preferences with their parents are markedly more stable in their electoral behavior than those who deviate from the preferences of their parents. In other words, a voter's susceptibility to deviation from his current partisan preference is influenced by the extent to which his preferences are "anchored in his primary groups, especially his family."[72] In addition, stability of partisan preferences is increased to the degree that the family preferences have remained consistent over time and the degree to which they have been reinforced by the family.[73]

The group concept is also applicable to the study of political participation. Substantial numbers of studies report relationships between categoric groups and rates of political participation. For example, levels of education, income, occupation, age, and sex are all related to participation.[74] Following the example we have been using, we may inquire if there is any research which demonstrates connections between group membership and levels of efficacy. Evidence of this type would lend plausibility to the argument that attitudes relevant for participation are developed in part through experiences which are group-related. One prominent relationship which has been widely reported is that between education and efficacy: "Several studies in several nations have shown that upper socio-economic status (SES) persons, especially the better educated, are more likely to develop efficacious feelings."[75] We can understand this relationship if we hypothesize that education will increase understanding and information relative to the political world, which in turn potentially increases effectiveness. In addition, since education is correlated with social position and income, factors which increase political effectiveness,

---

[69] *Ibid.*, p. 255.

[70] For example, see studies cited in *ibid.*, p. 255, n. 2.

[71] *Ibid.*, p. 258.

[72] *Ibid.*, p. 259.

[73] *Ibid.*, pp. 260–61.

[74] Milbrath, *op. cit.*, chap. 5.

[75] *Ibid.*, p. 57.

we would have even more reason to expect people with more education to experience effectiveness or to anticipate effectiveness. Finally, we may speculate that education is also related to the development of a sense of personal effectiveness. Thus, we arrive at the possible relationships illustrated in Figure 9–5.

FIGURE 9–5
Possible Relationships: Education, Personal Effectiveness,
Political Efficacy, and Participation

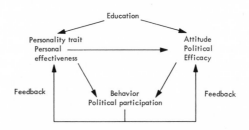

Group (sociological, categoric)

In the preceding paragraph, we reported relationships between categoric groups and political participation. We should also note here that there are relationships between interaction group memberships and participation. One of the clearest relationships is revealed by the simple dichotomy between those who belong to organized groups and those who do not—the sheer fact of belonging to a group or groups increases rates of participation.[76]

Although our major concern in this section has been the influence of groups on micro political behavior, the group has an importance in political science beyond these concerns in relationship to the explanation of the outcomes of political conflicts and to the stability of political systems. In particular, the argument has been advanced that multiple group memberships enhance the stability of democratic systems. The argument can be summarized in the following way: multiple memberships in groups which have conflicting interests lead to political moderation on the part of the members involved and their groups. Why should this be the case? The case is made that conflicts are moderated because individuals are cross-pressured. Too, groups must recognize the legitimacy of their opponents if their own members are also members of the opposition group. In contrast, a situation in which there are clear-cut divisions between members of opposing groups "produces conflicts so intractable that they undermine the legitimacy of opposition, and . . . this in turn leads to the destruction of democratic political organization."[77] From

---

[76] Milbrath, *op. cit.*, p. 17.

[77] Douglas W. Rae and Michael Taylor, *The Analysis of Political Cleavages* (New Haven: Yale University Press, 1970), p. 14.

this theoretical perspective, what would we predict about the *attitudes* of individuals who have multiple group memberships which conflict?

After this brief glimpse at the use of the group concept in studying micro political behavior, we will make some summarizing and evaluatory comments. First, we obviously do not consider "group" to be *the* central concept in political science. In fact, we would not select any concept or approach we have discussed (or could discuss) as the most significant. In particular, it is worth noting that attitudes and behavior often deviate from what we expect, given that we know the group or groups to which an individual belongs. For example, we know that as a general proposition, wealth is correlated with political conservatism. There are, however, many deviant cases such as John Kennedy and Averill Harriman.[78] This leads us to repeat the observation that it is the group or groups that the individual identifies with psychologically that are most likely to be influential in terms of his behavior. Further, membership in groups with conflicting positions creates the potential for conflicts in identifications and attitudes which may result in "deviant" behavior. Thus, Milbrath reports: "Persons belonging to more than one group may find their groups pulling in different directions, or some groups may urge political action while others urge inaction. Such persons may be thought of as cross-pressured. It has generally been found that persons in group cross-pressure are less likely to participate than those not cross-pressured."[79] A single group membership, then, is inadequate to account for political behavior.

In terms of our evaluative criteria, we believe that: (1) the group concept is useful for the communication of important ideas relative to micro political behavior, (2) the organizing power of the group concept is not particularly strong, (3) useful research has been stimulated through group and sociological approaches to micro political behavior,[80] and (4) in combination with psychological concepts, group concepts can provide the basis for explanatory and predictive statements. In short, although we reject the primacy of the group concept, it is hard to conceive of explanations of micro political behavior which could ignore the group context of such behavior.

POLITICAL SOCIALIZATION AND
MICRO POLITICAL BEHAVIOR

We have made direct and indirect references to the phenomenon of political socialization throughout our discussions of psychological orienta-

---

[78] For a discussion, see Gabriel A. Almond, "The Political Attitudes of Wealth," in Polsby *et al., op. cit.,* pp. 278–97.

[79] Milbrath, *op. cit.,* p. 132.

[80] Some of the recent research is summarized and discussed by David Truman in *The Governmental Process* (2d ed.; New York: Alfred A. Knopf, 1971), pp. xvii–xlvii.

tions and group approaches to micro political behavior. These references were the result of two assumptions made earlier which we call to your attention again: (1) psychological characteristics of individuals are largely learned predispositions, and (2) individuals in similar social circumstances tend to have similar learning experiences. The study of the process by which political predispositions are learned is the study of political socialization. This, then, is the most important reason for the concern of political scientists with the study of political socialization: it focuses on how and why people acquire the political predispositions they have.

In the most general sense, political socialization may be viewed as the induction into the *political culture* of the society of which the individual is a member. Thus, we expect that dominant modes or patterns of orientations toward politics in a society are transmitted from generation to generation through the socialization process. This leads us to a consideration of a second reason that political scientists have been concerned with socialization. Since political scientists are often interested in questions of stability and change in political systems (macro questions), and since we have earlier identified political culture as a concept which has been used in explanations of stability and change, it follows that the socialization process may have something to do with these macro questions. David Easton, for example, has argued that socialization develops a set of attitudes supportive of the political system which constitute a reservoir of attachment. This support is latent—it is not contingent upon the satisfaction of particular, immediate demands. As an illustration, students of political socialization have found that many children in the United States develop a "benevolent image" of political authority.[81] Although this uncritical attitude toward authority tends to alter in adulthood, the argument is that these attitudes and beliefs regarding the political system, inculcated early in life, color the remaining socialization experiences and influence long-term support for the political system. Socialization, however, need not inevitably result in attitudes supportive of the political system. In contrast to the research which turned up the "benevolent image" of political authority, research on members of an American subculture (Appalachian) found children with distinctively more negative and cynical attitudes toward the political system.[82] It is easy to speculate that individuals who have socialization experiences leading to these kinds of attitudes may later be politically apathetic or actively hostile to the political system.[83]

---

[81] David Easton and Jack Dennis, "The Child's Image of Government" in Roberta Sigel (ed.), *Learning About Politics* (New York: Random House, 1970), p. 31.

[82] Dean Jaros *et al.*, "The Malevolent Leader," *American Political Science Review*, Vol. 62 (June 1968), pp. 564–75.

[83] Political socialization research has only recently turned attention to American blacks.

It may also be suggested that the patterns of political socialization within systems may influence the kind of political system which is maintained. In our discussion of personality traits and political behavior, we introduced the concept of the authoritarian personality—an individual with a desire to uncritically submit to strong leaders and to dominate those weaker than himself.[84] A controversial proposition in social science would link authoritarian personalities in large numbers with authoritarian political regimes. As a corollary to that proposition, there is the question: "Are the societies which have a long history of democracy peopled by a majority of individuals who possess a personality conducive to democracy?"[85] A central element in the democratic personality would be a degree of independence from authority. The adult democratic citizen has a healthy skepticism of authority.[86] In addition, he has no need to excessively dominate others. Now both of these related hypotheses are by no means confirmed, and there are many reasons to be skeptical of a direct relationship between personality and political system characteristics.[87] Nevertheless, the possibility of such links calls attention to the significance of socialization for the political system, for we expect such traits as authoritarian and democratic character to be molded in the family and related socialization processes.[88]

The hypotheses relating political socialization to system maintenance and the kind of system maintained are examples of generalizations which link micro and macro political problems. We will take up these kinds of questions directly in Chapter 10. In this chapter, we want to concentrate attention on links between socialization and micro political behavior. First, a few general comments about the phenomenon of socialization. Socialization involves individuals interacting with agents from whom they learn appropriate attitudes, beliefs, and patterns of behavior relative to politics. This learning may be either intended by the agent or the by-product of other experiences. An example of intended learning would be civic education in the schools. An example of unintended learning would be where a child adopts the partisan identification of the parents by imitation. The study of political socialization is concerned with the learning of those patterns of orientation to the political world, which we earlier labeled the political culture. From the point of view of the

---

[84] Alex Inkeles, "National Character and Modern Political Systems" in Polsby *et al., op. cit.,* pp. 180–84.

[85] *Ibid.,* p. 184.

[86] *Ibid.,* pp. 185–186.

[87] These problems are discussed in some detail in Chapter 10.

[88] Fred Greenstein, "Personality and Political Socialization: The Theories of Authoritarian and Democratic Character" in "Political Socialization: Its Role in the Political Process," *Annals of the American Academy of Political and Social Science* (September 1965), pp. 81–95.

individual, these orientations constitute a view of the self in relationship to the political world. In terms of the content and timing of the socialization process, one salient finding is evidence that emotional and nonrational political identifications and attachments are developed in childhood. For example, second graders have been found to identify with a particular political party, although, of course, there is no issue content to their attachments.

It has been traditional to stress the significance of the early family experiences for the socialization process. There can be no question of the importance of the family. At the same time, it must be stressed that political socialization continues throughout the life of the individual. Other agents of socialization include the school, occupational groups, the mass media, and so on. Recognition of this fact allows for the possibility of discontinuities in the socialization process. What is learned in the family may or may not be reinforced in the school. Obvious hypotheses result: (1) homogeneous (reinforcing) socialization experiences will strengthen initial predispositions, and (2) discontinuous socialization experiences may lead to attitude conflict or change of initial predispositions.

As a final general comment, the concept of political socialization may also be used to investigate the ways in which political institutions develop and maintain a set of operating norms and role conceptions. For example, political scientists have investigated the ways in which legislative bodies develop expectations of behavior on the part of their members and the ways in which new members are socialized into these expectations.[89]

To illustrate the socialization perspective, let us turn to a study by Fred Greenstein on "Sex-Related Political Differences in Childhood."[90] The observation of one stark fact prompted Greenstein's concern with differences in political socialization by sex: "At the mass level, women are less likely than men to engage in the whole range of activities available to the politically interested citizen."[91] In reviewing older studies and more current research on the political attitudes of children, Greenstein consistently found differences which suggested more political interest and awareness on the part of boys than of girls.

Greenstein offers the following explanation for these differences. In general, males are socialized into roles which emphasize dominance and aggressiveness and females are not. For example, Greenstein notes that the reading matter for girls emphasizes "milder stories of home and school," while that for boys explores "violence or outdoor adventure, sports, travel, exploration and war."[92] These nonpolitical roles are then

---

[89] John Wahlke *et al.*, *The Legislative System* (New York: John Wiley & Sons, 1962).

[90] In Polsby *et al.*, *op. cit.*, pp. 244–54.

[91] *Ibid.*, p. 245.

[92] *Ibid.*, p. 252.

generalized into the political realm. Greenstein summarizes his argument as follows:

Children's political sex differences do not flow from a rationalistic developmental sequence in which the girl learns "politics is not for girls," hence "I am not interested in politics." Rather there is a much more subtle and complex process in which, through differential opportunities, rewards and punishments which vary by sex, and through mechanisms such as identification with one or the other parent, sex identity is acquired. Among other things this learning process associates girls with the immediate environment and boys with the wider environment. Political responses, developing as they do relatively late in childhood, fall into the framework of already present non-political orientations.[93]

An important point should be stressed here. We are discussing general tendencies, and there are obviously many exceptions to the general sex differences in political participation.

Since the continuing example we have been using of micro political behavior has been political participation (who participates and why), we may ask if a socialization perspective sheds any more light on that micro problem. We will turn to Gabriel Almond and Sidney Verba's investigation into the question of whether participation in decision making in nonpolitical units (such as the family, the school, the work situation) increases the probability of participation in political decision making. As they phrase the problem, "the essential question is whether there is a close relationship between the roles that a person plays in nonpolitical situations and his role in politics."[94] They suggest that an individual may generalize from roles played in the family, the school, or the job to politics. In addition, skills developed by participation in one arena may facilitate participation in others.

The actual research they report examines the relationship between the individuals' perceptions of participation in decision making in nonpolitical realms and their "sense of civic competence."[95] The "sense of civic competence" is very much analogous to the attitude cluster we earlier called a "sense of political efficacy"—the feeling of competence to participate in politics. The findings were that individuals who perceived that they had a participatory role in nonpolitical units tended to score higher on the measure of civic competence than those who perceived that they had nonparticipatory roles.[96]

---

[93] *Ibid.*, p. 253.

[94] Almond and Verba, *op. cit.*, p. 271.

[95] *Ibid.*, pp. 284–99.

[96] *Ibid.* Their summary statement is: "The data presented in this chapter suggest that there is indeed a generalization from the nonpolitical sphere to the polity" (p. 300).

In addition, the impact of the socialization experiences, in line with a hypothesis we suggested earlier, is cumulative: "If one finds oneself *consistently* in social situations where one has a voice over decisions, this is more likely to result in a general sense of competence than if the experience with participation in one area is not matched by similar experiences in other areas."[97] The most interesting aspect of this research is the provocative connection which is drawn between the impact of nonpolitical experiences and political attitudes and behavior. It may be useful now to expand our sketch of factors influencing political participation to include socialization experiences (see Figure 9–6).

FIGURE 9–6
Groups, Socialization, Attitudes, and Participation

Categoric Group Membership	Socialization Experiences	Attitudes/Personality Traits	Behavior
Education	→ Participation in decision making (school)	→ Sense of competence or efficacy	→ Political participation

Before we leave this research, it is necessary to make a couple of methodological observations. First, it should be clear that the dependent variable in the research, sense of competence, is an attitude, not a behavior. The assumption, which we believe is warranted, is that a sense of competence is associated with behavior—political participation.[98] Second, the measure of decision making in nonpolitical areas is also indirect. It depends on the recall of the respondents. Therefore, the causal direction is not at all clear from the data. Could it not be that the memory of past decision-making experiences could be influenced by one's current assessment of decision-making competence?[99]

We turn now to a brief evaluation of the socialization perspective for the study of micro political problems. A very important qualification is that ". . . investigators cannot make a priori assumptions about the stability over the life cycle of psychological dispositions and political orientations found in childhood."[100] Thus, we must be prepared to deal not only with stability over the life of an individual, but also with changes

---

[97] *Ibid.*, p. 301 (emphasis ours).

[98] In fact, there is considerable evidence to support this assumption. See Milbrath, *op. cit.*, pp. 56–57.

[99] The authors are, of course, aware of the limitations of their data. See Almond and Verba, *op. cit.*, pp. 273–74.

[100] Kenneth P. Langton, *Political Socialization* (New York: Oxford University Press, 1969), p. 18.

in orientations. A good example of this is the work on voting behavior. The standard literature gives us a general model of voting behavior which stresses the early learning of partisan identity in the family. Nevertheless, we know that individuals do change their partisan identities and do waver in their voting support for one party or the other. The socialization perspective must be broad enough to allow for political learning and change to occur throughout the life of the individual.

In terms of our criteria for evaluation, we make the following observations: (1) the socialization perspective does communicate an important set of ideas relating to the fact that political predispositions come from somewhere (they are acquired) and that there is a pattern or regularity to the acquisition process; (2) socialization does not provide much by way of organization schema, although several organizing principles may develop from such a perspective;[101] (3) there is a rapidly expanding body of research employing this perspective[102]; and (4) in general, socialization is not a theory which provides for explanations and predictions, but it is an orientation which suggests a place to look for more complete explanations of current behavior—the history of the organism under study. In short, the study of political socialization has been and promises to continue to be a fruitful area of inquiry for those interested in micro (and macro) political behavior.

ROLE THEORY AND MICRO POLITICAL BEHAVIOR

Particularly in our discussion of political socialization, we used the term "role" without stopping to define it. We are now going to explicitly discuss the relevance of the concept of role for the study of micro political behavior. As a point of departure, we may note that role, like group, has both a sociological component and a psychological one. The sociological component is that roles are attached to socially defined categories or positions, e.g., the role of policeman. At the same time, the definition of role which we will adopt stresses the psychological expectations of the occupants of the role and others. From our perspective, then, role is a psychological orientation which is learned through the socialization process. The role perspective seeks to account for uniformities in behavior by pointing out that individuals who occupy similar positions in society come to have similar conceptions about what behaviors are associated with that position. More formally,

---

[101] For example, one may divide the process into time segments or the study of the process by socialization agents. It would appear that many students of socialization have adopted some kind of systems or functional (input-output) scheme of organization (*ibid.*, pp. 5–8).

[102] See, for example, the bibliography included in Langton, *op. cit.*, pp. 185–210.

role . . . refers to a coherent set of "norms" [or expectations] of behavior which are thought by those involved in the interactions being viewed, to apply to all persons who occupy the position. . . . It is the normative aspect . . . which gives psychological validity to the concept: the concept postulates that individual[s] . . . are aware of the norms constituting the role and consciously adapt their behavior to them in some fashion."[103]

The role concept, then, is used to help explain the fact that individuals in given settings (such as groups, institutions, and so on) behave in regular patterns. Also, inherent in the perspective is the relationship of a given role to other roles. "Any role . . . can analytically be divided into role sectors, each sector comprising those norms appropriate to some particular 'counter-role,' i.e., to encounters with persons occupying some particular counterposition or status."[104] For example, talking about the role of teacher makes little sense unless we place that role in the framework of significant counterroles such as student or administrator.

Mentioning counterroles leads us directly to the next important consideration—role consensus. The extent to which role conceptions will lead to similar behavior depends on the extent to which there is consensus about the appropriate norms. Two forms of consensus are involved. First, there is the question of the degree of consensus among those who occupy a given role. Second, there is the question of the degree of consensus on the role between the occupant of a given position and a significant counterposition.[105] The first kind of consensus raises this sort of specific question: Do all teachers agree on what the teacher role is? The second raises another question: Do teachers and students (or administrators) agree on what the teacher role is?

It is important, also, to note that a given individual may be expected to occupy a number of different roles simultaneously. An individual may be both a teacher and an administrator, both a legislator and a family man, both a judge and a presidential adviser. Both within a given role and between roles, there is the potential for role conflict. This simply means a conflict in expectations arising from: (1) conflicting expectations applied to the occupant of a given position or (2) conflicting expectations applied to the occupant of more than one position. In the first case, an example would be a legislator whose constituency expected him to vote one way on a bill while his political party expected him to vote another way. In the second case, an example might be an individual

---

[103] Wahlke *et al.*, *op. cit.*, pp. 8–9. Another way of putting Wahlke's conception of role is to think of a role as having three psychological subcomponents: (1) how I believe I should behave in this position or situation, (2) how I perceive others think that I should behave in this position or situation, and (3) how in fact others do believe I should behave in this position or situation.

[104] *Ibid.*, pp. 10–11.

[105] *Ibid.*, p. 15.

who is both a politician and a family man facing a conflict (for example, how to allocate his time) in which his political role leads to one set of expectations about behavior and his family role leads to another, contradictory, set. As with attitude conflict, the idea of role conflict may help to explain unusual or deviant behaviors.

It is also worth noting that, as with political socialization, the concept role is sometimes used as a link between macro and micro political problems. For example, social systems are often described in terms of networks of interrelated roles. Thus role is, on the one hand, a psychological predisposition of individuals and, on the other, an interdependent part of a social system.

Perhaps the outstanding illustration of the application of role concepts in political science has been in the study of legislative behavior.[106] The ideas of representation, as in the situation of a legislator representing his constituency, employ concepts readily translated into role perspectives: Should legislators represent their districts' wishes literally, the *delegate* concept of representation; or should they represent what they conceive to be the best interests of the constituency regardless of what the constituents feel at the moment, the *trustee* conception?[107] Given these polar conceptions of legislative roles, questions can be raised: (1) Do legislators in fact hold role conceptions such as these? (2) With what frequency? and (3) Do these role conceptions have anything to do with legislative behavior? Research on the representational role orientations of state legislators turned up an affirmative answer to the first question. In responding to open-ended questions about the nature of their role, legislators did express role conceptions which fit the trustee-delegate typology. In addition, an intermediate type, called a "politico," was uncovered. The politico was an individual who adopted a trustee orientation in some circumstances and a delegate orientation in others.[108] In terms of frequency, the most frequently adopted orientation was that of trustee. The delegate was the least frequently adopted orientation.[109] There is as yet little convincing evidence of the relationship of these role conceptions to actual legislative behavior.

In effect, we have already illustrated the use of the concept of role in the study of political participation by our discussion of Greenstein's work on sex roles and political participation in the section on socialization. It is sufficient to point out here that certain social positions may carry with them the expectation of higher rates of political participation, while other roles may have the opposite expectations. Part of the cultural definition of the role of lawyer, for example, may be an expectation of attention

---

[106] *Ibid.*

[107] *Ibid.*, pp. 268–72.

[108] *Ibid.*, p. 277.

[109] *Ibid.*, p. 281.

to and participation in politics. In contrast, as part of the cultural definition of the role of sharecropper there may be an expectation of parochial political orientations and, consequently, extremely low rates of political participation.[110] We have reached the point in our discussion of approaches to micro political behavior where we can put all of the parts we have discussed back together in a general sketch which resembles our original framework (Figure 9–7). Clearly, an important segment

FIGURE 9–7
Illustrative Sketch: Antecedents of Political Participation

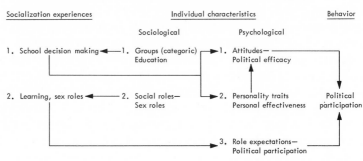

which is left out of this figure is the immediate environmental conditions. Also left out is the perceptual screen which filters responses to these conditions.

A major problem to keep in mind in using a role approach is to distinguish carefully between the role expectations and role performance (or role behavior). Failure to make this distinction will result in conceptual confusion. If we define a role in terms of the pattern of behavior of individuals who fill the role (role performance), we cannot turn around and use that to explain role behavior. They are, in effect, the same thing. At the same time, it does us little good to study role expectations (attitudes) if we do not ultimately intend to relate them to behavior. A second problem is that individuals who occupy the same role often behave differently—that is, the expectations are ambiguous enough to allow variations in role performance. We must look elsewhere (personality?) for factors to explain these differences.

Our general evaluation of the utility of the concept of role makes the following points: (1) role does communicate an important idea about micro political behavior, namely, that much of social and political behavior can be understood in terms of *patterns* of expectations of behavior for the occupants of particular social and political positions; (2) the concept has little organizational capacity as such, although organizational

---

[110] To be sure, there are other constraints, both legal and extralegal, on participation.

schemes may be developed on the basis of the concept; (3) a rather modest amount of research has stemmed from the perspective and has tended to center in the legislative area; and (4) role theory is not one coherent theory. The theories and the conceptual work orient the observer to a class of observations which may help to explain behavior. The concept has utility for political science, particularly as it is understood and used in the context of the other approaches we have discussed.

CONCLUSIONS

In this chapter we have examined a number of approaches to the study of micro political problems. We have examined the concepts and assumptions associated with each approach, we have illustrated the approaches via research examples in political science, and we have evaluated the approaches. In addition, we have stressed the interconnections between the various approaches. Much of this discussion is summarized in Table 9–2.

In our concluding comments, we wish to reemphasize several general points about the study of micro political problems.

First, we think it is useful to think of the factors involved in the

TABLE 9–2
Review of Selected Approaches to the Study of Micro Political Problems

Approach	Major Assumption	Key Concepts	Problems
Attitudes	Attitudes related to behavior	Attitude Intensity Salience Cross-pressures Object appraisal Social adjustment Externalization Political efficacy	Attitudes do not always predict behavior
Personality traits	Personality related to structure and content of attitudes and behavior	Personality trait Authoritarian personality Dogmatism Personal efficacy	Personality does not always predict attitudes, ideology, or behavior
Groups	Groups influence attitudes and behavior	Categoric group Potential group Interaction group Institution Group identification	Distinguish "objective" from "subjective" group membership
Socialization	Political attitudes are learned	Socialization	Socialization is ongoing
Role	Individuals in same role behave similarly	Role Role consensus Role conflict	Individuals in same role behave differently

study of micro political problems in terms of: (1) environmental characteristics and (2) characteristics of the individual. Although we have not paid much attention to the former in this chapter, both sets of factors are needed to explain micro behavior. Second, we think it is important to be aware that the characteristics of the individual, particularly the psychological ones, will influence what and how stimuli are received. There is a good example of this latter point in the voting literature. In the 1948 presidential campaign, voters favorable to a particular candidate but opposed to that candidate's stand on a particular issue tended to distort their perception of his stand in line with their own position.[111] Third, as part of the explanation of why people behave the way they do, we will often want to find out how and why they acquired the predispositions that they have. This concern will direct attention to the life history of the individual. Fourth, implicit in what we have been saying is that the explanation of individual political behavior is likely to be multivariate—involving a number of variables. Finally, we wish to stress the complementary nature of the approaches which we have mentioned. Group explanations which do not take account of the socialization experiences and psychological predispositions of individuals are not likely to be very satisfactory. Psychological explanations which ignore the social context of behavior are not worth much either. Approaches must be selected which are appropriate to the problem at hand, and the investigator must be aware of the factors which impinge on behavior, but which are not given primary consideration in a given approach. Some of these factors will come from other levels of analysis, and it is to the problems of linkage that we turn in the next chapter.

---

[111] Bernard Berelson *et al.*, *Voting* (Chicago: University of Chicago Press, 1954), p. 220.

10

Integrating approaches
to the study of politics: The
individual and the system

We have considered both micro and macro concepts, questions, and approaches and some linkage problems in previous chapters. We will draw these together with many of the examples in this chapter as we discuss (1) the need for explicit integration of different levels when dealing with most questions, (2) the basic problems associated with such integration, and (3) a number of linkage concepts and cross-level generalizations. This discussion will also make clearer the reasons for organizing the substantive material into micro-macro categories rather than into the subjects of American, state and local, comparative, and international politics.

THE NEED FOR EXPLICIT INTEGRATION

Most questions about politics, whether about the family or international alliances, require either assumptions about conditions at another level or the introduction of concepts from other levels. Consider the question of whether the congruity of parents' and children's political party preferences is related to variations in family authority patterns.[1] Are the children of an authoritarian home more likely to agree or disagree with their parents' party preferences? We will have to assume that the political system offers more than a one-party choice; otherwise, in a one-party forced-choice system, there will be no variation in party preference with which to relate variation in family authority patterns. Thus, we are assuming something about the presence of a macro level concept, the type

---

[1] For a discussion of this question, see Kenneth P. Langton, *Political Socialization* (New York: Oxford University Press, 1969), chap. 2.

of political party system. We may also find in exploring the problem further that the relationship is affected by the presence or absence of consistency of parents, friendship, and peer group party preferences; the school experience; mass media exposure; and party support. If the relationship between family authority patterns and the congruence of parent-child party preferences is affected by school socialization experiences, mass media exposure, or party support, we would be linking macro level concepts to our micro level concepts.

Going beyond this example, Figure 10–1 shows an individual linked via a number of processes to different levels of politics.[2] Given the level of concepts indicated in a particular question, it is possible to locate

FIGURE 10–1
Levels and Linkages of Political Components

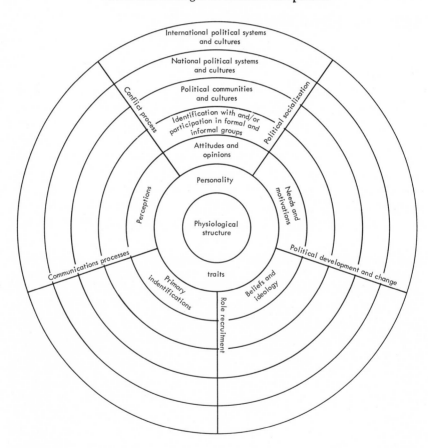

___
[2] The figure only includes the processes we have discussed; political scientists also study integration, power, influence, decision making in low-conflict situations, and other processes.

the level or levels that are immediately relevant. The levels contiguous to these levels are the ones about which assumptions will be made.

Lest these possible relationships and associations imply a necessary one-to-one patterning between levels, we hasten to say that variations between variables within one level will not necessarily be associated with variations between variables in another level. People with different types of personality (variation) may exhibit similar attitudes and opinions (no variation); in this case, however, we may find that they similarly interact with groups of individuals having consistent attitudes or opinions (no variation). Thus, the absence of expected variation between two levels may be explained through reference to another level. This possibility both introduces uncertainty where we might prefer order and allows us to show that implicit assumptions about the conditions at another level have to be made explicit even when addressing a question 'that appears to involve concepts at the same level. Figure 10–2 illustrates a

FIGURE 10–2
Micro Level Assumptions about Macro Level Relationships

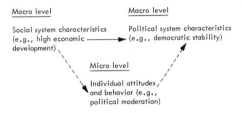

very simplified example of this argument.

Investigations of the preconditions of democratic stability may focus largely on system level characteristics, such as economic development,[3] but a basic assumption is that these characteristics have an impact on individual attitudes and behaviors, which in turn have an impact on the political system. Explanations of individual political behavior (e.g., voting) typically focus on other individual characteristics but make references to environmental conditions. One such generalization is Lipset's argument that we should expect greater working-class participation in a political system that has a rigid class structure than in one that does not have an integrated working-class structure.[4] Both of these examples show that it is not just questions characterized by mixed concepts that involve references to other levels, but questions that link micro to micro and macro to macro concepts that require the consideration of the "setting" at other levels.

---

[3] Seymour M. Lipset, *Political Man: The Social Bases of Politics* (Garden City, N.Y.: Doubleday & Co., 1960), chap. 2.

[4] *Ibid.*, p. 209.

THE PROBLEMS OF LINKAGE

Despite the manifest necessity of linking levels of analysis in tackling significant political questions, the problems associated with linkage can appear to be formidable when taken together. However, we shall separate them here, even though any one question may involve more than one problem.

Frequently, we are tempted to reason about a political problem by saying, "Since I accept a and b as valid empirical statements, I conclude that x is true." If x is a statement about a level different from a and b, we are more apt to be wrong than right in our conclusions. A police chief in a large midwestern city recently was reported as recommending changes in police procedures and expenditures. He based his recommendations on the FBI's annual report of crime statistics, which presented aggregate data on the relationship between race and major crime rates. His reasoning was equivalent to saying, "Since I know the relationship for the United States, I also know it for my city, and therefore I recommend changes in police procedures and expenditures to decrease the major crime rate in my city." In other words, he accepted without question a conclusion about his city derived from a valid statement about another level, the nation. It is in fact not very likely that the relationships for his city will be precisely the same as those for a whole heterogeneous nation. It is even possible that these variables are not related at all or are negatively related for his city.

We would be involved in a similar fallacy of reasoning if we attempted to infer an individual level relationship between literacy and violence, i.e., that illiterates were committing the acts of violence, from a valid macro level statement relating literacy rates and the rate of political violence within a political system (the more literacy, the less violence). Given the frequency of intellectual and middle-class participation in political violence and revolutionary activities, such an inference could be highly misleading with respect to individual political behavior. Relationships or associations discovered at a macro level may suggest hypotheses for testing at another level, but they cannot be accepted as true for that level without testing.

In a case where the accepted statement is a statement about the association or relationship between factors at a micro level, we can also be incorrect in inferring that these statements will hold for a more macro level.[5] Concluding that "In these times of emphasis on urban violence and the need for law and order, many individuals appear to find it easy to forget that the vast majority of Blacks are loyal Americans who see their personal future and the future of their nation and community as

---

[5] This is called the individualistic fallacy, a fallacy of composition.

inseparable" (from research findings gathered to test hypotheses in the city of Buffalo) is an example of this type of reasoning error.[6] Is the relationship between race and support for the American political system and government the same at the national level as in the city of Buffalo? The answer must be that we don't know. The findings in Buffalo suggest a hypothesis for more widespread testing but do not provide a basis for concluding that the relationship will hold for blacks in different political-social-economic groups, blacks with different types of experiences in obtaining what they want from governmental agencies, or blacks in communities and states of different sizes and characteristics.

Both of these fallacies of reasoning alert us to what must be avoided in integrating or linking different levels when predicting and explaining behavior at one level from what is known about other levels. The third problem area is related to these two by way of our recommendation that hypotheses be tested at each level to avoid erroneous conclusions. This problem is that the hypothesis changes (the empirical indicators or the procedures for measuring the concepts change) as the level of analysis changes. In Figure 10–1 the levels are linked by processes such as conflict, socialization, communications, etc. Even though the concept names do not change with the levels, the variables that we define as indicators of these concepts do. We may speak of personality conflict, urban conflict, race conflict, East-West conflict, or international conflict. Personality conflict is typically defined, by questionnaire responses, as involving contradictory traits or drives all of which the individual cannot satisfy; while international conflict is sometimes defined as troop movements, casualty rates, accusations, and sanctions. Although the concept of conflict is used in both cases, its definitions are quite different. There are many examples of this, but ones about overlapping memberships and national character should show what can happen to our hypotheses as we move up and down the levels of analysis.

Studies in American politics indicate that people are expected to withdraw or avoid political participation, particularly voting, when they belong to a number of formal and informal and/or potential groups[7] that give them contradictory or conflicting cues. Such an individual might be Jewish, have parents that have consistently voted for Democratic Party candidates, be a college graduate, and now earn a high income. He has Jewish friends who express consistent and strong preferences for Democratic Party candidates, while his work associates, who are college graduates

---

[6] E. F. Cataldo *et al.*, "Political Attitudes of Urban Blacks and Whites: Some Implications for Policy-Makers" in Jack R. Van Der Slik (ed.), *Black Conflict with White America* (Columbus, Ohio: Charles E. Merrill Publishing Co., 1970), p. 61.

[7] We defined potential groups previously as sets of individuals who share one or more characteristics in common (specifically, attitudes) but are not organized to achieve goals.

and make similarly high incomes, express strong Republican Party preferences. Cross-pressured by conflicting exhortations, he is likely to vacillate
or lose interest in politics. On the other hand, overlapping memberships
in the international system may be defined as the presence of ideological
similarities, economic and military dependencies, and memberships of
nations in different international organizations and alliances. The leaders
of the nations that share such similarities, dependencies, and memberships
with both parties to a conflict are expected at least initially to offer
"good offices" or other aid in resolving the conflict as a means of avoiding
choosing sides. Notice in the American voting example that individuals
are expected to be inconsistent in behavior, lose interest, perhaps not
participate at all when they are cross-pressured by overlapping memberships. On the other hand, the national political leaders are expected to
participate, but participate differently, in a conflict when their overlapping memberships involve both parties to a conflict. Could a theory of
overlapping memberships and cross pressures subsume both of these levels
by including the conditions appropriate to the different levels, or does
the change in concept definition and the corresponding change in hypothesis necessitate a subdivision into two separate theories? Before suggesting an answer to this question, we will describe an example from
the "national character" literature.

A popular proposition in this research area suggests that a congruence
exists between the personalities of individuals and the "fundamental character" of the political system in which they reside. To put it another
way, comparatively, one would expect that democratic political systems
would have more people with democratic personalities and authoritarian
political systems would have more people with authoritarian personality
traits.[8] If we are to treat this as a testable hypothesis, as we indicated
earlier the statement cannot be true by definition. That is, we do not
define a democratic system as one in which there are large numbers of
people with democratic personalities, nor an authoritarian system as one
in which there are large numbers of people with authoritarian personalities. We mean something different when we speak of an authoritarian
or democratic system than an aggregation of personalities in the system—
we would have to or the question would be trivial. But this also means
that we are using the terms "democratic" and "authoritarian" in different
ways when we refer to persons than when we refer to system properties,
and that the hypothesized connection is not a necessary one. In fact,
critics of the "national character" literature have made strong arguments
against the simple assumption of correspondence between personality traits
and political system characteristics.[9] It is logically possible, although we

---

[8] Alex Inkeles, "National Character and Modern Political Systems" in Nelson
Polsby *et al., Politics and Social Life* (Boston: Houghton Mifflin, 1963), pp. 172–92.

[9] R. Bendix, "Compliant Behavior and Individual Personality," *American Journal
of Sociology,* Vol. 58 (1952), pp. 292–303.

do not think it likely, that there is complete independence between personality characteristics and political system characteristics, as would·be the case if personality types were regularly and normally distributed in all systems.

Again, it is possible to see that although the terms remain the same, the concept definitions, the operational definitions, and the hypotheses change. We then come back to our previous question: Is it possible to subsume multiple levels under the same theory? This is not a trivial question nor a question of concern only to political scientists, for the answer that one gives will determine the applicability of what is known or theorized at one level to other levels. The answer we suggest is yes. Since theory is empirically testable theory only when some of the concepts are defined by their empirical indicators or variables and the procedures necessary for measuring them and these are linked in hypotheses, the concepts have no "stand-alone" true meaning. Therefore, the theory can subsume more than one level by specifying the levels to be included and the concepts' empirical indicators appropriate to the different levels.[10] If conditions vary from level to level, the theory would also include the concepts and assumptions linked to each level included.

In the latter case, the level specific concepts added to the theory may not be simply additive aggregations (lower level concepts combined by adding them) of the values of the micro units, as when we aggregate individual personality characteristics in the definition of modal personality. It may be appropriate sometimes to assign differential weights to the individual or micro units or to combine them using a rule of multiplication. For example,

. . . American nomination politics is organized in such a way that the views of active partisans have greater weight than the views of independents in the selection of the presidential nominee. Hence, one would commit the individualistic fallacy if he predicted the identity of the nominee on the basis of individual attitudes among the general population without giving due weight to the particular persons who are likely to be convention delegates.[11]

It is also possible that the same concepts are not relevant to all levels subsumed by the theory. The type of political party system may make a difference in our hypothesized expectations about the development of domestic conflicts, but we may not be able to show that international

---

[10] It is important to remember that independence is not maintained when one variable in a hypothesis is related to a second macro variable that aggregates the first micro variable with other micro variables. The hypothesis that gross national product will vary with the rate of change in gross national product is an example of failing to maintain independence.

[11] John H. Kessel et al., "Introduction" in John H. Kessel et al., *Micropolitics* (New York: Holt, Rinehart and Winston, Inc., 1970), p. 11. Used by permission.

conflict varies with the types of party systems characterizing all nations or even the nations directly involved in the conflict.

Sometimes we will want to add concepts whose empirical indicators are not observable on the more micro levels subsumed by our theory. This gets us into a long-standing argument in philosophy and the social sciences. Can concepts "emerge" at a more macro level, the components of which are not present on the micro level?[12] Cohesion is usually offered as an example by those taking an affirmative position. Does it make sense to talk about cohesion outside of a group context? And in the group context is cohesion defined as an aggregation of individual level characteristics or behaviors? And what about relational concepts, e.g., subordination and superordination? If we say that a political party is more powerful than the government because it has more men and arms in its paramilitary force than the government has in the military, we are using a relational concept—more powerful than—to link two objects generally defined as being at different levels of analysis. It seems to us that this is a special case of the general question of whether several levels can be linked within the same theory. Since we define emergent properties to be emergent concepts, our answer to the general question dictates our answer to this particular question. Not all concepts, whether they are aggregates of micro concepts or emergent concepts, will be relevant to all the levels on which a question can be stated or to all levels subsumed by a theory.

LINKING CONCEPTS AND GENERALIZATIONS IN POLITICAL SCIENCE

We are interested in generalizations which will link macro level concepts to micro level concepts. Figure 10–3 diagrams some of the logically possible ways. The direction of the relationship chosen will depend upon the question asked. We have chosen problems in urban, legislative, and comparative-international politics, which take up examples we have discussed in earlier chapters, as vehicles for identifying and exploring some linkage concepts and generalizations integrating various levels of political science.

---

[12] We are not discussing here the question of whether properties emerge in a group or political system which cannot be defined in terms of individual behaviors and are, therefore, left undefined (e.g., the state as something more than the sum of its parts), because we take the position that we cannot talk about anything left undefined. Rather we are talking about concepts whose defined indicators can be observed at one level but not at another level. For contrasting discussions of the question we are dealing with here, see May Brodbeck, "Methodological Individualisms: Definition and Reduction," in May Brodbeck (ed.), *Readings in the Philosophy of the Social Sciences* (New York: Macmillan Co., 1968), pp. 280–303; and Robert Dubin, *Theory Building* (New York: Free Press, 1969), pp. 122–25.

FIGURE 10–3
Micro-Macro Linkages

micro—macro
macro—micro

micro-micro ⟷	micro-macro; macro-micro; macro-macro
micro-macro ⟷	micro-micro; micro-macro; macro-micro; macro-macro
macro-micro ⟷	micro-micro; micro-macro; macro-micro; macro-macro
macro-macro ⟷	micro-micro; micro-macro; macro-micro

Linkages in urban politics

One of the major contemporary concerns in urban politics is the question of where people in the cities are going to get "proper" financing to meet the demands for services associated with increasing urbanization. Increasing urbanization is found all over the world, from Tokyo, Calcutta, Paris, and London to Los Angeles. The legal status of cities with regard to the amount of autonomy in decision making and revenue raising powers varies with the type of political system—unitary, mixed, or federal. In the United States, the different state legislatures have set down the requirements for the incorporation and functioning of cities within their boundaries.

National population increases and technological and industrial development have increased the number of urban areas.[13] One can look at the city as offering one type of opportunity structure to its residents. This opportunity structure—sanctions and rewards given to individuals by others for different types of behavior—is thought to differ from that found in rural areas, small towns, or other less urbanized areas. Among other things, cities may provide a greater choice of cultural, economic, and social opportunities than do other political units. Some have argued, however, that the family and church have declined as socializing agencies as urbanization has increased in the cities. Increasing size, decreasing distance, and a shift from the individual's reliance on his primary group (extended family and friends) to a reliance on secondary groups have been associated with changes in individual behavior, e.g., alienation and ethnicity,[14] and with increased demands on the cities' political leaders to obtain funds from other sources—particularly the state and federal governments—to meet these demands.

Urban political leaders argued for reapportionment and one-man, one-

---

[13] Urban areas are often defined as geographical units characterized by a population density equal to or greater than 150 people per square mile, high levels of industrialization, and specialization of tasks.

[14] The failure of different ethnic groups to melt into the American pot in the cities has been seen as a set of individualized responses aimed at protecting the primary group and culture against depersonalized larger political and social units. We wish to thank John Baker for calling our attention to some of these factors.

vote court decisions; because state legislatures and Congress had more representatives from the rural areas, who were believed to be unsympathetic to the demands of the cities. With the Supreme Court decisions, more representatives perceiving themselves as dependent upon urban constituencies for reelection and therefore willing to act on behalf of the urban areas were expected to be elected to the legislatures. Once elected, the funds were expected to increase. Increasing at the same time, however, were demands for national military expenditures, roads, education, and medical care. Appropriations priorities of the state and national executives and legislators changed. Although funds from these other sources increased, urbanization did, too, along with demands and burdens on urban resources. Increasing urbanization now may be changing individual behavior further. An increasing concern with law and order may be another characteristic of individuals who are looking to secondary groups and agencies (e.g., the schools and police) to socialize their children and others as well as punish them when they break the rules.

These hypothesized linkages are shown in Figure 10–4. These are divided into individual, urban, state, and international concepts. It is a simplified sketch, since it omits individual variations in learning, socialization, and participation. It does, however, include perception. Perception is a linkage concept in that it joins "what is happening out there" to

FIGURE 10–4
Some Urban Politics Linkages

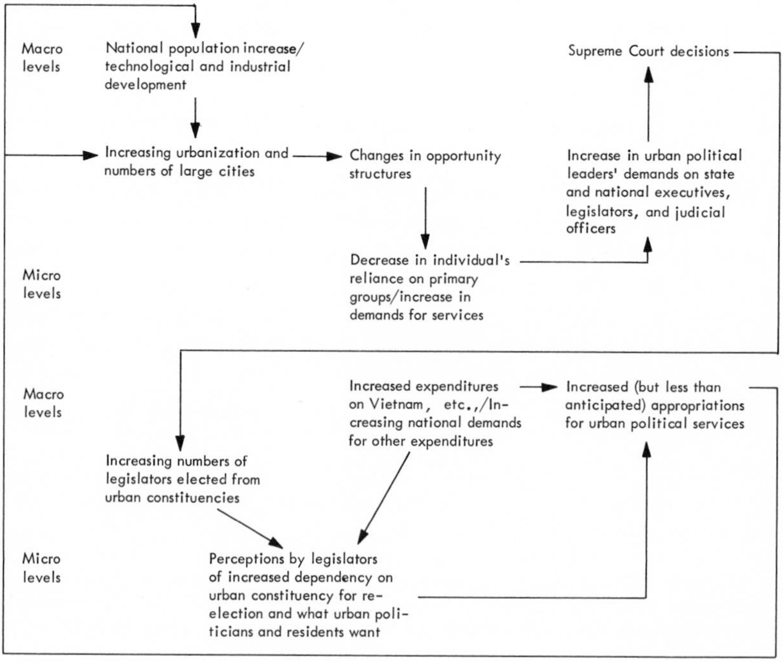

the individual. Perception refers to the individual's conscious, but perhaps erroneous, characterization of his environment, the source of demands, supports, rewards, and costs. Perception then links changes in urban areas to the legislator's voting behavior, which, when all legislators' votes are aggregated by majority rule, is linked to a national policy outcome.

Linkages in legislative politics

Role and political culture are often used as linkage concepts when someone is interested in legislative behavior. We can begin with the deceptively simple question: Why do legislators vote as they do? Some legislators appear to vote as an opinion poll might tell them their constituencies' voters would choose; others may vote more regularly with their party leadership, particularly if their party is in power. Some may trade their votes on some issues in return for others' voting to support their favored policy positions on future votes (logrolling). Still others seem to step to drummers of special interest groups, ideology, or ambitions for higher political office. Many do different things at different times. How do we begin to identify the sources of these variations? Figure 10–5 suggests the beginnings of an answer.

FIGURE 10–5
Linkages in Legislative Politics

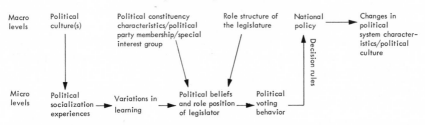

The individual—taking into account variations in capacity, motivation, opportunity, and reinforcement—learns about what he ought to believe and how he ought to behave in various circumstances from informal and formal agents of socialization. Socialization, therefore, links the individual to political culture. If the legislature has been around a while, the person also learns how individuals have behaved in their legislative roles and how others have reacted to their behavior (criticism or reelection). In other words, the legislative position has attached to it the beliefs of the legislator about how he ought to behave, his perceptions of how others believe that he ought to behave, and how in fact others believe that legislators ought to behave. Role, then, combines the micro beliefs and perceptions of the individual role occupant with the beliefs and

expectations of others about the people in the role position. A role structure combines a set of such positions.[15]

The legislator can also learn on the job; that is, new information from
other legislators, political officials, citizens, or events may lead him to
change his beliefs or perceptions, particularly if he wants to be reelected.
The decision rules (e.g., the procedures routing bills in the legislature
before voting on the floor, majority rule, and the President's signature)
aggregate individual voting behavior into national policy. The national
policy, if it is a change from previous policy, will change the distribution
of resources—money, position, and opportunity—to the general population. When combined with higher weights attached to more powerful
individuals, individual responses to this may produce uneven change
in the political culture and the political system.

Linkages in intra—interconflict processes

Political culture, role, perception, and reference group are important
linkage concepts in conflict, which itself is a linkage concept. As we
indicated in Chapter 8, several types of conflict patterns may characterize
a political system at any level. The one that we will consider here is
a cleavage conflict pattern; there have been several conflict issues that
have repeatedly divided the attentive population in this way. Such would
be the case in the United States if, for example, Vietnam, race, poverty,
and law and order issues made allies and enemies out of the same people.
In this hypothetical example we might have primarily white, pro-Vietnam, pro–law and order, rugged individualist leaders of one faction and
primarily black, anti-Vietnam, anti–law and order, and antipoverty leaders
of another faction.

The primarily black, anti-Vietnam, antipoverty, and anti–law and
order faction is formed of people who feel that the distribution of costs
and rewards in the political system repeatedly gives them more costs
than rewards compared to people who are white, pro-Vietnam, pro–law
and order and rugged individualists but who have similar formal status
and skills. The disproportionate rewards to the one group cannot be
justified by the other group on the basis of criteria acceptable to them.
On the individual level this means that blacks leading or supporting
change compare themselves with reference groups—whites they went
to school with, work with, observe or hear about from the communications media. This "unfair exchange" leads certain individuals to form
an opposition group.[16]

---

[15] John Wahlke *et al., The Legislative System* (New York: John Wiley & Sons,
1962).

[16] This is basically the process described in abstract terms by Peter Blau, *Exchange
and Power in Social Life* (New York: John Wiley & Sons, 1964), pp. 224–52.

Provided that there are no formal or informal constraints on participation, each set of leaders and supporters would be expected to place conflict demands on groups, parties, legislatures, executives, judges, and nongovernmental groups. We might find that each of these groups did not have equal access to all governmental and nongovernmental agencies and groups. The composition of some groups and governmental agencies might make the members more receptive to the demands of one group than another group. For example, a part-black and part-white legislature might mean that the legislators would bring the conflict into the legislature, while an all-white judiciary would be perceived by the blacks as making more decisions favoring the all-white faction.

Assuming that race determines receptiveness and that the ratio of blacks to whites in the general population and governmental agencies was favorable to the whites, the black have-nots would have little chance of getting their policy choices selected as governmental choices. Depending upon personality predisposition, the possession of skills, and the effective limits on alternative behaviors, the black political leaders might withdraw from the contest, choose what are considered by the majority to be nonlegitimate kinds of behavior, or seek another political arena perceived as being more receptive to their demands.

Pursuing the latter possibility, we have primarily black have-nots looking for another arena where their supporters might influence the white political leaders to choose more of their policy choices. The international arena, specifically the United Nations, might be considered. What would be the characteristics of the international system that would make it attractive to the temporary losers? A responsive international system might be one with a cleavage pattern dividing the leaders of two strong nations, one of which is supported by the leaders of other nations with predominantly nonwhite populations.[17]

The blacks go to the United Nations to argue that the United Nations should intervene in the racist domestic situation. The leaders of the U.S. white faction argue that the issue is a domestic issue not within the proper jurisdiction of the United Nations.[18] Given the beliefs and characteristics of the U.N. delegates, a large number are inclined to support the black have-nots, while the U.S. white faction attracts delegates from Western European nations to its position. The leaders of the other strong nation decide to direct the cause of the losing U.S. faction. Such behavior is expected to embarrass the United States while improving the strong nation's relations with the leaders of the nonwhite have-not nations.

---

[17] This type of international system is called a bi-polar system. We cannot conclude that an international conflict cleavage pattern implies national cleavage patterns or we would be guilty of a reasoning error, the ecological fallacy.

[18] The procedural question of jurisdiction requires a two-thirds vote before a substantive issue can be considered by the United Nations delegates.

The white have-nots, the delegates representing political leaders of Latin American nations, are pulled both ways. However, the delegates are instructed by their political leaders to vote with the U.S. delegates, because they are members of alliances with the United States and are dependent upon white U.S. leaders for military and economic aid. This determines the outcome; the U.S. black have-nots fail to obtain a two-thirds vote allowing the United Nations to deal with the substantive issue.

Depending upon the number of alternative arenas available and the psychological effects of failure, the black leaders might withdraw to await change in presently available arenas or the identification of new arenas, or they might choose other behaviors. If the conflict continued and was given international publicity, it might lead to conflicts between the United States and its supporters, thereby contributing to changes in international behavior and the international system.

In this hypothetical example, we can see how the perception by individuals of the structure and characteristics of different political systems is linked to the choices of arena they might make. Political culture is also linked, via socialization, to the choices, for it defines for both sets of political leaders and supporters the alternative behaviors and plays some part in their assignment of preferences to the identified alternatives. Role structures of the various nations are relevant insofar as they limit the voting choices of the delegates to the United Nations by making them disregard their own individual voting preferences when they are so instructed by the leaders of their own nations. Reference group is also an important linkage concept in this example. It is defined as the group of individuals with which a person compares "how well he is doing."[19] If he can discover no differences that he accepts as justifying their being better off (however that is defined) than he is and given the opportunity to participate, the reference group will be the spur to his political participation.[20]

This example, like the others, shows how certain concepts—role, perception, political culture, reference group; and the process concepts: conflict, socialization, exchange, integration, etc.—link the individual to a variety of groups, systems, and settings. The statements that connect these concepts to micro and macro concepts also point to the development of hypothesized cross-level generalizations and, we believe, make clear the reasons for avoiding the inflexible compartmentalization of questions into subjects such as state, national, or international politics.

---

[19] For examples of applications of reference group theory, see Herbert H. Hyman and Eleanor Singer, (eds.), *Readings in Reference Group Theory and Research* (New York: Free Press, 1968).

[20] On the other hand, a comparison that leads him to perceive that he is doing better than most of the people he perceives as similar to himself is apt to mean a continuation of his previous behavior pattern.

SUMMARY AND CONCLUSIONS

Clearly, we have taken controversial positions in this chapter: (1) it is permissible to link concepts defined at different levels via cross-level generalizations; (2) to the extent possible, one should look to contiguous levels for possible variations that one should assume will affect the relations between concepts defined at the same level and between concepts defined at different levels; (3) empirically testable theories may subsume many levels and conditions while keeping the abstract concept definitions constant; (4) the relationships between concepts operationally defined differently at different levels will not necessarily be consistent, and (5) each level(s) must be treated as a different situation necessitating the testing of hypotheses. With care, however, we can develop a better predictive and/or explanatory capacity by considering these additional complexities.

It may appear that this chapter (as, perhaps, the previous two) has suggested more substantive questions than answers about why people behave as they do politically and how their behavior may determine why and how the organization of political systems will change drastically or minimally. Like everyone else, we prefer answers to questions, but present knowledge in political science gives us only bits and pieces of answers. To pretend otherwise would not only be dishonest, but it would veil one of the most attractive aspects of studying political science—its challenge.

chapter

11

Political science and public
policy analysis

Political scientists, in the company of many social scientists, have become increasingly sensitive to the charge that their discipline is irrelevant for the urgent problems of the day.[1] Probably a number of things are meant by this charge; among them would be the following: (1) that there has been an overemphasis on theoretical questions as opposed to practical (or applied) questions,[2] (2) that the emphasis on science and quantification has directed the attention of political scientists toward trivial rather than major questions, and (3) that the stance of value neutrality of social science is false—that social scientists are in fact committed to values and, too often, the value commitments have been to the status quo.

It is not our purpose in this chapter to refute or support the assertions about what the impact of the so-called "behavioral revolution" in political science on the study of socially significant questions has been. Clearly, some topics of relevance and urgency are being addressed systematically by political scientists.[3] The argument which we wish to advance in this concluding chapter is simply this: the approach to the study of politics outlined in the foregoing chapters is compatible with, and indeed necessary for, the application of the knowledge of politics to the analysis of public policy alternatives.

---

[1] See, for example, the presidential address to the American Political Science Association by David Easton, "The New Revolution in Political Science," *American Political Science Review*, Vol. 63 (December 1969), pp. 1051–61.

[2] The dichotomy between practice and theory has been responsible for a great deal of confusion. Empirically testable theory is directly related to the real world and, thus, to the world of practical problems.

[3] For example, the growing literature on the political alienation of American blacks. One example is Joel D. Aberbach and Jack L. Walker, "Political Trust and Racial Ideology," *American Political Science Review*, Vol. 64 (December 1970), pp. 1199–1219.

First, a set of comments must be made about what we are not asserting here. We are not asserting that political science alone can tell us what policy alternatives to prefer. We are not asserting that political science will provide certain, final solutions to urgent questions. We are not asserting that political scientists will agree on what is to be done in any given circumstance. Nor are we asserting that for any given problem, there is a body of available political science knowledge and techniques for the solution of that problem. What we are claiming is that applied political science, the application of the knowledge and techniques of the study of politics to public policy questions, is intimately connected to and flows directly from the characteristics of a systematic study of politics; in this sense, the sharp division between pure and applied science is false.[4]

To buttress this argument, this chapter will undertake the following tasks: (1) to show how the general problem-solving model which we introduced in Chapter 4 is relevant for public policy analysis; (2) to show why it is that public policy analysis requires the use of such problem-solving techniques, and (3) to illustrate with specific examples the uses and limitations of such problem-solving techniques for contemporary public policy questions.

In his introductory remarks in a book entitled *An Introduction to Social Research*, the sociologist Hubert M. Blalock, Jr., notes the following:

After the disastrous riots of the summer of 1967, President Johnson appointed a commission to conduct a crash study of the causes of these riots and to make policy recommendations of major importance. In the aftermath of the Martin Luther King and Robert Kennedy assassinations he appointed a second blue-ribbon commission to study the causes of assassinations. These important groups contained a majority of politicians representing both parties, plus a few black leaders, clergymen, and labor representatives. But interestingly enough, no social scientists were named, in spite of the fact that there are hundreds of social scientists who have devoted their careers to careful, objective studies of social problems.[5]

There are, of course, many ways to interpret this. It could be the considered judgment of decision makers that social science is irrelevant for the making of public policy recommendations concerning the important questions that these commissions were asked to study. It is our contention that *in fact* the findings and methods of the social sciences are not irrele-

---

[4] To be sure, there may be constraints (see pp. 279–81) in the applied situation which do not apply in the pure situation. All we are arguing here is that the decision-making model regarding matters of fact is the same in basic outline.

[5] Hubert M. Blalock, *An Introduction to Social Research* (Englewood Cliffs, N.J.: Prentice-Hall, 1970), p. 3. This is not to say that the commissions did not use social science and social scientists in their work; however, the noninclusion at the commission level is symbolic of the relatively low status of social science.

vant, but that this fact has not been well communicated to decision makers and to the public at large. Thus, we argue that the problem-solving orientation of the social or political scientist is critical for attacking policy problems. It follows, then, that theory and findings are equally important for these questions.

In Chapter 4, we outlined and discussed a general, scientific, problem-solving model in the context of "academic questions." The steps in this model may be summarized as follows:

1. Statement of the general problem.
2. Formulation of hypotheses relating to the problem.
3. Defining the concepts which appear in these hypotheses.
4. Operationalization of the hypotheses: making the hypotheses disconfirmable, falsifiable.
5. Designing research to collect data relative to the hypotheses.
6. Collecting the data.
7. Analyzing the data.
8. Interpreting the data.

And now we add:

9. Applying the findings and interpretations to public policy problems.

One may well inquire: why is this orientation necessarily better than a political problem-solving model which relies on other, less systematic, procedures? If our general argument in this chapter is sound, we must confront this question directly.

To start, we ask: What are the purposes of the scientific problem-solving technique? Surely, one purpose is to arrive at information (data, generalizations) which is less dependent upon the way we want things to be than on the way things are. One purpose, then, is to reduce the amount of subjectivity in the conclusions which we reach.[6] Less systematic methods of problem solving are subject to biases resulting from our preferences for the way things ought to be or from sometimes unconscious manipulation of the evidence to give a distorted impression of reality. Again, this is not to claim total objectivity for the social sciences. It is to claim that the scientific problem-solving technique is a check on the influence of subjective factors by making subjective decisions and their consequences explicit.

Second, the scientific problem-solving technique is desirable precisely because the explanation of human phenomena is complex. Common sense

---

[6] The word "reduce" is deliberately chosen to indicate that the subjective element is probably never removed.

or intuitive "truths" about human behavior often turn out to be incorrect under examination. Scientific problem solving is a good way to try to manage the understanding of a complex problem—and the method also alerts us to the limitations on our ability to deal with such problems. An example may help to illustrate this point. In the study of political phenomena, we frequently sense that multiple factors are at work in producing certain consequences, but we simply do not know how to go about untangling the influence of one factor from another. Thus, we may feel that issues, parties, and candidates all have something to do with the way voters ultimately vote. But two questions immediately arise which cannot be answered by mere speculation:

1. How important are the various factors?
2. Are these factors interrelated, and which factor or factors influence the other or others?

Use of the techniques of systematic inquiry and evaluation may help to untangle such relationships.

Or, take another example. Words are frequently used to describe individuals and groups in the population with the implicit (if not explicit) implication that the words describe things which have political consequences. Among such words are "alienation," "racism," "establishment," and many others. As long as the concepts suggested by these words are not defined precisely and as long as no attempt is made to measure (at least, in some rough sense) the frequency with which such stereotypes conform to actual attitudes or behaviors, the policy suggestions which flow from the assumption that such words describe attitudes and behaviors with significant political implications might be completely off the mark. Moreover, as long as concepts are imprecise, there is no way to refute statements which contain such concepts. Thus, definition and measurement are key aspects of the problem-solving method.

Later in this chapter, we will illustrate the use of problem-solving techniques in the study of a public policy problem. Before we do that, however, it is appropriate to review and elaborate some points made in the first chapter of this book. A skeptic may well ask: What good are the theories and findings of the social sciences to policy makers? The skeptic may have in mind the following objection: the theory and findings of social or political science are not directly translatable into decisions about public policy, because the real world is much more complex and unpredictable than the world in which the social scientist operates. "It sounds good in theory, but will it work in practice?" In a (methodologically) more sophisticated way, critics may question the reliability and validity of the findings and recommendations of a social science of collective events for a specific, single policy decision.

We do not deny that there are problems with applying theory and findings of the social sciences to particular problems. We do assert, however, that the accumulation of reliable and valid findings is an important condition for rational decision making in public policy terms, and that the orientations and methods we discussed above are more likely than other (more haphazard) techniques to achieve reliable and valid findings. However, there is no assurance that we will find what we are looking for, and there is the real possibility that "you [and we] may not like the answers that you get. . . ."[7]

In order to substantiate our assertion that the theory and findings of political science are potentially important requisites for decisions regarding public policy, let us examine the components of a public policy decision. Ideally, those components would seem to be:

1. A definition of a problem and a description of the problem.
2. A set of alternative solutions to the problem.
3. A set of predictions about the probable consequences of the various alternatives (i.e., whether they would solve the problem).
4. The selection of the alternative which resolves the problem in the most satisfactory manner.

Unfortunately, this set of components is an oversimplification of the reality of the policy-making process in that "it fails to evoke or suggest the distinctively political aspects of policy making, its apparent disorder, and the consequent strikingly different ways in which policies emerge."[8] Nevertheless, the listing of these ideal components allows us to point out the relevance of political science for policy making.

In the first chapter of this book, we asserted that political scientists engaged in the following activities: description, analysis, and evaluation. We further asserted that the recommendation of policy alternatives was predicated on these three things that political scientists do. Most importantly, the specific facts and generalizations which political scientists discover form the basis for policy recommendation. Specific facts and generalizations aid us in describing problems and selecting among alternatives. For example, the choice of one alternative over another is based on the *prediction* that that alternative is more likely to lead to the desired consequence than the other alternative. As we discussed earlier, this prediction undoubtedly will be based on a generalization of the form: if A, then B. But how do we know that "if A, then B" is true? Although we never know certainly that the statement is true, we will have more confidence if we have examined the validity of the statement using the procedures

---

[7] Blalock, *op. cit.*, p. 5.

[8] Charles E. Lindblom, *The Policy-Making Process* (Englewood Cliffs, N.J.: Prentice-Hall, 1968), p. 4.

of the scientific problem-solving method and if the statement is in accord with our theoretical expectations.[9]

Of course, as we mentioned a moment ago, the components of the policy-making process as we have described them are idealized. We should mention several of the realities which intrude on the process to make the *simple* translation of social scientific findings into public policy an impossibility.[10] At the same time, these difficulties seem to us to argue even more strongly for the use of scientific problem-solving techniques wherever applicable in public policy making.

First of all, there is the problem of the complexity of social and political issues. There are very few problems of social significance where the relationships involved are simple and easy to untangle. In most instances, social and political scientists will probably disagree on what to do, even if they agree on what the facts are. Consider for a moment the question of whether the government should ban the advertising of cigarettes from television, because smoking is harmful to health.[11] In this area, experts have disagreed on what the facts are (whether there is an association between smoking and cancer), how to interpret the facts (whether smoking "causes" cancer), and what to do about it if smoking is harmful to our health.[12] A policy recommendation to ban cigarette advertising might be based on the prediction that to do so would reduce the incidence of smoking in the population at large. At this juncture, a social scientist might have a contribution to make, particularly someone interested in the effects of the mass media on behavior. The more general point is that the status of theories, findings, and interpretations in a wide variety of substantive areas may affect the choices which policy makers perceive as viable.

Second, a policy maker operates in a real world in which there are limitations on information and time. The scientist may say, "It will take 10 years and $10 million to answer the question that you ask me"; the policy maker may have to reply, "But I need to do something now!" To suggest that policy making must wait until all the facts are in is to suggest that policy making cease. As Lindblom notes: ". . . for complex policy problems, analysis can never be finished; it will always there-

---

[9] And, of course, if the weight of the evidence supports the generalization. An additional complication is, as we noted in the first chapter, that social science generalizations are likely to be probabilistic. Thus, the decision maker faces a situation in which he must decide, not on the basis of certainty but of uncertainty.

[10] These comments roughly parallel those of Lindblom, *op. cit.*, chap. 3.

[11] Note that this problem is not even a social scientific one exclusively, because some of the evidence is in the realm of the biological sciences.

[12] For a discussion of the disagreements which have raged over the relationship of smoking to lung cancer, see Jerome Cornfield *et al.*, "Smoking and Lung Cancer: Recent Evidence and a Discussion of Some Questions," in Edward R. Tufte (ed.), *The Quantitative Analysis of Social Problems* (Reading, Mass.: Addison-Wesley, 1970), pp. 68–96.

fore fail to prove that the right policy has been found and will always be subject to challenge."[13] Thus, the relationship between political science and policy making must be seen as ongoing and two-way, rather than temporary and one-way. The "ideal" solution for a policy problem is one which is unlikely to be available and, if available (for reasons we will discuss below), likely to be impractical.

Third, the policy-making process inevitably involves questions of values as well as questions of fact. In this connection, we have previously noted that political scientists as scientists cannot decide value questions: value statements cannot be, in our view, refuted by reference to the way things are. Moreover, in any concrete policy situation, conflicting values are likely to be at issue. Whatever solution is desirable from the point of view of one value may turn out to be undesirable from the point of view of another. For example, if we decide to place stringent controls on industrial pollution (and thus maximize the value of a clean environment), we may, at the same time, raise the level of unemployment (harming the value of full employment). It is probable that the rewards and costs of any social policy are differentially paid by different sectors of the population. Given that we cannot prove the rightness of our values and given that values will often be in conflict in situations where there may be real difficulty in deciding which values should predominate, we may anticipate that "some values have to be sacrificed to achieve others. . . ."[14]

This brings us squarely to the next complication. If scientists cannot decide which values are right, or which values ought to be sacrificed in given circumstances, who does decide? Our answer is that these decisions are political decisions, and therefore political criteria also count heavily in the making of public policy decisions. In a democratic system, this means simply that the decisions resolving value conflicts must somehow be in accord with an acceptable decision-making rule, e.g., majority rule.[15] We may disagree with the majority and think that the decision is irrational, immoral, unscientific, or contrary to the best interests of the majority; but if we are committed to a democratic decision-making system, we must accept the consequences of decisions made by the majority with whom we may disagree.[16] This last complication means that public policy analysis takes the value question as given, and then seeks to find the most desirable (efficient, socially acceptable) way of achieving

---

[13] Lindblom, *op. cit.*, p. 14.

[14] *Ibid.*, p. 17.

[15] We do not pause here to list all of the many qualifications which have to be attached to such a statement as this. Suffice it to say here that we agree with Robert Dahl's analysis of the operation of the majority principle, which he presents in *A Preface to Democratic Theory* (Chicago: University of Chicago Press, 1956), chap. 5.

[16] In fact, when many citizens decide that they cannot accept such decisions, democratic systems are in for trouble.

the objective. The political decision, however, may severely constrain the limits within which the policy analyst can function. He may, for example, be told to "solve" the water pollution problem but not given the financial resources or the clout necessary to do so.

Finally, what does the policy analyst do when his values conflict with those of the political system?[17] What if the ends political decision makers have specified are regarded by the policy scientist as irrational or even immoral? There are even more subtle problems. What if the policy scientist does not know the ends to which his research is directed? To what extent should policy analysts be involved in promoting the foreign policy objectives of their government in terms of intervention in the affairs of other nations?[18] There are no ready answers to these questions.

All of the foregoing points lead to the conclusion that the application of political science to public policy problems is a difficult and complex task. Even if a science of politics were realized, this would be true; given the fact that the state of reliable and valid theory and generalizations in the discipline is not what we would like, we must recognize that it is utopian to expect policy analysis to provide "the answers" to our pressing social problems.

Nevertheless, it is our contention that the systematic approach to the study of politics has much to offer those confronting problems in policy formulation.[19] Foremost among the contributions is the critical analysis of alternatives which are available: (1) What is the impact of current policy? (2) Will the suggested alternative lead to the desired result? (3) What other consequences follow from the selection of the alternative? To illustrate this approach to policy making and analysis, we will now turn to a policy-related example concerning suggested structural changes in the U.S. Congress which are expected to yield substantive policy changes.

Public policy analysis: An illustration

One area of public policy analysis which is particularly appropriate for scrutiny by political scientists is that of *political reform*. The example is drawn from this area. Political reforms are often suggestions for changes in the institutional structure which derive from the following analysis: institution X exists in a particular form and has certain undesirable consequences, Y. Therefore, we change (manipulate) X in order to change

---

[17] This is, of course, a more general problem for the so-called pure scientist, who also must be aware that his work can be used for either "good" or "bad" ends.

[18] See, for example, Irving Louis Horowitz, *The Rise and Fall of Project Camelot* (Cambridge, Mass.: M.I.T. Press, 1967).

[19] And no one has discovered another method for dealing with policy problems and questions that promises greater reliability and validity than the method we are outlining in this chapter!

Y. Put in this form, it is easy to see that a political reform is both a prediction and (when put into effect) a natural experiment. Often, although not always, what is ultimately expected to change is some aspect of public policy output. Thus, advocates of more equitable apportionment were not only concerned with equality (one-man, one-vote) in the abstract but also with the public policy consequences of having urban districts more heavily represented in legislative bodies.

Now if a political reform is in the nature of a prediction, and when put into effect a natural experiment, then we can subject reforms to critical scrutiny both before and after they are adopted. We are going to focus here on the former, although the latter is equally interesting. How can we examine the predicted impact of reform? In short, two major questions emerge: (1) Will the reform produce the intended objectives? and (2) What other, perhaps costly, consequences will the proposed change have?

To answer the two questions cited above, we must engage in systematic inquiry. In the study of political reform, we suggest the following general paradigm for analysis:

1. We inquire as to the objectives of the reform: What exactly is it intended to accomplish?
2. We examine the basic assumptions which underlie the objectives. For example, are certain values assumed, are certain descriptive statements assumed, are certain causal statements assumed?
3. We inquire into the logical consistency of the argument which is advanced. For example, are the objectives compatible in a strictly logical sense?
4. We examine the validity of the assumptions which can be examined empirically.
5. We estimate the probability that the cited objectives will in fact be achieved by the reform (will or does a change in X usually lead to a change in Y?).
6. We try to determine what other consequences the reform will have (will a change in X lead to Z?).
7. We try to estimate the feasibility of the proposal in terms of the probability of its being adopted.[20]

These, then, constitute the steps in making a critical analysis of recommended changes. The reader should recognize that to carry out these steps, we would have to engage in the systematic techniques discussed earlier and throughout this book.

---

[20] There may be some who would argue that feasibility is not relevant here; our point is that even if the reform would accomplish its objectives, if there is no chance of getting the change made we would be better off expending our efforts in other directions.

Let us now turn to a specific illustration: the problem of the seniority system in Congress.[21] The seniority system is a method of selecting the chairmen and ranking minority members of the committees of the United States Congress. The selection is based on the seniority rule, with length of service on the committee as the criterion of seniority. Obviously, such a system places a premium on longevity in the Congress in general, and on the committee in particular, as a method of leadership selection.

We may safely infer that critics of the seniority system ultimately hope that by reforming the system there will be a change in the product, the policy outputs, of the Congress. And, in particular, we may suppose that those critics by and large would like to see Congress move in a more liberal direction in terms of policy outputs.[22]

What assumptions do the reformers make? The following observation suggests some of the empirical assumptions made by critics of the seniority system:

By stipulating long congressional service the seniority system benefits certain one-party areas of the nation at the expense of others, overrepresenting in the committee chairs rural and conservative interests: Democrats from the South and Republicans from the rural Midwest and the Northeast. It obstructs party cohesion in Congress by creating independent power centers, a cadre of chairmen not responsible to party leaders since those leaders do not control their selection.[23]

The argument may be phrased as follows:

Descriptive assumption 1: The seniority system disproportionately rewards one-party areas.

Descriptive assumption 2: One-party areas are more likely to elect conservative legislators than competitive areas.

Therefore, descriptive conclusion 1: Committee leaders are likely to be more conservative than the other members of the Congress.

And:

Causal assumption 1: The fact that committee leaders are not chosen by the party leadership causes them to be less supportive of their party when voting on policy questions. This implies:

Descriptive conclusion 2: Committee chairmen are less supportive of their party than other party members.

[21] Much of what follows is dependent on the fine analysis of Barbara Hinckley, *The Seniority System in Congress* (Bloomington: Indiana University Press, 1971). Also see George Goodwin, "The Seniority System in Congress," *American Political Science Review*, Vol. 53 (June 1959), 412–17.

[22] Many, if not most, of the critics are liberals. See, for example, Joseph Clark, *Congress: The Sapless Branch* (New York: Harper & Row, 1964).

[23] Hinckley, *op. cit.*, p. 3.

Causal conclusion 1 (giant causal conclusion!): If the seniority system were changed, there would be more party cohesion on the part of the committee chairmen and more liberal legislation produced by the Congress.[24]

Of course, causal conclusion 1 is the ultimate payoff for the reformers, but it is important to realize the extent to which that contingency is tied to the other assumptions and conclusions.

In this instance, given the empirical validity of the assumptions, the logic of the argument seems sound.[25] Therefore, it would seem necessary to turn to the problem of converting the assumptions into empirical questions. The first one concerns the seniority system and one-party areas. However, when we examine this hypothesis, the most striking initial finding is the extent to which the members of Congress as a whole, not just committee chairmen, are elected from noncompetitive districts. As Hinckley documents:

The congressional seniority requirement presupposed by the seniority system does not appear sufficiently restrictive to screen out of the selection process more than a fairly small minority of states and districts. Thus the traditional argument that the system benefits only the safest states and districts may have to be reversed to read that the system penalizes only the most competitive—a reversal in emphasis of considerable importance.[26]

What this means is that the seniority system is not one which is significantly biased compared to the representation of the rest of Congress.

This same point can be illustrated by looking at the assumption of regional overrepresentation. Again, Hinckley summarizes the findings:

Much of the 'overrepresentation' cited in criticisms of the seniority system is not overrepresentation at all; the number of committee leaders from a given state or region is roughly proportional to the size of its delegation in Congress. Committee leaders may represent areas of traditional party strength not so much because the seniority rule favors them as because those

---

[24] Buried in these assumptions is the further assumption that committee chairmen are powerful influences on the outputs of the Congress, an assumption we are willing to make.

[25] To illustrate that the consistency of reform arguments is not always impressive: The reforms for the Democratic convention in 1972 were supposed to make the convention more representative (of certain groups such as women, young people, and blacks) and more democratic. But what would happen if the people in the party elected a nonrepresentative slate? What would happen if a credentials committee rejected a democratically elected slate as unrepresentative? Is a democratic slate the same thing as a representative slate?

[26] Hinckley, *op. cit.*, p. 33.

areas electing over time the largest number of congressmen will stand the best chance of gaining committee posts.[27]

As an illustration of this point, Hinckley shows that a distribution of chairmanships by lot (randomly) would not be markedly different from the distribution under the seniority system. Table 11–1[28] summarizes that

TABLE 11–1
Comparison of Senate Democratic Leaders
as Selected by Seniority
and by Lot

Region	Number by Seniority	Number by Lot	Difference
East....................	5	6	−1
South...................	35	30	+5
Midwest...............	1	6	−5
West...................	21	14	+7

observation. The data indicate some overrepresentation of the South and (somewhat surprisingly) the West. The Midwest is underrepresented. Nevertheless, the salient impression of the table is the extent to which the seniority system yields chairmanships approximately equal to the regional representation in the Congress.

Are committee leaders more conservative than the other members of their party (descriptive conclusion 1)?[29] Hinckley's data do suggest that Democratic Party leaders are more conservative than their cohorts. In addition, Democratic Party leaders are less likely to support their party than their colleagues.[30] Although clear, these differences are not of exceptional magnitude. This finding supports descriptive conclusion 2. Finally, although committee leaders resemble party leaders in most respects, they differ from party leaders in their support of their party as well.[31]

It is important to note, however, that Hinckley does not believe that these findings can be entirely due to the effect of the seniority system. In effect, she denies causal assumption 1:

In the Democratic Party, the requirement of congressional seniority gave to the South and the West, regions of greatest Democratic strength to start

---

[27] *Ibid.*, p. 52.

[28] Data taken from Table 7 in *ibid.*, p. 39. Used with permission.

[29] We will not examine descriptive assumption 2 here, because, for our purposes, examining 3 will suffice: How could you go about examining assumption 2?

[30] The same data is used to support both assertions (*ibid.*, pp. 64–67).

[31] *Ibid.*, pp. 101, 106.

with, an increased advantage, and these areas tended to be weakest in "liberalism" and support for presidential Democratic programs. But congressional seniority is only one factor contributing to the conservative cast of Democratic chairmen. Most notably conservative Democrats, weakest in support of party programs, were more likely to stay with their committees than their more liberal colleagues—suggesting that patterns of initial assignment or subsequent changes also influenced the results.[32]

To be more precise, Hinckley is suggesting multiple causation for the phenomenon of the conservative cast of Democratic chairmen.

Let us summarize the findings: (1) the fact that members of Congress as a whole are elected from relatively noncompetitive areas means that many congressmen are eligible for committee chairmanships; (2) chairmanships are distributed in a manner roughly proportional to the numbers of representatives elected by a party from a region or state; and (3) while chairmen as a group, in the Democratic Party, are more conservative and less supportive of their party than their fellow party members, not all of these differences can be traced to seniority.

Thus, we come to the "jackpot" question: Would changing the seniority system alter the policy outputs of Congress in a more liberal direction? In the face of the evidence presented by Hinckley, a policy analyst might conclude that no significant changes would likely be forthcoming if the seniority system were changed to say, some method of selection by the party or the party leadership. Hinckley summarizes her findings as follows: "Perhaps the single most important finding of this study is that the effect of committee chairmen selected by Congress is at most a limited one."[33] If that is the case, then elimination of the seniority rule and substitution of another is likely to have only marginal impact on the policy output of Congress.

What other, perhaps undesirable, consequences might a change in the seniority system bring about? We may suggest one hypothesis. As matters now stand, advancement on committee is automatic—not a matter of intraparty conflict. Some of the other systems which might be selected could be expected to increase intraparty conflict over committee rankings. If intraparty conflict increased, a change in the seniority rule might decrease party cohesion. This would be exactly the opposite of what the reformers intended.

What about the feasibility of change? The analysis suggests that if the conditions emerge which make Congress as a whole more responsive to demands for change, then the seniority system may be changed. At present, the system could be changed by a majority in either party. That it is not is ample evidence that the Congress does not desire to

---

[32] *Ibid.,* p. 82.

[33] *Ibid.,* p. 108.

change the system. Therefore, the best available means to change Congress is to elect different Congressmen.

CONCLUSIONS

The main theme of this chapter has been the significance of systematic political analysis for public policy decisions. In effect, we have argued that the ultimate payoff from the systematic study of politics comes in the application of that knowledge to the problems of the political world. The analysis of public policy alternatives involves making predictions about the consequences of alternate policies, and, therefore, generalizations are used (if only implicitly) by policy makers. To the degree that political scientists can supply more reliable generalizations, policy making will be more effective. At minimum, systematic political inquiry may suggest to the policy maker that a given policy will not produce the expected consequences or will have other consequences not previously considered. In the area of political reform, the seniority system example is a good illustration of how a little careful inquiry can provide a check to commonly held beliefs.

At the same time, we must caution that policy making is not a purely rational or scientific process, for several reasons. First, the state of knowledge in the discipline is not sufficient to allow us to make confident predictions about the consequences of many policy changes. Second, political scientists cannot tell us which values to prefer. Third, policy making is a political process, which means that political realities intrude upon decision making in such a way as to constrain the alternatives available. Finally, there is always a limit to time and money and other resources which can be used to implement any given decision.

We end this book where we began. We do not offer or believe in panaceas or magic recipes. We would not even predict that political man is going to be able to survive the manifold problems which face him. We do, however, offer a constructive and tested orientation to the world: a skeptical, empirical, independent, and hopeful orientation. Science cannot save us. Social science cannot save us. But social science can be a useful tool for attacking the crucial problems that we face. It seems to us that we cannot ask for more than that from an imperfect human invention.

Indexes

Author index

291

Subject index

293